HEADING HOME

HEADING HOME

Motherhood,
Work, and the
Failed Promise
of Equality

SHANI ORGAD

Columbia University Press / New York

Columbia University Press
Publishers Since 1893
New York   Chichester, West Sussex
cup.columbia.edu
Copyright © 2019 Columbia University Press

Library of Congress Cataloging-in-Publication Data
Names: Orgad, Shani, 1972- author.
Title: Heading home : motherhood, work, and the failed promise of equality /
    Shani Orgad.
Description: New York : Columbia University Press, [2019] | Includes bibliographical
    references and index.
Identifiers: LCCN 2018024035 (print) | LCCN 2018025997 (e-book) |
    ISBN 9780231545631 (e-book) | ISBN 9780231184724 (cloth : alk. paper)
Subjects: LCSH: Work and family. | Working mothers. | Stay-at-home mothers. |
    Women in the professions. | Women executives. | Sex discrimination
    in employment.
Classification: LCC HD4904.25 (e-book) | LCC HD4904.25 .O74 2019 (print) |
    DDC 331.4/4—dc23
LC record available at https://lccn.loc.gov/2018024035

Cover design: Lisa Hamm
Cover illustration: © Sharon Webber-Zvik, *The Operator*

Contents

Preface and Acknowledgements

The two women I have been closest to in my life, my paternal grandmother and my mother, I have always known as both mothers *and* workers. My grandmother immigrated to Kibbutz Kinneret (in what is now northern Israel) from Zilupe, Latvia, in 1935, and as a Zionist kibbutz pioneer, worked alongside her male and female peers on road construction, in agriculture, and milking cows. It was precisely as she was milking cows while heavily pregnant that she began to have her first contractions, heralding the birth of her first child, my father. She continued to work for many years afterward, until the age of 79, as one of the kibbutz's clothes storage managers, as a cook in the communal kitchen, and later, as a packer in the kibbutz's date factory. She had four sons, who, from the day they were born, were all raised in the kibbutz's communal children's houses. When my father and his brothers came to visit their parents in their small apartment, my grandmother would bake them their favorite cakes and biscuits, an act through which she expressed the immense pleasure and joy she took in motherhood (despite having always yearned for a daughter!). Although the different jobs she did throughout her lifetime were physically very demanding, she never complained. I have vivid memories of my grandmother's cheerful attitude and incredible energy—of her rising at 5:30 every morning and working long hours, often in the scorching heat.

My own mother, who at the age of four had lost her mother, to this day takes pride in motherhood as being her "number one occupation."

She trained as a teacher, and after marrying my father, she moved with him to the kibbutz. Since there were no jobs for her as a teacher, she undertook whatever jobs were available. When I was born, my mother led a successful campaign to abolish the kibbutz's communal sleeping system, where the children slept in the children's houses, which were monitored at night by rotating shifts of night watchmen and watchwomen who, using an intercom system, were supposed to locate and respond to the children's nighttime needs. For my mother, the thought of not having her baby sleeping beside her was unbearable. Later, our family left the kibbutz and my parents divorced. Although she had trained as a teacher, my mother never worked in her profession. She had always worked in administrative and sales jobs that had kept her afloat financially—and proved crucial following her divorce. "Make sure you always have enough money of your own to enable you to stand on your two feet," she repeatedly urged me when I was a girl and later when I became a young woman.

My relationship to work and family has been shaped, deeply and profoundly, by these two dear women and the models of womanhood, work, and family they presented to me. It was also significantly shaped by the promises of the 1980s and early 1990s. As a teenager, the popular culture I consumed was heavily influenced by messages of "girl power" (*Charlie's Angels*, Cyndi Lauper, Madonna, and Tina Turner posters were plastered all over my bedroom walls), and by depictions of empowered women who "just do it" in the spheres of both paid work and family (I remember enthusing about the films *Working Girl* and *Baby Boom*).

I started my first paid job in an advertising agency during the last year of my undergraduate studies, and I have been in paid employment ever since, including various part-time jobs during my master's and PhD studies, and the full-time academic employment I entered since completing my PhD in 2003. Like my grandmother, baking my two sons their favorite biscuits and cakes gives me immense pleasure, as do many other aspects of motherhood. Like my grandmother and my mother, for me being in employment was never a question. However, unlike them, with my mother's incredible support, I was fortunate that I could pursue a career in a profession I chose and about which I am passionate. Also unlike them, I do complain about work!

The women I interviewed for this book chose a path that is significantly different from mine: to leave paid employment and become stay-at-home mothers. However, there are also many commonalities between our experiences. Though I grew up in Israel and they grew up mostly in Britain, and some in the United States, Europe, and Latin America, we were exposed to similar messages and promises, and often to similar popular representations of femininity in the 1980s and 1990s. We belong to a generation that has experienced both the benefits and the fault lines of growing up in the wake of the feminist movement and the increasing dominance of neoliberalism— with the profound challenges and painful emotional injuries their imbrication has produced. This book tells the story of the conditions that have shaped these women's—and to an extent their generation's—experience of family and work under neoliberal capitalism.

I am deeply indebted to the women and men who shared their intimate experiences with me. This book could not have been written without their generosity and candor.

I am also very grateful to several people who assisted with the research for this book. Sara De Benedictis provided invaluable research assistance at various stages and was a real pleasure to work with. Gillian Paull at Frontier Economics conducted a statistical analysis of the UK Labour Force Survey and generously shared her expertise on aspects of UK labor policy. Richard Stupart worked persistently to secure the copyrights for use of images for this book. I also thank James Deeley for administrative support during different stages of the research project, and to Hila Shkolnik-Brener and Eleanor Cartwright for their help with the book's cover.

I want to express my gratitude to several people who read all or parts of the manuscript in draft form and offered constructive feedback. My heartfelt thanks go to Rosalind Gill for her insightful, inspiring, and generous feedback and continuous encouragement, and to Catherine Rottenberg for her detailed, incisive, and always encouraging and constructive comments. Special thanks go to Shai Aran, who read parts of the manuscript and gave excellent comments on both content and form. I owe thanks also to Nick Couldry and Jan Radway, and to the members of my book group—Bart Cammaerts, Lilie Chouliaraki, Ellen Helsper, Sonia Livingstone, and Peter Lunt, who commented on chapter drafts.

Several friends, including Natalie Aran, Keren Darmon, Dina Domb, Milly Marr, Lisa Roberts, Alex Simpson, and Kate Wright, helped by referring me to interviewees and/or places where I was able to recruit interviewees—I am deeply appreciative of their help. My deep gratitude goes also to Svetlana Smirnova, who spent hours meticulously formatting the manuscript, and to Cynthia Little, whom I have been extremely fortunate to have scrutinize and edit the manuscript (including this acknowledgement!).

I am grateful to the LSE Department of Media and Communications Research Committee Fund and the LSE REF Fund, which helped cover some of the costs involved in conducting the research. Thanks also to Saskia Sassen for her support of the project, and to LSE librarian Heather Dawson for her very helpful advice and suggestions.

At Columbia University Press, special thanks are due to Eric Schwartz for his enthusiasm about the project from its early stages and his offer to publish the book. Thanks also, Eric, for accommodating my various requests regarding the book cover. Thanks are due also to Caroline Wazer and Lowell Frye for their most valuable assistance, to Lunaea Weatherstone for copyediting the book so meticulously, and to Ben Kolstad for overseeing the production.

My dear friends Maya Becker, Rosalind Gill, Catherine Rottenberg, Avital Shaal, Hila Shkolnik-Brener, and Sagit Schneider have given their unstinting love, care, and encouragement and supported me in countless ways. I am blessed to have the wonderful friendship of these wise, brilliant, and immensely generous women.

My beloved sons, Yoav and Assaf, have been my anchor: always embracing, loving and forgiving, they have helped me see through the big bluff of work-life balance, and find joy in our many fantastic family imbalances. They were also wonderful (voluntary!) research assistants, constantly searching for films and adverts depicting mothers. Huge thanks to my husband, Amnon Aran, for his support, care, and love and the many nourishing and delicious meals he has cooked for us. I am fortunate to have the support of my loving mother, Atalya Wolf, my dad, Nechemya Orgad, Kobi Wolf, and my darling brother, Itamar Orgad, and his family.

The book is dedicated to Eileen Aird, who is a huge source of inspiration, guidance, care, and incredible feminist energy. I am hugely indebted to her.

Abbreviations

BA	British Airways
BBC	British Broadcasting Corporation
CEO	chief executive officer
CFO	chief financial officer
CMI	Chartered Management Institute
COO	chief operations officer
GDP	gross domestic product
GMMP	Global Media Monitoring Project
GP	general practitioner
ICT	information and communication technology
IGM	Initiative of Global Markets
IPSE	Association of Independent Professionals and the Self-Employed
IT	information technology
KPMG	Klynveld Peat Marwick Goerdeler
MBA	Master of Business Administration
MP	Member of Parliament (UK)
NGO	non-governmental organization
PSA	public service announcement
STEM	science, technology, engineering, and mathematics
UK	United Kingdom
US	United States

HEADING HOME

Introduction

L aura was born in the 1970s. One of four children, she was brought up in a council house[1] in the north of England by her bricklayer father and a mother who worked as a night nurse, a job that allowed her to take care of her children during the day. "My mom never stopped. Both my parents always worked and worked really hard, and financially things were a struggle when I was young," Laura recalls. "They didn't particularly have any leisure interests or any spare money to pursue any leisure interests. They worked hard so that we could have our holidays in the caravan. Bless them!"

As a teenager, Laura remembers watching the 1984–85 miners' strike that dominated Britain's television screens. The 1980s, she says, ushered in "kind of a different, new era." Neoliberalism was fast advancing as the UK government designed and implemented aggressive policies geared toward intensified privatization, market deregulation, and the opening of the national market to international trade and capital. The withdrawal of the state from many areas of social provision proceeded apace. Under Ronald Reagan in the United States and Margaret Thatcher in the United Kingdom, the Fordist model gave way to downsized industries, the manufacturing base declined, and the economy became increasingly dominated by the service sector. As a consequence, there was massive male unemployment alongside the opening up of formerly male-only sectors of the labor market to young women, which offered them an array of new opportunities.

Messages about women's choice, empowerment, and independence began circulating widely in popular culture, and there was a growing emphasis on girls' academic attainment. Young women like Laura encountered discourses of "girl power," which insisted that they could not only do whatever they wanted in the labor market but that they could also combine a profession with motherhood.[2] The image of a "self-assured, attractive, middle level [female] manager, with two happy children (in school or day-care), a smooth functioning household (thanks to all the new labour-saving household technology), and blessed with a supportive husband"[3] populated American and British women's magazines.

It was amid these images and cultural ideas, and the broader social, economic, and cultural shifts in the 1980s and 1990s, that Laura and most of the other women I interviewed for this book came of age. In the wake of these changes in the global labor market and the British economy, and excited by the prospect of "girl power," Laura's parents were keen for their daughter to do better than they (could) ever have done. They pushed her to succeed at school and to go to university. As Valerie Walkerdine, Helen Lucey, and June Melody note, for the working-class families at that time, "higher education and the subsequent possibility of entrance into a profession offered an escape from the grinding facts of ordinary-working class life."[4] Laura did well at school and in 1992 went to study at the University of Oxford—the first member of her family to go to university. After graduating in classics and English at the highest level, Laura became a successful software programmer in an international firm based in the southeast of England—a job she enjoyed and which she performed very successfully for nine years. Then she married a floor trader and moved to London, and at the age of thirty-six, after the birth of her first child, she left paid employment. Over the past seven years Laura had (as she put it) "reinvented" herself as a stay-at-home mother.

Laura had never envisaged life as someone who "juggles her job with small children and has a full-time nanny." The models of mothers in full-time paid employment she encountered were not ones that she wanted to emulate. Her own mother was a "positive role model," but Laura "did not want to be as harried and permanently exhausted" as she had been. Her mother-in-law, whom she described as "an aggressive career woman," "was never there for her children." The women at the global firm she worked for appeared to be "frazzled, stressed, and often frustrated," struggling to combine their childcare responsibilities with their career demands. And those other women, who inhabited magazines, fiction, advertisements, films, and television shows, who appeared to juggle career and motherhood seamlessly, Laura said, were "just too perfect" and "unrealistic." Later images of those "juggling women," especially from the mid-1990s onwards, did not appeal to Laura either: they were women who wrestled to "have it all," never quite managing to achieve the desired work-life balance[5]—Allison Pearson's 2002 bestselling novel *I Don't Know How She Does It* (later adapted to a film) being one of the most popular portrayals of this.[6] Laura "never wanted to go down the road" pursued by any of these women.

Yet Laura had not imagined becoming a full-time stay-at-home mother either. She was typical of many working-class young women in Britain who, in the late 1980s and early 1990s, were buoyed by the idea that a woman could do anything she wanted.[7] She had pursued higher education with a genuine desire to develop and realize herself professionally. Unlike her mother, Laura *could* afford high-quality childcare and pursue a fulfilling career and had quickly become aware of what was expected of her as a reinvented middle-class woman: "Society expects you, especially middle-class educated women, to be able to do it all. You're expected to be able to have a family and work. I can rationalize that to myself and say, that's complete rubbish!" Laura mused, but quickly dismissing the thought, she said, "But I can't really [ignore what society says], can I?"

Laura was unable to shake off these powerful societal expectations; they are not simply external messages that exist "out there." Rather, as feminist scholar Rosalind Gill eloquently observes, "what is 'out there' gets 'in here' to reconstruct our deepest yearnings and sense of self."[8] The dominant messages and ideas about women, work, and family that circulate in media, policy, and everyday life had profoundly shaped Laura's thinking and feelings. So, after "all those bloody qualifications" for which she had studied so hard, Laura had expected to "become something," *not* a stay-at-home mother.

When I first met Laura in a small café in north London in the course of researching for this book, I asked for permission to record the interview. "That's OK," she said, giggling, "I don't think I have anything really shocking to tell you!" This book is premised on the view that there *is* something shocking, or at least deeply puzzling, about the decisions made by women like Laura. Even though today, in contrast to the 1960s, this group of women is a minority, an astounding 20 percent of stay-at-home mothers in the United Kingdom are highly educated, while in the United States, a quarter of stay-at-home mothers have college degrees.[9] Why, then, do educated mothers who grew up in a cultural and policy climate that champions women's successful combining of motherhood and economic activity, and who can afford the help that would allow them to stay in paid employment, make this retrogressive "choice"?

More than half a century ago, Betty Friedan was baffled by a similar puzzle. Why, she asked, "did so many American women, with the ability and education to discover and create, go back home again?"[10] Friedan found the answer in the prevailing "feminine mystique": the oppressive image of the "happy housewife" which in the 1950s and 1960s "hardened into a mystique"[11] and forbade women's career dreams. The women who answered Friedan's questionnaire in 1957 were frustrated, unsatisfied, and unhappy. They experienced a sense of emptiness deriving from the "uneasy denial of the world outside the home."[12] Some sixty years on, however, this mystique has been widely challenged. Today's cultural landscape is full of images and stories celebrating real and fictional women who "lean in," as Sheryl Sandberg's bestseller cajoles them to do—that is, to assert themselves and achieve leadership positions, as they combine professional ambitions with motherhood.[13] In the wake of "feminist" manifestos such as Sandberg's (and Anne-Marie Slaughter's, which is discussed later), and the growing visibility of feminism in the cultural landscape in the West,[14] there has been renewed lively debate in the media and in policy discussions about the obstacles preventing women from "having it all" and how these obstacles could be overcome.[15] Work-life balance, flexibility, and gender diversity are terms *du jour* in discussions about women in the workplace. Governments and businesses in the West champion women's participation and entrenchment in the workforce. Furthermore, encouraging women to remain in and return to the workplace and achieve senior leadership positions is regarded increasingly not just as "right" but also as profitable—indeed, more and more business leaders, business schools, and politicians are passionately advocating the business case for creating and maintaining a diverse workforce.[16]

Like Laura, the other women I interviewed for this book were well aware that the choice they had made was fundamentally incongruent with contemporary dominant cultural ideas about desirable femininity. The messages they grew up with and are surrounded by are very different from the ones their mothers—the generation of Betty Friedan's women—received about a woman's "proper" place and role. Many of them (Laura included) had read *Lean In: Women, Work, and the Will to Lead* or similar contemporary "feminist" proclamations, and are well versed in the debate about women's equality in the workplace; some identify as feminists. They know that today, not only are women who combine careers and motherhood statistically the norm but also that the normative view is that a woman can only really achieve fulfillment if she is simultaneously a paid laborer *and* a mother, abiding by what feminist scholar Angela McRobbie calls the "new sexual contract."[17]

Thus, when I asked these women the question Friedan had asked her respondents some sixty years earlier, namely what they found satisfying in their current lives, their reaction was frequently puzzlement, sometimes even embarrassment. "Satisfaction is a strange word," Tanya, a former lawyer, told me. "It's a tricky question," former journalist Maggie responded. Susan, a former medical doctor, first fell silent and then, a minute later, said with discomfiture, "Oh, I should have something straight out, shouldn't I really?" Sara, a former financial director and a stay-at-home mother for the past three years, admitted pensively that it was "a good question," to which the "awful reality" was she had no answer. The discomfort, puzzlement, and embarrassment with which the women I interviewed reacted to my question derived, at least in part, from knowing that unlike their mothers, many of whom had had either to give up their jobs to look after the children or could not afford to quit their jobs, they *did* have a choice.

Indeed, the women I interviewed belong to a generation that has reaped the fruits of the long and ongoing feminist struggle to create the social conditions that should enable women to pursue their choices across all areas of daily life. In particular, the women's liberation movement of the 1970s propelled a dramatic rise in enrolment in higher education and participation of especially middle-class women in the workforce. In the United Kingdom, women's participation in the labor force rose from 52.8 percent in 1971 to 71.2 percent in 2018, while in the United States it increased from 43.4 percent in 1971 to 56.8 percent in 2016.[18] However, while overall the story of women's participation in the labor force is often celebrated as a success,[19] its heroines are women but not necessarily mothers. In the United Kingdom, despite relatively high female employment rates, maternal employment rates are lower than the international average.[20] Almost three-quarters (72 percent) of women outside the labor market are mothers, and mothers are almost twice as likely as women without children to stay at home (11 percent versus 6 percent for professional women; 24 percent versus 13 percent for non-professional women) (table 1).[21]

The trend in the United States is similar: mothers are almost twice as likely to leave the workforce as women without children.[22] Women in the United States participate in the workforce at high rates in their twenties, but fewer are working in their thirties and early forties, a period that normally coincides with raising young children.[23] Furthermore, while the share of mothers in the US labor force increased steadily from 1975 to 2000, it has leveled off since.[24]

Table 1 Comparison of Mothers and Women Without Children Outside the UK Labor Market*

Percentage of Mothers and Women Without Children Outside the Labor Force		Distribution of Women Outside the Labor Force	
Mothers:		*Mothers:*	
- professional	11%	- professional	12%
- nonprofessionals	24%	- nonprofessionals	38%
		- never been employed	22%
Women without children:		*Women without children:*	
- professional	6%	- professional	4%
- nonprofessionals	13%	- nonprofessionals	11%
		- never been employed	12%
		Total	100%**

*Prepared by Gillian Paull, Frontier Economics. Figures are based on Q1 in the 2017 UK Labour Force Survey. The sample is restricted to women under the age of fifty to create a more comparable age profile between mothers of non-adult children and women without children.

**Columns may not sum to 100% due to rounding.

Overall, then, as the British economist Gillian Paull points out, "the likelihood that a mother will remain in work is much lower than would be expected from normal labour market dynamics."[25] Furthermore, as Anne-Marie Slaughter, an American foreign policy expert and president and chief executive officer (CEO) of the think tank New America notes, "motherhood is now a greater predictor of wage inequality than gender."[26] The majority of mothers return to paid employment but see the gains made before having children (education, early career achievements) dissipate after they become mothers. Their time out of the workforce interrupts their peak earning years and is both financially and emotionally costly. Thus, between university entry and childbirth, women achieve relative equity in the public world of work, but then this equity seems to stall.

Today, there are just over two million stay-at-home mothers in the United Kingdom, of whom approximately 340,000 (17 percent) are former professionals.[27] Recent studies suggest that among UK families that are in the top 20 percent based on income, increasing numbers of women leave the workplace to look after their children and do not engage in any formal paid work.[28] An astounding 25 percent of UK mothers with partners in the top earnings quartile are stay-at-home mothers—a substantial percentage of whom are highly educated.[29] In the United States, 14 percent of women trained in managerial and professional occupations are outside the labor force.[30] So why do highly educated women who could afford childcare give up education and successful careers and "return" home, seemingly to embrace motherhood as a full-time occupation?

A myriad of explanations have been offered, purporting to explain this puzzle. Some argue that, like all other work- and family-related decisions, women's decisions to leave paid employment are personal choices based on their individual preferences, psychological factors, and biological differences.[31] For instance, British sociologist Catherine Hakim's "preference theory" posits that in advanced capitalist countries such as Britain and the United States, the key driver of women's employment patterns is lifestyle preference.[32] According to Hakim, some women prefer "work-centered" lives, while others prefer a "home-centered" model or want to combine work and family ("adaptive"). This view is echoed in various popular outlets. For example, a 2015 Gallup poll reported that more than half of American women who have a child younger than eighteen "prefer" to stay home and care for their house and family.[33] The blogosphere and social media are replete with accounts of women describing their decision to become a stay-at-home mother as a private, personal, and positive preference-based choice.[34] Similarly, interviews with and books by celebrities turned stay-at-home mothers typically cast these women as freely choosing individuals who are driven by innate maternal feelings and a "natural" preference to pursue motherhood as a full-time career, and who feel comfortable and true to their preferences in their new role.[35] The gender essentialist flavor of these accounts also can be found in abundance in evolutionary psychology and neuroscience-based explanations of men's and women's work-related trajectories. A typical example is the ten-page "manifesto" written by a Google software engineer, which was leaked to the public in August 2017 and which explained the dearth of women in tech and leadership as the result, at least in part, of innate biological differences between men and women.[36] While its publication provoked public outcry, it simultaneously received an outpouring of support on social media.[37]

Other accounts suggest that motherhood is accompanied by loss of confidence and reduced commitment to a career. Confidence is "one of the top three barriers to returning to work,"[38] avers a study conducted by the website Workingmums.co.uk, while another study, reported in the *Huffington Post*, found that "mothers on maternity leave suffer a major crash in confidence when their babies are eleven months old" and that they feel they "can no longer cut it in the world of work."[39] Discussions in the media, workplaces, and policy circles about gender equality in the workplace regularly debate women's tendency to suffer from "impostor syndrome" and "ambition gap"[40] and ways to tackle the problem of women's lack of confidence and poise. Others, including a leading study by Harvard Business School, argue that women's sense of what constitutes success and power differs substantially from that of men.[41] Still others describe women's "flight" from the workplace as a nostalgic return to traditional gender roles or as a rational response to increasingly demanding workplace conditions. *New York* magazine, for example, describes the choice of some women to become the "retro wife" and embrace domesticity as a feminist "solution to resolving the long-running tensions between work and life."[42] Echoing this view, in 2017, *Guardian* commentator Victoria Coren Mitchell asked whether happiness and confidence would return "if full-time motherhood became the normal expectation again," and cited the "horribly convincing" argument that "at least when women mainly aspired to have children, most of them could achieve it. But now they're expected to want to complete professional fulfilment, when only a fraction can even hope for a secure job."[43]

At the same time, some—although few and far between—policy and media stories and images call into question these popular explanations. For example, the 2017 film *The Wife*, an adaptation of feminist author Meg Wolitzer's novel of the same name, centers on the complex story of Joan (Glenn Close), whose promising writing career ended early so she could support her Nobel prize-winning writer husband and raise a family. HBO's 2017 television drama *Big Little Lies*, based on the novel of the same name by Liane Moriarty, is another example of a popular representation that potently punctures the notion that educated stay-at-home mothers made a personal choice, derived from lack of ambition and confidence, and driven by their innate feelings and personal preferences for motherhood and domesticity over career. Set in gleaming Monterey, California, the show centers on four mothers, two of whom are educated stay-at-home mothers: gorgeous former corporate lawyer Celeste (Nicole Kidman) and chirpy, high-strung Madeline (Reese Witherspoon). (Although Madeline has a side gig in community theater, she dismisses its significance compared to mothers who have careers.) Building on the thrust of previous shows such as *Desperate Housewives*, and on broader changes in the depiction of motherhood in popular culture (discussed in chapter 4), the show exposes these mothers' deep unhappiness in their marriages and their subjection to male violence beneath the veneer of their stunning, expansive beach houses, moneyed lifestyles, and "perfect" families. In particular, glamorous Celeste, the envy of the American suburban town, with her "perfect" husband and twin sons, is revealed to be the victim of violence and abuse from her husband. In episode 4, in a meeting with the mayor, Celeste represents Madeline against the mayor's threat to ban her theater play. Celeste is in her element, commanding the case, attracting everyone's awe. After the meeting, she honks the horn of Madeline's car, screaming ecstatically, "I felt alive!" Then bursting into tears, she declares, "I feel so ashamed for saying this, but being a mother is not enough for me. It's just not. It's not even close!"

However, accounts of the lived experience of *real* educated mothers who left paid employment are still largely and glaringly absent from current debates on women, work, and family, as is an understanding of how their private choices are situated within and shaped by social and cultural contexts and pressures, economic structures, and employment norms.

One exception is the 2007 book *Opting Out? Why Women Really Quit Careers and Head Home*, by American sociologist Pamela Stone.[44] Drawing on in-depth interviews with highly achieving women who graduated from Ivy League universities, held senior management positions in their workplaces, and quit their jobs after having children, Stone highlights the detrimental impact these women's workplace conditions had on their decisions to quit their jobs.[45] However, *Opting Out?* is now more than a decade old—a decade that has seen major events and changes: the global economic crisis and ensuing recession, the rise of conservative forces and far-right politics across the globe, and an intensifying backlash against feminist gains and rhetoric. Concurrently, over the last decade there has been a resurgence and growing popularity of feminism,[46] manifest in the heightened visibility and popularity of the #MeToo campaign, a surge of high-powered women and men publicly and unabashedly identifying as feminists, and in a flurry of cultural representations, many of which are explored in this book. In addition, Stone was not interested in whether and how the experiences of the women she interviewed were shaped by media and policy constructions of women, work, and family. In equal measure, much of the scholarly research on media discourses and depictions of gender, work, and family does not look at people's lived experience.[47] Recent studies mostly look at *either* experience *or* representation, not the connection between the two, and none explains directly *why* educated women leave the workplace after having children and with what consequences.

What, then, is the relationship between cultural and policy representations of women, work, and family, and the decisions of educated women like Laura to quit their careers? What are the consequences of this choice? In *Heading Home*, I address these questions by exploring the uncharted territory of the lived experience of educated mothers who left paid employment, juxtaposing these women's firsthand accounts against an analysis of contemporary narratives and images of gender, family, and work in UK and US media and policy.

THE RELATIONSHIP BETWEEN LIVED EXPERIENCE AND REPRESENTATIONS

The relationship between women's lived experience and cultural representations has been a central concern of feminist scholarship since at
least the late 1960s. In particular, studies of earlier eras highlight how
representations of motherhood and work often fail to correspond with
and mask women's lived experience, thus supporting the reproduction of
patriarchal structures and relations of gender inequality. Betty Friedan
famously exposed the stark mismatch between the quiet desperation of
American women and the oppressive 1950s image of the happy modern
American housewife. Later, Arlie Hochschild with Anne Machung, in the
United States, and Rosalind Coward, in the United Kingdom, observed
the blatant incongruence between women's experience and media
images (especially in women's magazines) of successful career mothers
that dominated the popular imagination in the 1980s.[48] Happy images of
career mothers hid "intricate webs of tension, and the huge, hidden emotional cost to women, men, and children, having to manage inequality,"
wrote Hochschild.[49]

However, feminist media studies since the mid-1990s seem largely to
have moved away from studying women's lived experience and everyday
lives to focus more on the analysis of media texts. There has been little
empirically based research into whether and in what ways the meanings
of media representations correspond to women's lived experience.[50] In
particular, since the turn of the century, the relationship between contemporary representations of motherhood and work and women's experience
of these two domains has remained largely unexplored.[51]

In this book, I refocus attention on the relations between mediated
and lived experience, and on the consequences of these relationships
for women's feelings and identities and for gender power relations more
generally. This exploration is animated and deeply informed by the 1959
project that renowned American sociologist Charles Wright Mills called
The Sociological Imagination.[52] The value of sociology, Mills contended, lies
in its capacity to make connections between "the personal troubles of
milieu" and "the public issues of social structure."[53] In a famous passage,
Mills explains that "Troubles occur within the character of the individual
and within the range of his [sic] immediate relations with others," whereas

"Issues have to do with matters that transcend these local environments of the individual and the range of his [sic] inner life."[54] For Mills, the task of the social sciences is to identify the larger social forces that furnish our most intimate personal troubles, and to connect the "personal troubles" of private individuals to "public issues" of history and society, in order to show both how we are produced as subjects and how we can be more than what we are already.[55]

Fourteen years later, sociologists Richard Sennett and Jonathan Cobb wrote in their seminal study *The Hidden Injuries of Class* that "there must be some compulsion, some magnet, from the larger society that enters and gives form to people's daily experience."[56] Cultural, media, political, and policy discourses constitute a central force of this societal magnet; they feed our imagination and lifeworld, and shape our daily experience.[57] The women I interviewed rarely reflected on the effect of this magnet on their thinking, desires, feelings, and sense of self. Yet their accounts bear the marks of these discourses, which seem to have entered these women's imaginations and shaped their experiences in profound ways. The women often related their experience and its sources as a private problem, but their most intimate "troubles" were significantly furnished and shaped by "the public issues of social structure,"[58] that is, by key structural forces and contradictions of advanced capitalism, and by media and policy discourses, narratives, and images that articulate, justify, perpetuate, and occasionally challenge these structures.

In exploring the intricate relationship between these women's lived experience and cultural and policy representations, I draw on the American feminist historian Joan Wallach Scott, who challenges the notion of experience as uncontestable authoritative evidence and as the point of origin of explanation.[59] Following Scott, I am interested in exposing the *constructed* nature of experience: how the subjectivities of the women I interviewed are constituted, how their visions, fantasies, and deepest desires are structured by (among other forces) media and policy representations and the cultural ideas they carry. Importantly, I try to avoid an opposition between cultural representations seen as a monolithic site where norms are reproduced versus subjects' accounts of their experience as a site of complexity, diversity, and change. Rather, I engage with the potentially contradictory, complex, and inconsistent character of both cultural representations *and* interviewees' accounts, and of the relationship between the two. Thus, my task in this book is to draw connections and highlight disjunctures between the realm of women's personal and private experience and the realm of public issues around women, work, and family, as portrayed and discussed in media and policy. It is by making these connections that we can recognize that "this is not just the private problem of each individual woman," as Betty Friedan put it more than half a century ago,[60] and look for social and structural ways of tackling these "personal troubles."

It is worth noting that this is *not* a study of audience reception of specific media or policy texts. Rather, I examine the far less direct, often intangible, but meaningful relations between women's lived experience and cultural and policy representations. In doing so, I was inspired and influenced particularly by feminist scholar Janice Radway's germinal book *Reading the Romance*,[61] which explores the connections between the world of the romance novel and the world inhabited by its women readers. I also build on the work of the feminist psychosocial studies scholar Valerie Walkerdine,[62] which cogently highlights how the social, cultural, and psychological are deeply entwined. Both Radway's and Walkerdine's studies underscore how media and popular culture in particular allow women to work through emotionally and resolve in fantasy painful experiences, longings, and contradictions that they are unable to resolve in reality. In turn, the fantasies and resolution offered by cultural representations play upon and mobilize desires already present in the lives of women, which are themselves shaped and influenced by wider cultural and social forces.

RESEARCHING EDUCATED STAY-AT-HOME MOTHERS' LIVED EXPERIENCE

Every morning when dropping off my children at the local school in our leafy north London neighborhood I would see these stay-at-home moms. Occasionally I might have a brief chat with one of them in the schoolyard, as we were waiting for the bell to ring and the teachers to come and collect the children. I always felt very conscious of these encounters as embodying the stereotypical distinction between "working" and "nonworking" mothers: the stay-at-home mothers would normally be in training outfits, ready for a jog after drop-off, or in jeans and a baggy T-shirt, whereas I was normally dressed more formally, on my way to a busy day of university teaching and meetings. However, even more than our dress, the tempo marked the difference between us: I was normally in a hurry because I had a lecture or a meeting starting at 10:00; thus, as soon as the school bell rang at 9:00, I would rush off to work. The stay-at-home moms would hang around and chat after the children went in or go for morning coffee at a local café or one of their houses. I never experienced the notorious "mommy wars"—a popular narrative that pits "working mothers" against "stay-at-home mothers,"[63] but I certainly felt there was something significant that distinguished us. Once, one of the stay-at-home mothers invited me to join them for morning coffee. When I thanked her and said I could not because I had to go to work, she gave me a pitying look and said, "You poor thing." I was perplexed by her comment and wondered why she felt sorry for me. Had her former experience in paid employment been traumatic or difficult? I often wondered why she and other women had become full-time mothers and what their lives looked like. However, like the sociologist Pamela Stone, whose study I mentioned earlier, I did not have the courage to probe, and I was acutely aware that any questioning might be perceived as judgmental and patronizing.

It was at a class parents' party that I had the opportunity to talk at more length to one of the stay-at-home mothers, and not about a school-related issue. She told me about growing up in the 1970s and 1980s in the north of England, dreaming of becoming something different from her working-class parents. She recounted with pride how she was accepted by and graduated from a good university, before beginning to work as an accountant in a London firm where, a few years later, she met her future husband (now a senior partner in a global accountancy firm). "Then we married, I got pregnant, and it stopped working," she said. "And look where he is and look where I am now!" she concluded sarcastically. My head was buzzing with questions that I never got to ask her: What did she mean by "it stopped working"? Why had she given up years of education, training, and a successful career, seemingly to embrace full-time motherhood? And, if this was the choice she had made, why was she bitter? I was curious about this particular woman's story, but more fundamentally about the group of women to which she belonged: educated women who left careers and did not return to paid employment after starting a family.

Why study privileged stay-at-home mothers?

In the course of conducting this research, colleagues and friends occasionally made cynical comments echoing popular disparaging sentiments about privileged women: "Why study this minority group of middle-class women who have everything they want and made a choice to quit their jobs?" Indeed, most of the women whose stories are recounted in this book are not simply middle-class mothers. Rather, by dint of their husbands' earnings, they live in single-income families, mostly in affluent suburbs of one of the most expensive capital cities in the world. Many of them do not have mortgage or rental obligations and are able to avail themselves of paid domestic help—luxuries that are unaffordable for the majority of the population in the United Kingdom. So why study their experiences? To address this question, it is useful to differentiate between the more general question of *why study the privileged* and the question of *why study privileged stay-at-home mothers* in particular.

Feminist accounts of "studying up" and Michèle Lamont's sociological study of the French and American upper-middle classes offer some helpful answers to the broader question of the reasons for studying the privileged.[64] First, Lamont observes, members of the upper-middle class (and by extension, the UK "established middle class," as defined by the Great British Class Survey,[65] to which many of my interviewees belong) tend to control the allocation of many of the resources most valued in advanced industrial societies. In the case of my study, many of the women I interviewed had once wielded considerable power and had played central roles—as senior lawyers, accountants, managers, journalists, doctors, or teachers—in framing other people's lives. Their husbands occupy powerful positions and control highly valued resources in their organizations and in society more broadly. Studying how these privileged men and women operate within, help sustain, and occasionally resist powerful institutions in contemporary capitalism—in particular, the family and the workplace—is critical in order to better understand these institutions and, crucially, how to change them. As American anthropologist Laura Nader (the first woman hired on tenure track at the University of California, Berkeley, Department of Anthropology) wrote in 1972 about "studying up," studying how powerful institutions work provides necessary information that generates feelings of indignation—an animating force of critical feminist research.[66]

Second, Lamont notes that the mass media and the advertising industry (and also, as I will show, policy discourse) offer upper-middle-class culture as a model to members of other classes, who often try to emulate it or define their identities against it. Indeed, as various examples of media and policy representations discussed in the book demonstrate, the lives of middle-class and upper-middle-class stay-at-home mothers are often presented by media and policy discourses as a model for the rest of the population (although not entirely without ambivalence).

Third, sociologist Arlie Hochschild observes in her study of American two-job and mostly middle-class couples that if *these* people find it hard to juggle work and family, many others, "who earn less, work at less flexible, steady, or lucrative jobs, and rely on poorer day care—are likely to find it harder still."[67] The study on which this book is based raises a similar issue to which I return in the conclusion: if the educated and privileged women I interviewed were unable to resist the patriarchal institutions they encountered, if *they* struggled to articulate and act on their desires, what might this tell us about women who lack education and privilege?

But why study highly educated stay-at-home mothers who are a clear minority both socioeconomically and in terms of their employment path (given that the majority of mothers in post-industrial liberal societies are in paid employment)? Why focus on these extraordinarily privileged women? Friedan helpfully noted about the middle-class American women she studied in the 1950s that their "hunger" was such "that food cannot fill"; it was "not caused by lack of material advantages."[68] Drawing on Friedan, I argue that to suggest that because the women in this book are privileged and chose to be stay-at-home mothers they do not suffer any problems—or that their struggles are entirely of their own making and thus irrelevant to others—fails to recognize that oppression can be experienced *alongside* privilege, that choice and inequality are *not* mutually exclusive.[69]

The historical example of Judith Hubback is useful here. In 1936, Hubback graduated with first-class honors (the highest grade in the British education system) in history from the University of Cambridge. She later married senior civil servant David Hubback, whose rewarding work she envied, and became a frustrated housewife and mother to their three kids. In 1957 (six years before publication of Friedan's *Feminine Mystique*) Judith Hubback published *Wives Who Went to College*, drawing on a survey she conducted of 2,000 women graduates. The book explored the derailment of the hopes that these full-of-potential, privileged women had had for emancipation, independence, and equality. Like Hubback herself, the majority of the women whom she studied bitterly regretted the waste of their potential. *Wives Who Went to College* "stirred up a hornets' nest in the press"[70] and led Judith Hubback to pursue a new career as an analytical psychologist. However, her husband, David Hubback, was unsympathetic: "How could she possibly be depressed when she had a good husband, a good home and three nice children, all doing well at school? Complaining in these circumstances was pure self-indulgence."[71]

Rather than lamenting the circumstances of educated women who left paid employment and became full-time mothers, this book seeks to expose the contradictions, ambivalences, and forms of oppression that these women experience *within* their privileged lives. Dismissing or marginalizing the importance of these forms of subjection because these women are privileged and have made a non-normative choice echoes David Hubback's voice and constitutes a failure to recognize that choices are always made within constraints.[72]

Hence, while the experiences of the women and men I interviewed are to an extent unique—indeed, living in a single-income family is unaffordable for most of the population—they simultaneously expose and resemble major challenges faced by educated women and their partners in post-industrial liberal democracies. To paraphrase Richard Sennett and Jonathan Cobb's observation about the American working men they studied in the 1970s,[73] the story that the women I interviewed have to tell is not just about who *they* are but also about what the contradictory messages, pressures, and experiences of "aspirational" women in their generation are. Therefore, the question of the representativeness of the sample of the women I interviewed is not whether other women's experiences replicate theirs, but rather how the lives of the women I study present "focused points of human experience that can teach something about a more general problem" [74] of women, work, and family. Understanding these women's choices and lived experiences and situating them in the context of the cultural landscape of gender, work, and family, spotlight central fault lines of the unequal structures that condition women's experience of work and family in advanced capitalist societies. In other words, as a woman, one does not necessarily have to be "headed home" in order to be interested in and/or identify with the issues raised by the accounts of the women in this book; they distill some of the pivotal facets of the broader crises of gender, work, and family in contemporary capitalism.[75]

THE WOMEN AND MEN WHOSE STORIES APPEAR IN THIS BOOK

It was challenging to find enough women willing to speak with me who had left paid employment after having children. There is not a clear institutional context, such as the workplace, from which to identify these women. Thus, looking for interviewees involved posting notes on various parents' mailing lists in schools in middle-class/upper-middle-class neighborhoods in London, on various London social media mothers' groups where there were likely to be a high concentration of highly educated mothers, and on notice boards in local libraries, community centers, and leisure/sport clubs in these neighborhoods.

I conducted thirty-five in-depth interviews with women who live in London and who had left paid employment between three and seventeen years earlier, eight being the average number of years outside the workforce. All except one were highly educated, and all had been professionals in a variety of sectors and at various levels of seniority: lawyers, accountants, teachers, deputy head teachers, artists, fashion designers, journalists, media producers, engineers, medical doctors, academics, social workers, and managers. I interviewed women across an age spectrum, though most were in their early forties; the youngest interviewee was thirty-five and the oldest fifty-one. They had between one and four children, aged two to twenty. The majority were white; three were mixed race and one was black. All interviewees were heterosexual and described their intimate lives and views as subscribing to heteronormative notions of family, parenting, and relationships. Most interviewees were British, but just over a quarter (ten) were immigrants who had moved to London in pursuit of professional and creative opportunities, often following their husbands' work relocation. They include six Europeans, three Americans, and a woman from Latin America. Apart from two divorced women, all were married to men who could financially support their staying at home—most interviewees' husbands were senior lawyers, bankers, financial directors, or senior managers in technology and media firms (appendix 1 lists the participants by key characteristics).

I also interviewed five male partners or husbands of women who were professionals turned stay-at-home mothers; however, none of these men were the husbands or partners of my women interviewees. I believe that the candor of the women I interviewed stemmed in part from knowing that I would *not* be talking to their husbands. The five men interviewed were all white, in their mid- to late forties, and in senior positions in technology and financial firms. I had hoped to interview more men, but accessing them proved difficult. Even those I accessed through friends and acquaintances were often "flaky" and would not commit to meeting me regardless of persistent attempts to arrange an interview. Despite the small number of men interviewees, I wove insights from these five interviews into the discussion to elucidate various aspects, such as their work routines and household division of labor, and show where they differed from or converged with the perspectives of women interviewees, and how they related (or not) to media and policy accounts. In particular, at various places throughout the book I gesture toward the husbands' sense of anger and resentfulness at what they depict as their wives' easy life—a broader theme that came up in my interviews with both men and women. However, since I interviewed only five men (compared to thirty-five women), and since the husbands' voices are mediated largely through the women's accounts, claims about what these men feel and how they think need to be carefully qualified. Fundamentally, the focus of this book is purposefully and centrally on women's accounts.

The interviews

Following Scott's critique discussed earlier, and sociologist Les Back's discussion of the interview as a sociological method rather than a resource to understand the nature of society or a tool to "give voice" to my subjects, I see the interview as a place where people make judgments and use tools as they attempt to make sense of their place within society.[76] I wanted to listen to the voices of women who had left paid employment not in order to gain access to some unmediated or authentic truth but to understand how they *accounted for* the decision to quit their job and the consequences of this decision for their lives and identities. I also wanted to explore what symbolic resources, judgments, and tools they appropriated and employed in seeking to make sense of their experiences.

Around half of the women invited me to meet them in their homes; the rest preferred to meet in coffee shops or other public places in the vicinity of their homes. Visiting women's homes provided invaluable insights into their lives as mothers, wives, and heads of the home—roles I explore in chapters 3 and 4. Most interviews were held during the day when the children were at nursery and/or school and the women's partners were at work, which allowed the women to speak openly and with little or no interruption. The interviews in coffee shops, and in one case in a community center, were more difficult because of noise, disruptions, and lack of privacy. Paradoxically, however, most of the interviewees I met outside their homes were extremely open, candid, and often emotional. Tears were frequent throughout the interviews; being away from the space of the home, the locus of unequal labor and many of the things women struggled with in their daily lives, seemed to afford them temporary respite and a space for emotional release and self-reflection. Indeed, at the end of the interviews, many said that it felt like therapy, and some voluntarily asked if they could suggest that friends, who were also stay-at-home mothers, contact me in order to be interviewed. About a third of the women emailed me later to say that the interview had caused them to reflect on their lives and futures in ways they had not felt able to before: "It's amazing what happens when the floodgates are allowed to open!" wrote one woman.

The objective of these interviews, which lasted between 90 and 150 minutes, was to explore these women's life trajectories and the factors that had influenced their decisions to leave their jobs. I wanted to allow my interviewees the space and time to describe what they considered most central, important, and/or difficult in their lives. Thus, I used open-ended questions to give my interviewees room to interpret them in the ways they felt were most meaningful and appropriate for them, and to enable as nuanced an understanding of their worldviews as possible (for more details, see appendix 3).

I was aware that because I had pursued a different path—working in full-time employment while raising children—I might unintentionally come across as judgmental of these women's choices, and that, as a consequence, the interview encounter could generate defensiveness, tensions, and antagonism. I do not deny that the context in which the interviews were arranged, the expectations of my interviewees, and our different work and family paths all had a bearing on the accounts the women gave.

Overall, however, I was immensely impressed and gratified by the ease, comfort, and honesty of the women's narratives. They articulated remarkably rich, reflective, and frank accounts; mostly I just had to listen.

The interviews were audiotaped and transcribed verbatim, including pauses, laughter, and word repetitions, all of which proved especially important in revealing interviewees' emotions and moments where discourse seemed to fail them. Details that might identify interviewees have either been removed or changed (for instance, names of firms or names of neighborhoods in London) to ensure confidentiality and anonymity.

JUXTAPOSING WOMEN'S LIVED EXPERIENCE AGAINST MEDIA AND POLICY REPRESENTATIONS

In the following chapters I focus on specific women's accounts, often going into some detail in order to contextualize and situate their stories as appropriately as possible. I made every effort to treat these accounts with sensitivity, empathy, and care. Yet I also tried to explain their experiences in ways that I felt they denied or could not express, to illuminate issues they never discussed in order to make sense of those they did. My analysis in no way constitutes a judgment or critique of the individuals whose stories I relate, but rather endeavors to provide an account of the conditions and contexts that have shaped these women's lives and stories. I seek to elucidate the connections and conflicts, the congruences and incongruences between their experiences and wider cultural and policy narratives and discourses.

In looking at media and policy representations of women, family, and work, my purpose was not to produce an exhaustive picture of the cultural terrain within which the subjectivities and experiences of the women I studied are situated. Rather, I wanted to produce a selective account of the cultural and policy representations that have a bearing on these women's lives. Thus, my objective has been to identify *illustrative examples* of media and policy representations and discourses (see appendix 2) that resonate with and/or are in tension with the accounts of these women's lived experience. By *cultural and media representations*, I refer to narratives and images that circulate in the contemporary media sphere, including magazines, film, popular fiction, self-help/guide books, celebrity, advertising, social media, and popular academic accounts. By *policy representations*, I refer to government policy reports, speeches, and announcements, and corporate and nongovernmental organizations' policy reports and papers, such as reports on gender equality policies in the workplace. In some instances, references are made to political discourse, for example, a political leader's speech. When such mentions are made, they are always related to policy discussions. In appendix 3, I provide additional details about the interviewee sample, how the interviews were conducted and analyzed, as well as how I devised the sample of media and policy representations and how they were analyzed, so as to juxtapose them against the interviewees' accounts.

When I began this study, I had felt that there was something quite significant that distinguished me from the women I interviewed. However, as I concluded the research, I came to appreciate both the differences *and* the pivotal commonalities and continuities between our experiences as well as our capacity to account for and transform them. It is for this reason that I deliberately avoid using the terms "working mothers" and "nonworking mothers," referring instead to women who are in or outside paid employment. The accounts of the women I interviewed highlight the huge amount of labor they perform, corroborating feminists' long struggle against the consistent devaluation of domestic, reproductive, emotional, and maternal labor, and the normalization of women's unpaid domestic labor.[77] If, as this book shows, discourse shapes identities and experiences in significant ways, then the terms we use matter a great deal.

OVERVIEW OF THE BOOK

Each of the following chapters is framed around a disjunction between a central aspect or trope of *representations* of gender, family, and work, and women's accounts of their *experience* of these aspects. This juxtaposition is signified by the chapters' titles, which are divided by a slash: the first part refers to the trope of cultural and policy representations, while the second part (after the slash) refers to a central aspect of women's experience. While each chapter centers on a particular theme, the chapters' different themes often overlap and are interconnected in both women's accounts and media and policy representations. For instance, chapter 2 explores how the "balanced woman" operates as a cultural ideal through which women read their own failure as personal pathology, notwithstanding the fact that their failure to be that "balanced woman" is due in large part to the deep forms of inequality in the home and their daily married life. The theme of inequality in the home is revisited in chapter 4, where women's experiences of wifehood are juxtaposed against the hypervisibility of motherhood in popular culture and policy discourses. Given these close and complex connections between the chapters' themes, in some instances I discuss the same media or policy example and/or the same interview account in more than one chapter. Additionally, central cultural points of reference, such as Sheryl Sandberg's influential book *Lean In* (which was mentioned by interviewees), appear in more than one chapter but are used to discuss different issues.

Part I, *Heading Home: Forced Choices* (chapters 1 and 2), focuses on women's leaving their careers: How do they and their partners account for this "choice" in a cultural and policy climate that encourages women to stay in the workforce after having children? Why did they fail to live up to the expectation that women should combine successful economic activity with being a "good mother"? How did they negotiate their decision *vis-à-vis* the demand to be a "balanced woman"?

Part II, *Heading the Home: The Personal Consequences of Forced Choices* (chapters 3 and 4), then looks at how, as a consequence of heading home, women have become *heads of their homes*, running their families as small enterprises. The discussion explores what women's lives look like in their roles as stay-at-home mothers, and how they negotiate their reinvented identities as full-time mothers, and crucially as wives, amid conflicting cultural messages about family, gender, and work.

In part III, *Heading Where? Curbed Desires* (chapters 5 and 6), I examine the future lives that these women envision for themselves and their children, and show how their desires and fantasies about their future selves and their children's futures are vague and inarticulate, an elusiveness that is animated by dominant contemporary narratives about the future of work and gender equality. In the conclusion, I reflect on how the disjunctions discussed in the book reveal what I describe, following Lauren Berlant,[78] as the cruel optimism of the contemporary imaginary of women, work, and family. This imaginary ignites a sense of possibility and inveigles these women into desiring the promises it holds out, while simultaneously impeding their addressing and challenging the very structural issues that obstruct their ability to realize their desires.[79] Crucially, it privatizes and individualizes women's "problems" and their solutions: despite women's clear identification of the various structural factors that affected their decision to quit their jobs, they continue to attribute their decision, which is fraught with ambivalence and pain, to personal failure whose source and remedy are to be found in the self.

I end by discussing the continuous and concerted hushing of disappointment and rage in the lives of the women I interviewed. I look at some of the structural conditions, specifically in the workplace and the family, as well as the necessary changes in cultural and policy representations that could help unmute these women's disappointment. Contra to popular calls for women to transform their feelings, states of mind, and behavior on the path to gender equality, the call emerging from the stories of the women in this book is for reinventing the social structures of inequality that condition their subjectivities.

PART 1

Heading Home
Forced Choices

CHAPTER 1

Choice and Confidence Culture/ Toxic Work Culture

At the age of twenty-two, after graduating in Russian studies and politics from one of the United Kingdom's leading universities, Louise got her first job as marketing manager in the UK headquarters of a Danish firm. The firm was quick to appreciate its bright, talented, ambitious, and fluent Russian-speaking new employee and, a few months into her job, Louise was promoted to manager of the firm's operations in Russia. The job involved extensive international travel and a two-year relocation, which Louise "enjoyed very much: it was very active, it was very challenging, it was very rewarding, on all fronts." For twelve years the company was like her "own family." "Scandinavian organizations are generally very progressive, very forward thinking," she told me. After reminiscing about this satisfying chapter of her life as a young professional woman during the late 1990s and early 2000s, Louise paused. "This was obviously [pause], not necessarily obvious, but it was before my daughter came along," she said.

Louise's pause and subsequent withdrawal of her initial statement, that enjoying a rewarding career was "obvious" so long as she did not have children, points to a deep contradiction. She had experienced the satisfactions, sense of empowerment, and independence that the "girl power" discourses and the "new sexual contract" had promised educated women in the West since the late 1980s.[1] Louise's generation of women were encouraged to achieve at school, at university, and in the world of work and to expect the norms of gender equality to prevail in each of these spheres.

The "new sexual contract," which rests on combining motherhood and successful career, was the hegemonic "obvious" contract to subscribe to. Therefore, it appeared obvious to Louise that—unlike her mother, a working-class woman who raised six children and never engaged in any form of paid employment—she *could* and *should* continue enjoying a financially and personally rewarding career after having children. Yet for Louise and other women like her, the alluring "new sexual contract" proved far from obvious in practice. Women of her generation "realized that it was totally ridiculous . . . [and] completely untenable," Louise reflected with deep disappointment.

The contradiction between the dictate of the "new sexual contract" to happily combine motherhood and a successful career and the failure to practice it is a contradiction between representation and experience. Like Louise, most of the women I interviewed experienced a stark discrepancy between their lived experience and the cultural, political, and policy messages to which they were exposed as young women in the late 1980s and 1990s, and in their later lives. In particular, women's accounts of their experience strongly challenged two key and related ideas in cultural and policy constructions of women, family, and work: choice and confidence. However, as I will show in this chapter and throughout the book, this disjunction between experience and representation has not led these women to reject the ideals to which they tried but failed to conform. Rather, the choice paradigm and the imaginary of what I will describe as the "confidence culture" have provided an enormously powerful framework for making sense of their experience. They struggle to justify their experience outside of and against the narratives of choice, ambition, and confidence.

THE CHOICE PARADIGM AND CONFIDENCE CULTURE

Since the 1980s, images of empowered women who juggle thriving careers with motherhood have largely replaced the image of the happy housewife that populated 1950s and 1960s American and British magazines, advertisements, advice books, newspapers, and television programs. The new images broke away from the rigid feminine mystique that marked previous eras in that they challenged the feminine postwar ideal role of the wife-and-mother whose good mothering was predicated on the fundamental prohibitions of sexuality and of work outside the home.[2] The "supermom" who effortlessly combines motherhood and career was the quintessential image of the late 1980s cultural landscape. Sociologist Arlie Hochschild describes her characteristics: "She has that working-mother look as she strides forward, briefcase in one hand, smiling child in the other. Literally and figuratively, she is moving ahead . . . She is confident, active, 'liberated.' She has made it in a man's world without sacrificing her femininity. And she has done this on her own."[3]

The child and the briefcase were the iconic symbols of the supermom in American popular culture. In *The Second Shift: Working Families and the Revolution at Home*, Hochschild describes the front cover of a September 1984 issue of the *New York Times Magazine*, featuring a young, good-looking, on-the-go working mother accompanied by her smiling daughter "as she lugs her mother's briefcase."[4] Similar images inhabited American and British women's magazines, the popular press, films, and advertisements throughout the 1980s and 1990s.[5] An illustrative example is a 1988 United Airlines commercial showing a briefcase-toting career mother dropping off her child at school, hopping on a plane and then dazzling her clients in a business meeting, and whooshing back in time to collect her child at the end of the day.[6] Such images of professional working mothers seemed both to reflect and reinforce a colossal historical change that has taken place since the 1970s, and most dramatically between the 1980s and the late 1990s, namely the substantial surge in—especially middle-class—women's employment in the workforce.[7] Thus, both representations and women's experience over the past decades seem to tell the same story: women now can make the choice their mothers' generation fought so hard for them to have, that is, to be good mothers *and* successful workers.

Ideas of personal freedom, choice, individualism, and agency increasingly animate the debate on and construction of women, family, and work. These notions more broadly have been central to the feminist movement and its political claims, and are tied to "a classic American belief that we are independent, free, and autonomous; that we have choices and choose among our options freely; and that as a result, we ourselves are solely responsible for the results."[8] However, as sociologist Shelley Budgeon observes, while second wave feminism focused on the constraints women faced in making free choices, from the 1990s onward, feminist politics have been reoriented toward what has come to be known as "choice feminism."[9]

One of the defining features of choice feminism, Budgeon writes, is "the notion that structural factors which once systematically ordered social relations to the detriment of women have now been largely overcome ... This implies that any differences which remain in the lives of women and men can be accounted for by choices knowingly made by individuals."[10] Thus, the fundamental aim of choice feminism is to celebrate and validate the individual choices of individual women.

The idea of choice feminism and the emphasis on individual responsibility gained particular currency in emerging postfeminist media discourses in the 1990s. Embracing feminist goals of gender equality, these discourses "present[ed] women as autonomous agents no longer constrained by inequalities or power imbalances whatsoever."[11] Feminist scholar Rosalind Gill demonstrates this construction in a range of Anglo-American media, from newspapers to advertising, talk shows, chick-lit, and popular fiction. Gill notes the striking degree of fit between the postfeminist discourses that have emerged since the 1990s that cast women as autonomous, freely choosing individuals, and the psychological subject demanded by neoliberalism—an entrepreneurial actor who is rational, calculating, and self-regulating. At the heart of both postfeminism and neoliberalism, Gill writes, "is the notion of the 'choice biography' and the contemporary injunction to render one's life knowable and meaningful through a narrative of free choice and autonomy—however constrained one might actually be."[12]

Thus, unlike the choiceless "captive wife" of the 1950s and 1960s,[13] the late 1980s and 1990s modern woman faced demands to make active choices in the various spheres of her life and, pertinently, in relation to family and work. British sociologist Catherine Hakim describes this in terms of a preference theory.[14] Hakim claims that discussion of women's paid work and family responsibilities focuses on what women are expected to do and are prevented from doing but fails to consider their preferences. She argues that in societies where genuine choices are open to women, the key driver of how work is divided is lifestyle preference. Women in these societies fall into three categories: work-centered, home-centered, or wanting to combine paid work and family (adaptive). Thus, for Hakim, women quitting their careers clearly make a preference-based, personal choice of a traditionalist home-centered lifestyle.

Notions of flexibility and work-life balance, which suffuse policy and media discussions of women and work (explored in Chapter 2), reinforce an emphasis on choice as compatible with feminist goals. "Mommy track" is a particularly popular term, especially in US public discourse, to refer to women's ability to choose to switch from time-intensive careers, either by scaling down into a flexible, balanced model that combines family and career (but necessarily sacrifices career advancement), or by opting out altogether to look after their children. While choosing to leave professional careers is often imbued with negative connotations, this decision is depicted mostly as a woman's personal choice whose consequences are private and personal, with little mention of the barriers, constraints, regrets, or broader social implications[15]—issues we examine in chapter 3. In short, unlike the historical housewife, the decisions of both the contemporary employed mothers and stay-at-home mothers are couched in terms of choice and female liberation.[16]

However, the 1980s and 1990s images of happy career mothers who "chose to have it all" concealed the difficult conflicts "and the huge, hidden emotional cost to women, men, and children of having to manage inequality."[17] They celebrated empowered women liberated by realizing their career dreams, but they neglected to address enduring inequalities at home, in the workplace, and in society at large—the very inequalities that stalled the revolution, as Hochschild famously argued.

In the twenty-first century, more complicated representations of motherhood and work gradually have emerged, partly as a response to critiques of the mismatch between such idealized images and women's and families' lived realities. The images that Louise and other women I interviewed had in mind are radically different from the postwar feminine mystique of "occupation: housewife," which reigned during their mothers' time in the 1960s and 1970s.[18] Nor are they similar to the late 1980s supermom images to which the women Hochschild interviewed related. Though neither the happy housewife nor the supermom has disappeared from the public imagination, in the second decade of the twenty-first century, other types of feminine ideals seem to have gained currency.

In particular, the notion that a woman can freely choose tracks based on her personal preferences and enjoy a flexible career and motherhood as she likes has come under increasing attack. A 2012 *Atlantic* article by American foreign policy expert Anne-Marie Slaughter, entitled "Why Women Still Can't Have It All," was formative in articulating this attack. Slaughter used her personal story (she decided to leave her workplace, the US State

Department, at the end of two years in office as the first woman director of policy planning) to elucidate the enduring obstacles professional mothers face in US workplace culture, which favors professional advancement over family. The essay garnered immense attention, controversy, and critique. It signaled the urgency of an honest debate to confront the structural barriers—specifically the social norms surrounding notions of success and inflexible workplaces—that stand in women's way to the top. Slaughter exposed the fictitiousness of the rhetoric of choice and called for an end to blaming women for failing to make and manage the right choices. Unless workplace norms and conceptions of successful career trajectories are radically transformed, Slaughter argued, we are likely to see ambitious women opting out of the fast track in larger numbers than men.

The following year saw the publication of a book that soon topped bestseller lists in both the United States and Europe, and injected the debate on women, family, and work with a revived energy. In *Lean In: Women, Work, and the Will to Lead*, Facebook's chief operations officer (COO) Sheryl Sandberg draws extensively on her personal experience as a successful professional woman and mother, to spotlight the "external barriers erected by society"[19] impeding women's success and progress in the workplace. In a confessional fashion similar to Slaughter's, she describes the insecurities, vulnerabilities, and challenges she faced as she made her way to the top in the corporate world. Relying heavily on psychological studies, Sandberg encourages a more open and honest conversation about workplaces' inflexibility, social norms, and entrenched different definitions of success and good management in relation to women and men. Sandberg highlights that "personal choices are not always as personal as they appear"[20] and goes some way toward exposing how women's work and family decisions are influenced by social scripts, pressures, familial expectations, and workplace norms.

Slaughter and Sandberg embrace and, to a large extent, represent women's freedom to choose to combine a successful career and motherhood. However, one aspect that distinguishes them significantly from the 1980s supermom is that they openly confront the tensions and costs of making this choice, and demonstrate how these obstacles can be overcome or, at least, substantially reduced. They promote a move away from idealized images of supermoms having it all to a more self-reflexive discussion that deliberately punctures the myth of having it all, and acknowledges that women's choices in relation to work and family are never completely free, autonomous, and theirs alone. They call for some changes at the structural, societal, and cultural levels, including the need to challenge gender stereotypes and develop alternative images of female success, and to design and implement organizational changes aimed at enhancing gender "diversity" (the term favored over "equality") in the workplace.[21]

However, notwithstanding this more honest, reflexive, and critical discussion, which acknowledges the influence of structural forces and the urgency of challenging them, the emphasis is still largely on women's onus to change themselves. So, for example, while *Lean In* identifies some changes needed in the workplace, it eschews tackling issues such as the absence of paid maternity leave for women in the United States, the need for employer-based childcare, or the extremely long hours demanded in order to survive—let alone progress and succeed—in the corporate workplace.[22] Rather, Sandberg centers on ways in which women themselves can challenge the big, complex structures and learn to "undistort the distortion."[23] She cajoles women to defy the "barriers that exist within themselves"[24] by working on their selves and monitoring their feelings, thoughts, and behaviors. Similarly, authors of self-help and business bestsellers such as *The Confidence Code* and *Getting to 50/50* state that while there is some truth behind concerns about sexism and institutional barriers aligned against women, the "more profound" issue is women's "lack of self-belief."[25] Even Slaughter, who in her 2015 book *Unfinished Business: Women, Men, Work, Family* distances herself from the (especially American) preoccupation with self-help and insists that it is not enough to tell women they need ambition and confidence, devotes a considerable part of her book to "turning the spotlight on ourselves,"[26] by which she means exclusively women. *Unfinished Business* is replete with instrumental do-it-yourself-type advice to women about how to change their talk, behavior, and self-expectations. Slaughter even calls upon women to take advice from "Let It Go," the theme song of the Disney children's movie *Frozen*, and let go of the suffocating expectations about how they should behave as workers, wives, and mothers.

The central premise of these current discussions and representations is that there is a crisis that is peculiar to women, namely self-doubt and an "ambition gap" that holds them back in public and professional working life (the latter understood primarily as the corporate workplace). Women's self-confidence and persistent ambition are seen as key to resolving the crisis and to realizing the project of gender equality at work and in public life. This message, which can be found in realms such as education, public health, finance, consumer culture, body image, and well-being, is embedded within a broader set of knowledges, apparatuses, and incitements addressed to women in the early twenty-first century, which Rosalind Gill and I call the "confidence cult(ure)."[27] The confidence culture circulates and materializes in a wide variety of media and cultural sites:

> Women's magazines celebrate a "confidence revolution," beauty brands hire "confidence ambassadors," and one can now even buy a "confidence mirror" from furniture store IKEA that will pay "compliments" and offer "inspirational" confidence messages [. . .] Academics and think tanks, politicians and newspaper columnists, call on women to recognise that they are being held back not by patriarchal capitalism or institutionalised sexism, but by their own lack of confidence [. . .] leadership programmes, mentoring, email add-ons such as Google's "Just Not Sorry" [. . .] promote the use of more confident language, and an ever-growing range of confidence apps designed to boost women's self-esteem and sense of personal efficacy.[28]

Firmly situated within the self-help and advice culture, a plethora of books, reports, blogs, training programs, experts, videos, hashtags, apps, advertisements, and television programs are invested in establishing women's lack of confidence as the fundamental obstacle to women's success, achievement, and happiness. They urge women to turn inward and—through individual, psychological self-work and self-monitoring—improve and strengthen their confidence and ambition as the ultimate solution.[29]

One of the all-time most viewed TED Talks offers a vivid example of this injunction. In "Your Body Language Shapes Who You Are," Harvard Business School social psychologist Amy Cuddy lays out her "power posing" theory. While she addresses both men and women, she explains that women in particular "often shrink in public settings," tend to touch their face or neck, or cross their ankles tightly when seated.[30] Such postures and gestures (which strikingly echo those Ervin Goffman identified in his well-known 1976 study of advertising's depiction of stereotypical gender roles),[31] are associated with powerlessness and constrain people from expressing who they really are, argues Cuddy.[32] Thus, she exhorts women to practice power poses daily, advice she accompanies with an image of Wonder Woman in her famous pose of hands on hips and feet wide apart, staring confidently forward. In similar fashion to the authors of *Lean In* and *The Confidence Code*, Cuddy compels women to "fake it till you make it" and ultimately, "till you become it." Faking self-confidence is recommended as necessary for women's advancement in the workplace.

Similar messages and constructions circulate in popular culture. On the one hand, more complex depictions of mothers who are professional workers proliferate—with characters such as Birgitte Nyborg, the Danish prime minister in the television series *Borgen*, Mackenzie Allen, the first female US president in ABC's drama *Commander-in-Chief*, and lawyer Alicia Florrick, lead character in CBS's show *The Good Wife*. On the other hand, in these and various other recent shows, mothers' professional success is depicted as depending significantly on their individual self-confidence, inner ambition, and ability to "lean in." Take, for example, *The Good Wife*. As its title suggests and as explained by its creators, the show seeks to un-silence the wife mutely standing beside her public figure husband as he apologizes for scandalous misconduct. Through its depiction of its lead character Alicia Florrick, the drama probes the myth of the woman who has it all and exposes aspects of the difficulty of striking a balance between competitive long-hours work and family life (an issue we look at in more detail in chapter 2). Her demanding job causes her to miss out on her children's experiences, including serious matters like her son's girlfriend's abortion, which she discovers only months later. Alicia's relationship with her children involves tensions, secrets, and disappointments but is simultaneously strong and intimate. Her maternal commitments at times affect her work performance: she sometimes misses important meetings because of attending to her children's issues and is criticized in her peer review for her "leisurely hours." These difficulties are compounded by the struggles in her collapsing marriage and her consequent yearning for romance and love outside her marital relationship.[33]

At the same time, ambition, assertiveness, and confidence allow Alicia seamlessly to reinvent herself from a submissive stay-at-home mother and wife—a role she performed for thirteen years—to a successful lawyer in the prestigious, bustling, dynamic American law firm, Lockhart/Gardner. Her wardrobe is ever-changing; she always looks beautiful and glamorous, but the extensive labor and expense involved in achieving this immaculate appearance are never shown or discussed.[34] Alicia is constantly busy and on the move—striding out as she enters the courtroom or the office, dressed in power outfits and striking all the Cuddy-recommended power poses. With every episode, she becomes more confident, outspoken, assertive, and determined to "kick ass," a phrase she uses repeatedly. She is extremely ambitious, taking on several, often very difficult cases simultaneously, and is unafraid of challenging both her legal opponents and judges—behavior that is rewarded by success, recognition, and promotion, ultimately leading her to found her own firm and then run for state's attorney. From time to time, she has moments of self-doubt about being a good lawyer and a good mother, but she quickly sloughs them off and "leans in."[35]

Policy discourses appropriate a very similar language and reinforce a similar emphasis. On the one hand, there is increasing discussion at both the workplace and national policy levels about issues such as sexism, institutional barriers aligned against women, the gender pay gap, paternal leave, and childcare. On the other hand, many of the proffered solutions focus on changing women's psyches and behavior, specifically by manufacturing self-confidence and fostering their leadership ambitions. For example, a report by Klynveld Peat Marwick Goerdeler (KPMG), a firm widely recognized for its innovative approach to gender diversity,[36] identifies boosting women's confidence in the workplace as top priority for businesses, through confidence-building, leadership, and performance reward programs, networking opportunities, and encouragement from role models.[37] Adopting Sandberg's language, KPMG recommends the provision of mentoring so women learn to "lean in and look beyond the immediate challenges of combining parenthood and career."[38] Similarly, the global consultancy firm McKinsey, another often-praised champion of innovative and progressive gender diversity programs, explains in one of its reports that what distinguishes women who have successfully entered leadership ranks is "their *strong belief* that they are making a difference, their *ability to turn adversity into learning opportunities*, their *persistence* in building relationships with sponsors and others, their *willingness to step outside their comfort zone*, and the *positive energy* that comes with loving their work."[39] Though the McKinsey report admits that cultural factors play an important role, ultimately, it argues, a woman's success and progression in the workplace are down largely to the woman's individual choice, inner drive, ambition, and determination.

European and UK gender equality policies also appear to be concerned about the problem of women's lack of confidence and seeking solutions to resolve it. For example, in 2015, the European Parliament Committee on Women's Rights and Gender Equality commissioned a study exploring the barriers and discriminatory effects hindering women's entrepreneurship, including access to finance in the European Union. One of the study's key findings was that levels of self-confidence and optimism, two factors claimed to substantially affect the ability to succeed as entrepreneurs, are considerably lacking in women in comparison to men.[40] Similarly, at the national policy level, in the United Kingdom, a 2013 white paper on women in leadership published by the Chartered Management Institute (CMI) stressed confidence as a crucial skill women needed to develop in order to "realise their potential."[41] Perhaps most remarkable was the French government's launch in 2014 of "Leadership Pour Elles," a smartphone app that aims to address the national gender wage gap by boosting women's self-confidence. Championed by the former French women's rights minister and later minister of education Najat Vallaud-Belkacem, the app invites women to take a self-assessment quiz. Based on their answers, it directs the women to the appropriate modules, simulators, and recommendations.

Media discussions of women's (lack of) confidence, and policies aimed at boosting their confidence and optimism, often draw on evidence from academic research, particularly business and management studies. Seeking to explain issues such as the poor representation of women on company boards, unequal progression of women and men in the workplace, and the "leaky pipeline" (a metaphor describing women's dropping out of science, technology, engineering, and mathematics [STEM] fields at all career stages), researchers find an answer in women's lack of confidence and the ambition gap between women and men. For instance, drawing on an analysis of data from a survey of economists in top US institutions by Initiative of Global Markets (IGM), economists Heather Sarsons and Guo Xu found that the problem of the gender gap lay in women being less confident than men. Sarsons and Xu argue that focusing on structural explanations for the "leaky pipeline"—such as motherhood penalty, everyday sexism in the workplace, and the old boys' network—leave "*a more fundamental question* aside," namely, "What if women behave intrinsically differently in competitive work environments?"[42] In similar vein, a Harvard Business School survey of 4,000 men and women found that men are driven by power in the workplace, while women have more life goals, but fewer are focused on power.[43] According to the researchers, "While women and men believe they are equally able to attain high-level leadership positions, men want that power more than women do."[44] The Harvard Business School researchers were not interested in asking why this is so. Their findings, they wrote, were "descriptive, not prescriptive"; they wanted to avoid making "value judgments about whether men and women's differing views of professional advancement are good or bad, rational or irrational, at any level of analysis."[45]

However, whether framing women's lack of confidence, ambition, and/ or optimism as a problem that has to be tackled, or stressing that women's aspirations, goals, desires, and self-esteem are inherently different from those of men, such studies, alongside policy and popular discourses, suggest that gender inequality in the public world of work is to do with *women as individuals.* They emphasize that both the problem of and solution to gender equality stem from women's personal choices, their innate preferences and goals, their attitudes and (poor) self-confidence, or their different understanding of power. So, while current debates on gender inequality recognize more than before that women's choices are influenced by structural, cultural, social, and economic obstacles, they simultaneously reproduce an individualized focus and revitalize notions of natural sexual difference. Thus, they reinforce "difference feminism"— a view that posits that "women really [are] more nurturing, more cooperative, more intuitive [and crucially] less competitive than men."[46]

TOXIC WORK CULTURES

The women I interviewed were at one level strikingly similar to the mediated—both real and fictional—characters I described in contemporary representations. They were lawyers, accountants, teachers, artists, designers, media producers, journalists, medical doctors, publishers, academics, and managers, with great professional ambition, self-confidence, and a strong sense of professional success. Many took considerable pleasure and pride in their professional accomplishments, in making progress at work, and in earning money. Some had been earning more than their male partners when they left the workplace. However, largely in contrast to these media and policy narratives, they were deeply disillusioned and disempowered by their attempts to combine motherhood with a high-powered career. The demanding long-hours work culture in which fictional characters such as *The Good Wife*'s Alicia Florrick or real women such as Facebook's COO Sheryl Sandberg and Yahoo's former chief operations/executive officer (CO/EO) Marissa Mayer seemed to thrive constituted one of the fundamental obstacles to my interviewees' ability and desire to continue their careers.

Tanya, a former law firm partner and now a stay-at-home mother of two children, describes her work experience before having children as very similar to that of mediated fictional and real characters—demanding, intense, all-consuming, with long hours. But it was also fun, interesting, rewarding, and "sexy":

> It was lots of fun . . . It's very sexy, there's lots going on . . . you're working in an environment that's in the news and it's great fun and lots of young people doing the same as you . . . You go to lots of events that are really interesting, you meet really interesting people and it was great. But it is a lot of pressure and it is a lot of work, and you have to work hard, but you don't mind that because everyone's doing that. And that's what you're used to, that's your life. I'd never leave work before eight or nine o'clock. I remember often, you'd be in until like midnight, and that was just normal.

However, the allure of these work cultures and norms dissipated dramatically after Tanya had children:

> Once you've got a life outside of that [work], you sort of take a step back and you realize that is a crazy way to live, and you can't live like that and be sane, and have a normal home life . . . There's lots of female partners at work who have two nannies, a day and a night nanny . . . so they'd see their kids at weekends or while they were asleep. I was just like: I really don't want to do that! There was a total mood shift from within me . . . And then at weekends you're exhausted. So then there'd be events that you

had to go to, which when you're twenty-eight, if someone says, "Would you like to go to a black tie event at a fancy place?" you go, "Yeah!" But when you want to go home and see your kids, or just go home, you just think, I can't think of anything worse. I've got to go home and get a dress on, I have to go and smile at people all night and make . . . and I've got to find a cab and get home, and you just have this sinking feeling of . . . that's not fun anymore.

Tanya's account of her work experience before having children as radically different from after having children, and the consequent "sinking feeling" she suffered, recurred in many of the interviews. Many of my women interviewees described similar feelings when they had to miss their child's school performance because of a work meeting, or came home late to find their young children already asleep. They experienced these feelings as difficult and unpleasant, yet as feelings that they *should* and *could* contain. The dominant message they were hearing—from family members, colleagues, friends, and professional women in the media speaking openly about experiencing similar feelings and offering strategies for coping with them—was that the difficult and painful feelings they experienced were legitimate, perhaps even inevitable, and that they needed to be worked on, controlled, and overcome.

Louise, with whose story I started this chapter, described how upon returning from maternity leave to her workplace, she had tried "really, really, really hard" for an entire year to manage working late hours. She had always been the ideal worker, who "gets on with stuff": efficient, rarely sick, focused, and always available. She truly wanted to continue getting on with stuff and not letting those sinking feelings interfere with her performance and satisfaction in her job: "I felt I needed to prove to myself that I could do it." She reflected:

I could see all these other women who worked late. Well, if they can do it, I can do it! [pause] . . . I felt a lot of pressure to conform to what these other women were doing. And I assumed they were seemingly happy with that situation, and their children were, I'm sure, thriving . . . I felt very strongly that I was expected to . . . conform to what the other women who had children were doing.

I asked Louise who were these "other women who worked late" and were "seemingly happy with that situation" of combining motherhood and working late hours. She struggled to answer: "Um, um, so . . . the women that work, yeah, I'm sure it's that . . . so, it's um . . . I'm trying to think now of who those women who work are."

Louise's stammered response and inability to recall particular examples of those other women is not atypical. Other interviewees also referred to that other woman who thrived as a professional mother, but when asked for a concrete example, often struggled to produce one. The other woman is a powerful fantasy produced and nourished by popular stories and images like those I discussed earlier. Crucially, it is a real enough fantasy to be believable, since it acknowledges the idealized perfections of previous fantasy figures—the 1960s happy housewife, the 1980s supermom—and appears to offer a more honest and authentic type of woman, in either the figure of real women like Sheryl Sandberg or fictional characters like Alicia Florrick who thrive on confronting their feelings and challenges. It is against such imaginary women that the women I interviewed often judgmentally compared and lambasted themselves.

This struggle might, of course, be read simply as a conflict in the individual personalities of women like Louise. Her strong feelings of needing to conform to those other exemplary women, and her struggle to cope with these feelings, might be the consequence of her psychological insecurities or, as Hakim would argue, her personal preference for a home-centered life. However, it would be more accurate to understand this struggle, which is experienced as private and personal, as a struggle produced, at least partly, by the contradictions between representation and experience. The stories of the women I interviewed were not just stories of who they are but stories of the contradictory expectations of women of their generation.[47]

So long as the clashes between family and work commitments, especially due to having to stay late hours at work, are neither consistent nor too frequent, so long as the childcare arrangements function relatively smoothly and the job continues to be satisfying and rewarding, these women clung on to living up to the "lean in" fantasy. They accepted and contained sinking feelings of distress, guilt, and loss, treating them as local, momentary, one-off feelings. However, the work cultures in which many of the women I interviewed participated were such that late hours and sleep deprivation were the norm, not the exception, and where commitment to career supposed that one never thought about, valued, or did anything else.[48] In *Unfinished Business*, Anne-Marie Slaughter calls it a toxic overwork culture, where working is continually in crisis mode, and the ideal worker is always on, always awake.[49] In such a work culture, isolated sinking feelings are impossible to continually suppress or regularly contain. The expectations of this workplace culture penetrated the women I met and became self-expectations; living up to these expectations became unbearable. Louise's sinking feeling became acute and constant: she fell into depression.[50]

After a year of ongoing "minor" incidents of having to stay late hours and work on weekends while caring for her young child, Louise reached a point where—although agonizing—she had to admit to herself and her workplace that she could not live up to the dictates and norms of her workplace and the confidence culture. "I can't live up . . . this is not what I expected. And this is not . . . I can't live up to . . . I can't," she stumbled. She arrived at this self-admission after an incident she described as the "heart meeting." When Louise's daughter was born she was diagnosed with a minor fault in her heart, which required Louise to take her child for monthly hospital checkups. As soon as these hospital appointments were scheduled, Louise would inform her boss—a mother of three who worked part-time—about the days and times she would have to leave work early. One of the hospital "heart meetings" happened to clash with an important work meeting, which Louise had to leave. She remembered she had "felt very conspicuous standing up and leaving in the middle of a . . . in the middle of a . . . in the middle of a meeting, which really I'd discussed [with my boss]." Later, in an appraisal meeting, her boss commented critically on her inappropriate and unprofessional conduct of leaving the meeting early. "To me that was a real shock," Louise recalled, "that she was so completely . . . I mean it wasn't a GP [general practitioner] appointment, it's a specialist heart meeting! Heart . . . heart . . . heart . . . consultant."

The heart meeting was a breaking point because it highlighted for Louise that she was no longer capable of being the ideal worker. "The ideal worker can jump on a plane whenever the boss asks because someone else is responsible for getting the kids off to school or attending the preschool play," writes feminist critic Joan Williams.[51] Louise recognized that she might have had the bad luck of having a particularly horrible boss (an idea popularized by movies such *Horrible Bosses*), but that the problem she fundamentally faced was cultural and organizational: "Everyone was kept on tenterhooks in that company." Louise's workplace conditions were utterly incompatible with family life (and perhaps with life more generally!). However, unlike the male heroes in *Horrible Bosses*, who plot to grind down their intolerable bosses, and unlike the many inspiring female figures who "made it" by learning how to play the corporate game deftly and to "lean in," Louise decided to quit her job. She concluded, "I took it *personally*. And to me that was incredibly difficult, because I'd been there for like twelve years and they were almost like my family. They were very . . . it was very difficult, but at the same time I really felt like the tables had turned on me so much, and um . . . and I didn't really have an option."

There is more and more evidence of the tables being turned on women, particularly mothers, in the modern workplace. Women continue to suffer the "motherhood penalty," and motherhood is now a greater predictor of wage inequality than gender.[52] The gains women make before having children (education, early career) dissipate once they become mothers. In the United Kingdom, 60,000 women a year lose their jobs because of pregnancy and maternity discrimination, a figure that does not account for women who suffer harassment, are demoted, overlooked for promotion, or lose contracts if they are self-employed.[53] In the United States, Pamela Stone's study of high-achieving women who graduated from Ivy League universities and quit their jobs after having children found that women's decisions to quit their job were forced by denials of requests to work part-time, the pay gap, and relocations.[54] Despite growing awareness of and debate about gender equality in the workplace, evidence repeatedly shows corporations hemorrhage talented women who reject lockstep career paths and question promotion systems that elevate the quantity of hours worked over the quality of the work being done.[55]

Like Louise, most of my interviewees were well aware of these systemic work culture issues from information they read and heard about and from their personal experience. They spoke about pay inequalities in their workplace, workplace norms that prioritize presence over quality and results—an approach commonly referred to as "presentism"—being excluded from significant and big projects as soon as they announced their pregnancy or soon after they returned from maternity leave, being required to relocate to another city or country in order to progress, and being refused requests to move to part-time work. Women's accounts also revealed the large extent to which their decision to quit was influenced by their husbands' high-powered, demanding, long-hours jobs—an aspect explored in chapter 2. Thus, women's accounts strongly challenge the mantra that leaving the workforce is a *choice* they made as a result of a personal preference and/ or lack of ambition, confidence, determination, and commitment to their careers. Rather, they reveal that these women's exit from the workforce was strongly influenced by a confluence of factors, key of which were their and their husbands' working hours and workplace conditions, which were deeply discordant with family life.

However, despite women's accounts of the huge influence of their and their husbands' work cultures on their decision to quit, they struggled to explain this decision outside of and against the individualized paradigm of choice, confidence, and ambition. Like Louise, many of the women I interviewed were able to provide a clear analysis of the impact of their workplace norms and cultures on their decision to leave, but at the same time, they made it *personal*. They explained to themselves and others that ultimately it was *they* who were not cut out for that type of ambitious, demanding job. "There's absolutely no judgment whatsoever, but for me it just wasn't right," Louise concluded somberly. Thus, media and policy representations that stress and celebrate confidence and choice failed to correspond with the lived experience of the women I interviewed, yet these women often judged their experience through these representations. The choice and confidence culture imaginary provided an enormously powerful framework for interpreting and judging their experience and for their subsequent self-denigration. Let me give two characteristic examples.

The first is that of forty-two-year-old Sara, who in the previous three years had been a stay-at-home mother of two, now aged four and six. At the start of our interview, Sara warned, "If I start to cry, I apologize. Stop [the recording] if I start to cry because I'm feeling a little sensitive talking about this." Sara quit her job after fifteen years as a financial director, first in an investment bank and later in a consulting firm. She used to work sixteen hours a day in an "unbelievably pressurized" environment where staying late, being always "on" and at your clients' and bosses' disposal, and having lunch at your desk were the norm. Ten years into her first job, in the aftermath of the 2008 financial crisis, the bank she worked for collapsed. "It was very stressful. We all picked up jobs very quickly because we were very cheap. They didn't have to buy us out of the share programs or anything. We were worthless," she recalls. Soon after the firm's collapse, like many of her colleagues, Sara had a nervous breakdown. She was on a two-month stress leave, after which she returned to work in another firm. "I was still working twelve-, thirteen-, fourteen-hour days, traveling all over the UK and partly Europe . . . Lots of early flights. You get up especially early, you might get home late, but at least you're there the following morning." She remembers the job as being stressful but satisfying, and a significant part of her former identity, which she still finds enormously difficult to withdraw from. "I found it satisfying: my client list, the amount of revenue that they were bringing into the company, winning a particular pitch." After the birth of her second child, Sara returned from maternity leave and asked to move to part-time, working four days a week. Her request was approved, "but the reality was my boss wanted me to be on call that [fifth] day. I needed to take calls, and I needed to be able to switch the days at his discretion. And I was only getting paid 80 percent and had a full-time nanny living with us." Her daughter was struggling at school, her husband (a banker) "never saw the kids," and Sara was "too tired and too stressed." Ultimately, "I just bit the bullet and quit. So obviously the levels of pressures and amount of stress were the main factor, or the only factor, to leave. I don't know if I didn't have kids whether I would have felt quite so pressured."

Sara's story is illustrative of the fundamental incompatibility of the toxic work cultures of two parents and family life, and its hugely painful impact on the woman's life. Her decision to leave the workforce was a bullet she had to bite and about which she has regrets; it was *not* a free choice based on her personal preferences. At the same time, notwithstanding her articulate account of the work culture and norms being the main or only factor causing her to leave, Sara resorted to personal explanations of the kind rehearsed in popular explanations of women's work- and family-related decisions. Toward the end of the interview she explained her decision to leave her job as due to her "personality type." In another part of the interview, Sara echoed popular ideas (expressed, for instance, in *The Confidence Code*) that it is women's perfectionism that paralyses their ambitions and stands in their way to success. "I was stepping over the threshold of perfectionism and just not being able to cope because you cannot provide the level of service that you feel you should be doing. So the reality was it made more sense for me to stop." Yet, in another moment, she explained that her decision to leave was due to the fact she no longer had "the huge ambition" that she had when she was twenty.

The experience of the women I spoke to often did not corroborate the notion that they lacked ambition or confidence and therefore quit their jobs, nor that quitting was a free choice they made willingly. Yet they justified and reconstructed this experience through the terms of the choice and confidence culture and its individualized and psychological language. The external barriers that the women faced and that pushed them out of the workplace were recast as internal barriers: I do not have the personality type of a professional mother, I suffer from perfectionism, I didn't have the ambition it takes.

A second example further illuminates the contradictory accounts women gave of their experience and how they drew on the ambition/confidence and choice discourses to reconstruct their experience and sense of self. Susan had studied medicine and begun training in clinical genetics, but abandoned her dream of becoming a geneticist and became a general practitioner (GP) in deference to her husband's demanding job in the financial sector. Following their relocation for his job to another country, she quit paid employment altogether and for the past eleven years had been a stay-at-home mother of three children. It was due largely to her husband's long-hours job that Susan left the workforce and has not returned to work. "He goes to work too early and comes back too late . . . we were always going to be driven by his job," she explained. Yet despite her clear account of the decisive influence of her husband's career on her work life, she repeatedly referred to herself as "never very ambitious." When I asked, "How come you're saying that you're not very ambitious, after studying for so many years, practicing medicine, and planning to become a clinical geneticist?" Susan replied:

> I think partly because that's what I [pause] . . . I mean, I think if I'd been really ambitious I wouldn't have given it up, really. But, yes, I suppose it is a bit contradictory. But [pause] . . . yes, it is a bit contradictory as well [laughter]. [Silence]. Yes, I think [pause], I think if I'd been really ambitious I would have, I would have . . . just said I wasn't going to go to take care [of the children] and I would have carried on, you know.

The many pauses, silences, incomplete sentences, and laughter in such a short quote capture the real struggle to articulate this experience outside of and against the "lean in" confidence/ambition narratives. Susan recognizes the contradiction between her big dream of becoming a clinical geneticist and her investment in making it happen, and the explanation she gives of her failure to realize it, namely lack of sufficient ambition. Yet she resolves or, rather, denies the contradiction by accepting the explanation that so many popular—including some academic—accounts promote: women are just not as ambitious as men. Rather than questioning the terms of the choice and confidence culture and why their lived experiences do not match these terms, women like Susan internalize these contradictions and blame themselves. The women I spoke to judged their experience through ideals and discourses that flew in the face of their lived experience. This sense-making strategy and its often painful consequences are further explored in chapter 2, by probing how the women account for their experience in relation to the work-life balance myth that dominates current discussions of gender, work, and family.

CHAPTER 2
The Balanced Woman/Unequal Homes

DICHTER'S BALANCED WOMAN

Advertisers, "the manipulators and their clients in American business," observed Betty Friedan in 1963, are a fundamental force in the creation, sustenance, and strengthening of the feminine mystique.[1] One of the masterminds of the "manipulation business" was Dr. Ernest Dichter, a pioneer of consumer market research, who in the mid-1940s directed the Institute for Motivational Research in Westchester, New York. Dichter saw the central role of advertising as giving the consumer the permission to "enjoy his [sic] life freely."[2] He believed that consumption, if properly channeled, became a form of therapy and self-realization. By conducting what he described as "depth" interviews, mostly with American housewives, Dichter and his motivational researchers sought to understand the deeper psychological needs that consumption served and how they could be exploited for consumer sale. "Properly manipulated," Dichter told Friedan when she visited his institute, "American housewives can be given the sense of identity, purpose, creativity, the self-realization, even the sexual joy they lack—by the buying of things."[3]

In 1945, studying the consumption of home appliances, Dichter conducted a survey of 4,500 middle-class, high school– and college-educated American housewives. Friedan observes: "It was a study of 'the psychology of housekeeping'; 'a woman's attitude toward housekeeping appliances cannot be separated from her attitudes toward homemaking in general,' [Dichter's report] warned."[4] The study classified American women into three categories, each representing a distinct psychological disposition. The first type (which according to Dichter matched 51 percent of women at the time) was the *true housewife*. She identified strongly with her role as guardian of the home, took the utmost pride and satisfaction in maintaining a comfortable and well-run home for her family, and reveled in domestic duties. At the opposite end of the spectrum was the *career woman* (or *would-be career woman*), who did not believe that a woman's primary place was in the home and considered "household chores as an inferior task in life."[5] She wanted independence and even if she lacked an actual career, she dreamed of one and felt bored and frustrated by housework. Neither of these two types of women was likely to be a receptive consumer of household goods, the study explained. The career woman was too critical and clearly unhealthy from the seller's standpoint, whereas the true housewife was committed to the doctrine of "do it yourself" and, thus, was reluctant to accept new devices.[6]

It was the third type, the *balanced woman*, who was the ideal consumer. She was the most fulfilled emotionally because she knew she was capable of both housework *and* career. She had a desire for creativeness, was interested in and engaged in some activities outside the domestic sphere ("in social action, in education, even in politics"),[7] and may have held a job before turning exclusively to housewifery. At the same time, she was committed to housekeeping and determined "to use her own executive ability 'in managing a well-run household.'"[8] The balanced woman was "becoming much more of a partner in the whole family operation,"[9] including areas and activities in which previously she was not interested or involved, such as operating and fixing household appliances or driving a car. "*The walls are going down in the homes*,"[10] Dichter noted. The new type of the modern balanced woman was a product of social, political, and economic transformations and the changing sexual division of labor and relations in postwar America. "In times of such deep insecurities," he wrote, men "don't want to marry a dear little creature who is just sweet and helpless"; rather, they want a confident and mature woman "who can be a partner."[11]

The balanced woman represented the market with the greatest potential because she could be enticed to be liberated from drudgery by trying some supposedly labor-saving products that would allegedly increase her free time, while at the same time playing on her guilt at not being a more dedicated homemaker and her desire to meld domesticity and creativity.[12] Dichter's study concluded with a clear message to advertisers and their clients:

> Make more and more women aware of the desirability of belonging to this [Balanced Woman] group. Educate them through advertising that it is possible to have outside interests and become alert to wider intellectual influence (without becoming a Career Woman). The art of good homemaking should be the goal of every normal woman.[13]

SLAUGHTER'S BALANCED WOMAN AND WORK-LIFE BALANCE IN POLICY DISCOURSE

Friedan vehemently attacked Dichter's motivational research and the business of hidden persuasion with its army of manipulators. She accused them of "persuading housewives to stay at home, mesmerized in front of a television set, their nonsexual human needs unnamed, unsatisfied, drained by the sexual sell into the buying of things."[14] Seven decades after Dichter's study, and more than half a century since publication of *The Feminine Mystique*, both the representations and the lives of women in developed countries have changed profoundly. The true housewife and the balanced woman no longer represent the ideal woman (though they may retain some force over the public imagination).[15] Since the late 1970s, new ideal feminine types have emerged. Most notably, the image of the career woman—the empowered, breezily confident "woman with the flying hair,"[16] carrying a baby in one hand and a briefcase in the other—has assumed center-stage in the Western cultural media landscape. The career women group, which back in the 1950s was a minority, is now the majority. In the United Kingdom, 70.2 percent of women between the ages of 16 and 64 are in employment (compared to 79.5 percent of men in the same age group), and in the United States, 56.7 percent of women participate in the labor force (compared to 69.1 percent of men in the same age group).[17]

However, these (relatively) upbeat figures obscure various enduring inequalities, including the high proportions of women in part-time, low-paid, precarious employment, persistent pay gaps between women and men, and low maternal employment rates compared to overall female employment rates. As noted in the introduction, while women's participation in the labor force has risen substantially over the past five decades, its beneficiaries mostly have been women in general rather than specifically mothers. Furthermore, mothers' labor participation rates are significantly lower than those of fathers. In the United Kingdom, 74.4 percent of married/cohabiting mothers are in employment compared to 92.6 percent of married/cohabiting fathers.[18] In the United States, 70.5 percent of mothers participate in the workforce, compared to 92.8 percent of fathers.[19] Similarly, the image of the career woman or supermom, which in the 1980s became the new normal, was an "upbeat cover for a grim reality."[20] Women were subject to the debilitating demand to live up to the expectations of both the public and private realms while keeping them separate and unchallenged.[21] Subsequently, as discussed in chapter 1, the cultural idea of the career woman and the image of the supermom who has it all came under fierce attack from scholars, policymakers, workplaces, and employees. Facebook COO Sheryl Sandberg's book *Lean In* popularized the call to challenge this idealized damaging image and "find a robust image of female success that is first, not male, and second, not a white woman on the phone, holding a crying baby." "Until we can get there," Sandberg warns, "women will continue to sacrifice being liked for being successful."[22]

Voices of popular feminist advocates of this kind represent a profound, if subtle shift toward a new conception of progress for white middle-class women in the West. They promote a new(ish) feminine ideal, namely the upwardly mobile woman crafting a felicitous equilibrium between work and family. Feminist researcher Catherine Rottenberg argues that earlier popular images of middle-class women in the public sphere, such as Ally McBeal in the American legal comedy-drama television series of the same name (1997–2002), or Carrie Bradshaw in HBO's popular television series *Sex and the City* (1998–2004), depicted them as liberated professionally and sexually, yet still longing for heterosexual love and marriage.[23] By contrast, the primary concerns of contemporary fictional characters, for example, Alicia Florrick in the television drama *The Good Wife*, Birgitte Nyberg in the drama *Borgen*, Kate Reddy in the novel *How Hard Can It Be?*, or real women such as businesswoman and mother of nine Helena Morrissey,[24] Sheryl

Sandberg, and Anne-Marie Slaughter "revolve around whether they will be able to negotiate the two spheres of their lives successfully."[25] The quest of the twenty-first century middle-class woman is for well-roundedness: "The dilemma and the ambivalence no longer seem to be about entering the public sphere, or about finding the right partner, but rather about the possibility of finding happiness through a balancing act, which itself becomes the sign of women's progress."[26]

The exemplary "well-rounded woman," who successfully manages the balancing act, is closely tied to the concept of "work-life balance." This latter has been at the forefront of policy discourse in developed countries since the late twentieth century. It emerged against a backdrop of globalization, rapid technological change, an aging population, and concerns over falling fertility rates and labor market participation rates, particularly those of mothers. The concept of "work-family balance" which preceded it, suggested that by giving equal priority to both work and family roles, individuals would be equally involved in and satisfied with both. However, work-family balance was criticized for focusing on employees with family responsibilities, and triggering a backlash in the workplace among nonparents. Consequently, the term "work-life balance" gained widespread use in research and policy arenas and has come to be associated with increased worker flexibility and autonomy for negotiating workers' attention, time, and presence in the workplace.[27]

As more women (and especially more middle-class women) entered the workforce during the 1980s, the issue of work-family conflict entered feminist discussion in developed countries, and work-life balance became the hegemonic solution, closely coupled with the notion of giving (female) employees greater choice. Numerous studies show that when work-life balance is achieved, employees demonstrate increased organizational commitment and job satisfaction, and improved mental health and well-being. It is linked to reduced absences and better integration of women returning from maternity leave. Unmet demand for work-life balance, on the other hand, is shown to have adverse consequences for employees' well-being and performance at work.[28] Thus, in national and workplace policy discourse in developed countries "it is often taken for granted that the work-life balance should be formulated in terms of a win-win situation, where employees' preferences coincide with their employers' desire for greater flexibility of working practices, particularly working time."[29]

Though formally including both men and women, work-life balance and its sister term "flexibility" commonly have been seen and continue to be discussed largely through the lens of female employment and framed as a women's issue.[30] As researcher Melissa Gregg argues, in both government policy and popular culture, work-life balance and flexible labor are constructed as ideal *for women*, "a commonsense manifestation of feminism's successful accomplishments in the public sphere of work."[31] However, policy and popular work-life balance discourses, which are equated with generous and progressive workplace arrangements, tend to take as given that women are the primary caregivers in the family, or what feminist author Rebecca Asher calls the "foundation parent."[32] The focus on celebrating women's choice to work when and where they want, Gregg points out, "reinscribe[s] women's 'natural preference' for flexible work."[33] A recent advertising campaign for the UK conference call service Powwownow neatly illustrates this. Women are shown as the exclusive beneficiaries of flexible work (and, thus, the beneficiaries of this service). In one of the ads (figure 2.1), the mother, in her gym outfit, is "flexibly" balancing her laptop, while stretching backward and speaking on the phone, her daughter staring at her with a puzzled look. In another ad from the same campaign (figure 2.2), a man is seen in a formal business suit, carrying a typical old-fashioned office file box, mesmerized by the "flexible" (and somewhat ridiculed) female workers:

FIGURE 2.1 Powwownow: "Here's to Flexible Working" (with mother), print advertisement, 2016. *Image courtesy of Powwownow UK*

FIGURE 2.2 Powwownow: "Here's to Flexible Working" (with man), print advertisement, 2016. *Image courtesy of Powwownow UK*

they are "liberated," engaging in what seems to be fun and playful physical exercise, rather than serious, important, or stressful work. The gender of the person in the middle of the group of three is not completely clear although s/he is dressed in a feminine gym outfit.

The take-up of work-life balance and flexible labor arrangements corresponds closely to the gender bias in policy and popular discourses. Women with dependent children are most likely to choose solutions such as part-time working and/or reduced working-hour arrangements, while men's take-up of such arrangements—even in countries with the most progressive gender equality policies such as Denmark and Sweden—remains very limited.[34] The most common type of flexible work available is part-time work. In the United Kingdom, 41 percent of all women work part-time, compared to only 12 percent of men.[35] More than two-fifths of those women who work part-time do so primarily to allow time to take care of children or incapacitated adults, compared to only 5.7 percent of men who work part-time.[36] In the United States, the number of women in part-time employment is almost double the number of men (17,716,000 women compared to 9,853,000 men).[37]

It is within this policy and cultural context that the balanced woman emerged as a renewed ideal feminine figure. She is situated squarely within the growing visibility of gender equality in public discourse and the development of fairer and more progressive policy and workplace practices. She acknowledges the falseness of the 1980s superwoman with the flying hair,[38] who seemed to seamlessly combine a successful career with being a good mother. The twenty-first century balanced woman tells middle-class women: I know how difficult it is negotiating work and home life; there are entrenched stereotypes and enduring perceptions about women's domestic responsibilities; workplace policies still have a way to go to become truly family friendly; and care is undervalued in our society. However, striking a felicitous work-life balance is possible and desirable. It is possible to craft a happy equilibrium between work and family, and between the private and public aspects of oneself.

This message reverberates through various recent bestsellers, including Sandberg's *Lean In*, Meers and Strober's *Getting to 50/50: How Working Couples Can Have It All by Sharing It All*, Morrissey's *A Good Time to Be a Girl*, and Slaughter's *Unfinished Business*. It circulates in advice columns in women's magazines, newspaper sections dedicated to women's issues (e.g., *Huffington Post*'s Women section, the *Guardian*'s Women in Leadership, the *Daily Mail*'s Femail), and in a surge of apps designed to help—especially women—strike the perfect work-life balance. Apps such as Cozi Family Organizer, Daily Routine, TimeTune, and ATracker[39] are marketed as effective ways for women to govern their conduct so as to make "work life balance a reality (not just a fantasy)"—as the online magazine *Working Mother* explains:

> Even if you love your job, you love your family and time for yourself too. Plus, too many extra hours of work can deplete the passion you went into the job with. So you have to strike an equilibrium between time at your desk and time away if you want to stay happy, healthy, productive and sane.
>
> If you need some help keeping things in check, these six apps offer unique and effective solutions. From blocking your email to staying calm, these mom apps will help you make work life fitness a reality—and not just something your friends (and magazines;) tell you to work on.[40]

Popular maternal characters iterate a similar conception of progress and the ideal of the upwardly mobile woman crafting a felicitous equilibrium between work and family. For instance, the television show *The Good Wife*, mentioned in chapter 1, depicts the difficulty of striking a balance between competitive long-hours work and family life. Lead character Alicia Florrick is often shown working in her apartment while her children eat dinner, or engaged in work-related phone calls that prevent her from responding even when her children seek her attention. Her demanding job causes her to miss out on her children's experiences; at other times, her maternal commitments affect her work performance. Nevertheless, ultimately Alicia manages to enjoy a successful career in a highly competitive, aggressive, and demanding work culture and be the "#1 Mom" as a pin on her office pencil cup states. The work is demanding but highly rewarding; Alicia is frequently praised by her employers, peers, family, and even her opponents for her excellent performance. On days when Alicia arrives home in the early evening, she is tired but de-stresses with wine and attends to her children with calm and patience. She shares intimate moments with her children, snuggling up on the sofa with them in front of the television, engaging in difficult but honest conversations (for instance, about their dad's scandalous affair), laughing with them, and comforting them emotionally and physically.[41] At work, although highly immersed in her job, she is on call for her children, the distinctive ringtone of her smartphone ("Hey, Mom, pick up the phone") interrupting even the most important work meetings—a sign of her uncompromised commitment as a mother. In the first two years of full-time work, Alicia benefits from help from her mother-in-law, Jackie. However, the contribution made by this free and always-available childcare to Alicia's ability to perform successfully and step up her career is marginalized by the depiction of Jackie as unhelpfully judgemental, bossy, and intrusive, and by the small impact her dismissal made on Alicia's continuing successful performance at work.[42] Hence, in many ways, Alicia embodies the balanced woman who manages to craft the difficult but desirable felicitous balance between good mothering and professional success.

However, Alicia lacks one significant ingredient of the ideal balanced woman: the right partner. In *Lean In*, Sandberg devotes an entire chapter to exhorting women to make their partner "a real partner"—the implied partner being a heterosexual man. From the beginning of a relationship, she contends, women have to establish the division of labor and encourage men "to lean in to their families."[43] *Getting to 50-50*, *Unfinished Business*, and numerous other similar "feminist" self-help/business books make a similar point about the woman's responsibility to choose the right partner and educate him from the outset, and throughout their couple life, to be a real partner.[44] Indeed, Sandberg, Slaughter (in *Unfinished Business*), and Morrissey (in *A Good Time to Be a Girl*) take pride in their partners, who supported and helped facilitate their high-powered careers and enabled them to make it to the top while pursuing their own satisfying careers (tragically, Sandberg's husband, Dave Goldberg, died a year after publication of *Lean In*).

Recent ads capitalize on this "progressive" message, which nevertheless is confined to a heteronormative view, showing men as active partners who participate in looking after the children and the household. In a Barclaycard advertisement (figure 2.3), for instance, a man is shown outdoors with his two children—the boy happily throwing a ball, the girl riding her scooter, while the dad is on the phone (supposedly on a work-related call), laden with shopping bags, flowers (presumably for the home), and dry cleaning. In an ad for a Legal & General life insurance product, a father is shown carrying his son on his shoulders, both wearing superhero costumes. The text reads, "Because not even superhero dads are invincible." In yet another ad, this time for popsicles, a man wearing a superhero costume with the letter D on his chest is playing with his son, the text to the side of the image written in comic style cajoling men to "become a superdad."

FIGURE 2.3 Barclaycard: "Today I Will Stress Less," print advertisement, 2015. *Image courtesy of BBH Partners LLP*

Governments have also joined the effort to encourage men to become more involved in family life. Social policy researchers Jonathan Scourfield and Mark Drakeford argue that during the 1990s, the UK New Labour government made explicit references to men in various areas of policy, the most high-profile of which was in relation to fathering (and the education of boys). New Labour sought to strike a more positive note than previous administrations in relation to involving fathers in the care of children. For example, *Sure Start*, which was launched by the UK government in 1998 with the aim of "giving children the best possible start in life," included several funded programs that made specific mention of interventions geared toward fathers; the Child Support Agency, which was set up as a delivery arm of the Department for Work and Pensions, emphasized the economic obligations solely of fathers.[45] In the United States, the Ad Council, the US Department of Health and Human Services, and the National Responsible Fatherhood Clearinghouse launched a series of public service advertisements (PSAs) aimed at providing men with tools and information to help them be more involved with their children. The ads encourage fathers to "Take Time to Be a Dad" and recognize the critical role they play in their children's lives (figure 2.4).[46]

Nevertheless, the focus in these ads and government messages continues to be on men as *fathers*, stressing their involvement in the fun and educational aspects of parenting. Men's contributions to domestic and household labor are still largely invisible,[47] and, as the evidence shows repeatedly, remain profoundly unequal, with women consistently bearing the brunt. In the United Kingdom, an Office for National Statistics analysis of time use data shows that women put in more than double the amount of unpaid work than men when it comes to cooking, childcare, and housework.[48] In the United States, for every two-and-a-quarter hours per day that women spend on household activities on average, men spend only one hour and twenty-five minutes.[49]

However, cultural and policy discourses often suggest it is the woman's onus to make her man "a real partner."[50] American foreign policy expert Anne-Marie Slaughter calls on women to overcome their "superwoman perfectionism," let their partners do it their own way, and recommends women: "close your eyes and imagine letting it all go—the expectations you imagine others have of you and that you have of yourself, your mate, and your house."[51] It is only then that it will be possible to become the balanced woman.

FIGURE 2.4 Fatherhood.gov, "Take Time to Be a Dad Today" advertising campaign.
Image courtesy of Ad Council and National Responsible Fatherhood Clearinghouse

So, in a strange and somewhat ironic twist, the contemporary "telos of the progressive narrative with respect to emancipated womanhood"[52] is remarkably redolent of the conservative feminine mystique. For example, there is a striking resemblance between Dichter's typology and Catherine Hakim's popular preference theory: the true housewife, career woman, and balanced woman in Dichter's classification, and the home-centered, work-centered, and adaptive woman who wants to combine work and family in Hakim's.[53] Today's balanced or adaptive woman is, of course, not bound to the domestic sphere like her idealized 1950s counterpart, and is in an allegedly more equal relationship with her partner. Nevertheless, she faces demands to fulfill a disturbingly similar psychological obligation: to achieve a fine balance between the private and the public aspects of her life while keeping them separate and unchallenged. The ideal of the truly liberated woman in the twenty-first century is of a woman who "can bridge private and public spheres simultaneously *without disavowing or disparaging either one.*"[54] In a slight twist on Dichter's words, one might say that a central message of both policy and popular discourses today is that the art of good balancing should be the goal of every normal (i.e., middle-class) woman.

UNEQUAL HOMES

The women's accounts reveal that their quitting their jobs and not returning to paid employment were influenced not only by their own workplaces but crucially also by their husbands'. Compared to their European counterparts, fathers in the United Kingdom work some of the longest hours.[55] Indeed, almost all the women I interviewed have partners in high-powered, demanding, long-hours jobs which allow the family to live on a single income. The partners' work conditions and the workplace cultures they operate in had a major impact on the woman's so-called choice to leave the workplace and also, to a large extent, prevented the woman's return to work. Let me give an example.

Paula is a forty-three-year-old mother of two children, aged ten and twelve. For eight years Paula worked as a solicitor in a law firm, then she married and soon after had her first child. She returned to work after a six-month maternity leave, but a year later was made redundant following her firm's takeover by an American company. She decided to scale down and took a three-days-a-week job as a legal adviser in a government service. A year later, her second child was born. Though she found the transition back to work after the birth of her second child difficult, she continued to enjoy her job. In particular, Paula cherished the feeling her job gave her of "being able to be in control of something," compared to parenting, which she found to be an experience where she frequently had very limited or no control. She used to look forward to Monday mornings after a busy weekend as a respite from the stress and demands of motherhood.

However, shortly after her second child's first birthday, Paula left her part-time job. She explains:

> A really major factor [for why I quit my part-time job] is that my husband's job is very stressful and very unpredictable so . . . I just at that point decided to not go back . . . My employer, they welcome people who want to work part-time. They're brilliant; they're a brilliant employer in that you can work part-time there and I worked hard to get that job and get through the interview and all of that sort of things and it . . . and it's a . . . and it's a very . . . it would've been a good thing [to return to work], really, but I just . . . I was feeling needed at home.

Paula met the requirements that policy and media representations outline as necessary to achieve the magical work-life balance. First, her former workplace had progressive and well-implemented "flex policies" (unlike many workplaces whose flexible policies remain largely on paper).[56] Second, the public and private aspects of Paula's self were "balanced": she is a talented, focused, and well-organized person, who was keen to realize herself as *both* worker and mother. She worked hard to get the job and enjoyed it, while at the same time she wanted to become a mother, and when she did, took much pleasure in it. She wanted to continue to pursue both career and motherhood. Thus, Paula's decision to quit her job was *not* due to some lack or loss of balance. Rather, as the quote above and her whole interview show, a major push for her quitting was her husband's job: he occupies a high-powered position in a media firm and normally does not get home until 10:30 p.m. It is the deep imbalance *in the home*, created largely by her husband's work culture and conditions, that forced Paula out of the workforce. For Paula, as for most of my other interviewees, the missing ingredient in the mix was not some kind of balance of personal preferences or personality: these women did not fall into Catherine Hakim's home-centered type, nor had they some kind of natural calling to be stay-at-home mothers. The crucial missing ingredient was the husband in the home.

It was not uncommon for the husbands of many of the women I interviewed not to see their children awake during the week; they left home early and returned after the children were in bed. Tanya, a stay-at-home mother of two girls, in her late forties, who previously was a partner in a law firm, occasionally told her husband that he should try and have breakfast with the children once a week. "And he goes, 'I know, I know.' It just doesn't happen, and I know why that is, because I had been a lawyer," Tanya explains. "Your diary gets filled up and you've almost got to block it out." Tess, formerly a senior news producer whose husband is a lawyer, observed somewhat sarcastically that her husband "spends more time sleeping in the house than he spends actually awake in it!"

Husbands' absence from the home—at least during weekdays—produces, sustains, and reproduces deep gender inequalities in daily married life, particularly (though not only) in relation to childcare and housework. Although the women I interviewed were able to afford childcare, and many were generally satisfied with the childcare arrangements they put in place, the burden of finding and managing childcare was almost exclusively theirs. Taking time off to nurse sick children, take them to medical appointments, attend their nursery and school activities, and ferry them to social activities were almost always the woman's job. Even if the woman occupied a similarly high-powered position as her husband, and earned the same or more than he did, the unequal distribution of domestic labor normally persisted. As Tanya, the former law firm partner whose husband does the same job, recalls:

> [At work], from 4:00 p.m. onwards you're just like, "Oh, my God, how am I going to get out of here?" And then suddenly I had to leave by 6:45 p.m. at the latest to get home. And my nanny worked until 7:30, so that was quite late. She'd been there since 8:00 in the morning until 7:30 at night . . . I could phone and say I need to work late, but it was always on me to sort out the childcare. You know, my husband just carried on in his normal life.

"Why is that?" I asked.

"Exactly!" Tanya exclaimed with anger, as if I enunciated the question she had been asking herself for a while, privately, in her head. She paused, sighed, and carried on:

> It's like, you know, that was my [sigh] . . . that was part of my role. So he wouldn't have thought, "Oh, I can't work late tonight, I've got to get home." And then sometimes we'd have a chat, you know, I'd be like, "Well, you need to get home because . . ." [and he would say] "No, no, well, I need

to do this" [imitating his voice with slight sarcasm about its earnest tone].
So I'd be like, "Well, no! I need to do this!" And so, I'd be the one who'd
call the nanny, "Oh, can you stay for another hour? I've just got to get this
finished." And [then] I'd go home, release the nanny, put my daughter to
bed, and then be on the computer for two hours or checking someone's
document . . .

Tanya's account provides a vivid glimpse into the routine bargaining
that goes on in the heterosexual marital life of two-job families, and the
tacit dynamic in which it is the woman who normally loses. Her state-
ments that her husband "just carried on in his *normal* life" and looking
after the family "was part of [her] role" alludes to the entrenched ideas
about "normal" gender roles and arrangements that underpin this recurrent dynamic. Tanya tried to challenge and resist this deep-seated "nor-
malcy": "Well, no!" she confronted her husband. "I need to do this!"
However, her resistance went unacknowledged, "And so, I'd be the one
who'd call the nanny," and the "normal" unequal division of labor was
reconfirmed and reproduced.

Tanya's experience is not unique.[57] Women of her generation who grew
up in Britain and the United States were encouraged by policies and cultural messages to combine careers with having children. At the same time,
as Angela McRobbie observes, these very policies and messages allowed
the husband "the chance to pursue his working life without female complaint, without the requirement that he curbs his working hours so that
he can play an equal role in the household."[58] Men are encouraged to "lean
in" to their families, and women are encouraged to encourage them to
do so, but the work cultures and norms in which these men work have
remained largely unchanged, as have many deep-seated conceptions of
what is the "normal" division of labor in the home. Thus, notions of the
ideal work-life balance and individual choice seem to have gained force
alongside the consolidation of deeply entrenched assumptions and tenacious structural obstacles.

A wealth of research has underscored the immense power of cultural
representations, and of media and policy discourses—from ads, news, dramas, magazines, books, films, and policies to social media platforms and
apps—to reflect, construct, and legitimize which social relations, arrangements, and gender roles are deemed normal, natural, and inevitable.[59]

Notwithstanding media responses to criticisms of stereotypical depictions of femininity and masculinity, and some significant changes in representations of gender roles, conservative constructions persist.[60] Research over the last decades has shown consistently the endurance of misrepresentation and underrepresentation of women in the media. In 2015, the Global Media Monitoring Project (GMMP), which takes stock of changes in dimensions of gender in news media content since 1995, revealed that "the rate of progress towards media gender parity has almost ground to a halt" since 2010.[61] For example, it found that "overall, women remain more than twice as likely as men to be portrayed as victims as they were a decade ago."[62] Echoing similar findings, the 2017 report *The Status of Women in the US Media* by the Women's Media Center, which is based on monitoring news outlets for three months, showed persistent gender imparity, regression, underrepresentation, misrepresentation, and outright pushback in news coverage across outlets.[63]

My interviewees rarely made explicit connections between media, cultural, or policy constructions of "normal" gender roles and their private experience. However, as Tanya's account reveals, public discourses and cultural constructions of what is deemed normal and taken for granted operate in their lives in subtle, often indirect and intangible, but meaningful ways.

One way in which conservative ideas about "normal" gender roles are communicated and powerfully regulate women's thinking, feeling, and behavior is through messages they receive from their parents, partners, friends, colleagues, and their children's schools. These messages frequently converge with and reinforce broader cultural ideas about gender, family, and work. For example, at an evening parents' meeting, to which Louise, a marketing director, went directly from work but for which her husband "couldn't get out of work," the teacher made a critical comment about the negative impact of two full-time working parents on children's well-being and performance at school, implying Louise's child's difficulties at school were Louise's fault. "I thought it was outrageous, absolutely outrageous!" Louise reflected, and yet, she admits, the message "gets inside [you]": "There's definitely a stigma if you work full-time." Most women talked about the judgments they felt were being made about their choice to work in full-time high-powered jobs by other mothers who were either not in paid employment or worked part-time. Several women reflected on their mothers-in-law's normally unspoken but very clear view that they (the wives of their sons) should quit their jobs and become full-time mothers to accommodate their husbands' demanding careers.

The husbands' views about women's appropriate and normal role in the home (and by implication their own) have had a major influence on the women, even if—and perhaps especially because—they were often conveyed latently. Take, for instance, Tim, CEO of a technology firm, whose wife is a stay-at-home mother. Tim takes genuine pride in what he describes as his and his wife's egalitarian "teamwork" relationship. Like many of the women I interviewed, he too masters feminist rhetoric. "We've gone further than our parents . . . who lived in a big suburban house, very conventional, very gender segregated life," he tells me. But there is still a long way to go, he professes passionately. "If you look at the gender distribution in the city boards, if you look at the gender distribution of politics . . . Ultimately, the point is that that's still worthy of comment, and as long as it's worthy of comment we haven't escaped gender politics, have we?" Facebook COO Sheryl Sandberg and president and CEO of Yahoo Marissa Mayer are "acting as models for a new employment paradigm," Tim comments with genuine optimism. However, when Tim describes his wife's former work as an art curator, he explains that "it was never a feature of the family's economic life, it was a feature of her self-actualization . . . [that] had no significant impact on our existence." By contrast, he describes his work as what supports the family's existence. Although he makes various references to the satisfaction he derives from his working life, he contrasts it with his wife's in describing it as *not* about self-actualization. Tim explains that since his wife was paid so little, when their first child was born it was "pointless" for her to return to work. "She's really not interested in what's necessary to climb up the greasy pole, which is good," he observed, "because if there were two of us [in demanding careers] it would be awful."

I asked Tim whether the issue of his wife's financial dependence had ever come up after she left her job. He replied, "Oh, sure! It comes up for everybody, doesn't it?" Thus, Tim critiques gender politics and sees himself as an egalitarian partner while simultaneously embracing in his own life the traditional male breadwinner/female caregiver model; he speaks the language of feminism but sees women's financial dependence as the norm. Such contradictions run deep in both women's and men's accounts;

such messages were frequently conveyed by husbands to the women I interviewed (as I explore further in the following chapters).

Workplace practices and messages, however progressive and flexible, also help to sustain conservative and patriarchal gender roles. Researchers Cécile Guillaume and Sophie Pochic show how firms' organizational and particularly human resources practices are based on an underlying set of traditional gender values that associate women with domestic life and men with public life, which help to sustain unequal household division of labor and career trajectories.[64] For example, career promotion is linked to employees' geographical mobility and ability to be always "on." Sheryl, who was a senior fundraiser for a large American university, told me in tears how her pregnancy had "completely derailed" her career. She had been "on the brink of a breakthrough" in her career, but when she became a mother she could no longer cope with the long commute and frequent business travels her job demanded. Although her boss never said this was why she was not promoted, Sheryl is clear it had played a significant role in torpedoing her career. My interviews with other women corroborated that such tacit criteria prevented some of them from moving up the career ladder as fast and as easily as the men in their organizations and, ultimately, contributed to their decision to quit their jobs. Yet like Sheryl, they would often internalize and personalize the blame. Sheryl owns the responsibility for her career's derailment: "My pregnancy completely derailed my career," she says. Thus, despite the new sexual contract becoming since the 1990s the primary social contract to which women are exhorted to subscribe (and men are encouraged to support), competing old contract messages continue to circulate and to have significant influence on women's and men's lives.

In addition to the very limited contribution of husbands to childcare, their demanding work conditions and absence from the home, coupled with the cultural perceptions I described above, reproduced unequal distribution of household labor, which further affected women's decision to quit their jobs. While almost all of them employed housecleaners, a luxury that many lower-income families cannot afford, the day-to-day management of the household was predominantly the woman's responsibility and was especially onerous at the end of the working day. For example, Helen, a former senior accountant, recalls how when she was in the workforce she "hated it, coming in to an absolute mess at the end of the day. The kitchen [had to be] cleaned, picking up after the children, so it's always an hour or so at the end of the day."

"How would you describe the distribution of labor at home between you and your husband when you were in paid employment?" I asked Paula, the former lawyer whose story I related earlier. She replied:

> Ah, mainly me. No, he does do . . . he, he, he does a lot of . . . he clears up the breakfast things in the morning so if . . . I would be busy, rushing around in the mornings normally so he will do all that, but then I do all the shopping, pretty much all the cooking, all of the laundry, and then I might, sort of, say at the weekend . . . I'll say, "Oh, can you put the clean clothes away or something?" I mean, he does do stuff, but not, not, not that much, really.

There is a struggle within Paula, between the image in her mind of the marriage she wants to be in, the partner she wants to be with, and the woman she wants to be, and her lived reality of deeply unequal relations in the home. She wants to be the balanced woman that Sheryl Sandberg and Anne-Marie Slaughter represent and urge women like her to become: the woman who strikes the magical balance and lets her partner take responsibility and do his share, the woman who makes her husband "a real partner." "He does a lot," Paula insists somewhat defensively; "he clears up the breakfast things" when she is busy rushing around, he puts the laundry away (at her request). However, this wishful image is shattered by admission of her lived reality: "He does do stuff, but *not, not, not* that much, really."

The conflict in women like Paula arises because, unlike their mothers' generation, these women grew up knowing that aligning with the patriarchal old contract sustains and reinstates the deep inequalities in their private lives and in society at large. The women I interviewed speak the language of *The Feminine Mystique* and *The Second Shift*, but seem incapable of using it to challenge the inequalities in their marital relations. Tess, a former news producer and a stay-at-home mother to two children, reflected with great sadness how even when both she and her husband had demanding full-time jobs, the division of labor was "very much pigeonholed along gender lines."

Laura, a former software programmer and a stay-at-home mother of two children, admitted that she does not "really like to have these rigid gender roles," but that "unfortunately, it is usually the husband that's working in the city and the mom that's looking after the children." Jenny, a former engineer and for the past three years a stay-at-home mother to two kids, described how the relations and division of labor between her and her husband started changing after their first child was born: "Suddenly, you know, we started taking on much more traditional gender roles and I was thinking, this isn't us! This is not us! So, you know, I was . . . I felt like . . . whether it was true or not, I felt like I was doing all the house things and, you know, but we don't do that . . . that wasn't us! You know, we, we share them!"

How can these women make sense of the conflict between the image of what they want to be (or feel they once embodied) and the image in their mind of who they are or have become? What kind of resolutions do the women caught up in this struggle try to make? One way to deal with it is by rejecting the feasibility and uptake of the desired image of the balanced woman. "I don't think anyone ever thinks they've done the right thing. I've never met anyone who said, you know what, I've got the perfect balance of work and children! No one has ever, ever said that," said Katie, a former accountant and a stay-at-home mother of two. "Work-life balance is a joke, nobody really has it," said another woman. Relatedly, the women I spoke to would refute the probability of husbands truly becoming "a real partner" (to use *Lean In*'s words): the man who works *and* shares the load of childcare and housework equally is a myth, they argued. Denying the possibility of realizing the idealized image of the balanced woman who manages the desirable "felicitous work-family balance" and makes her partner "a real partner," seemed to offer a resolution; if it is not possible for others, it is not possible for me.

However, this seemed to be only a very temporary and unstable resolution. The image of the balanced woman, and the idea of work-life balance whose feasibility women rejected, continued to haunt them and be desired as a possibility. Their resolution of the conflict they experienced was to criticize *themselves* for failing to live up to the ideal; they had appropriated the term "work-life balance" and measured themselves against the image of the balanced woman, to conclude that they had personally and privately failed to become that person.

Louise, the marketing director whose story we discussed in chapter 1, recognized that the problem she faced was largely to do with her workplace conditions, which were profoundly hostile to family life. She even took legal action against her workplace and was successful in demonstrating that she was subjected to sexual discrimination. However, while most clearly locating and legally proving her workplace's major responsibility for pushing her out of her job, Louise locates the responsibility in herself and her personal failure to get her balancing act right:

> I felt guilty . . . Some people are probably very good at just doing that, I mean, *without making a big deal of it*, but to me, it really put a strain on me. Some women hold down extremely high-powered jobs, their kids are fine, they are fine. And it's not . . . I know that people can do it, and they can do it well, but for me, I just needed to stop working . . . But I do have to find a job . . . I do have to find part-time work. I have to find a job, I have to find a part-time job, and I have to try again, just to get the balance.

Those other women, who felicitously manage a work-life balance without making a big deal of it, operate as powerful disciplinary figures over Louise's thinking and feelings. They perform the psychological obligation of women to be balanced: to do it, and to do it well and—crucially, as Louise points out—without complaint. Measuring herself against the benchmark of those other women who can do it well without making a big deal of it, Louise denigrates herself and, simultaneously, disciplines herself to try again and "get the balance" right; "I have to find a job," she repeats four times.

In contrast to the fantasy of the balanced woman, who smoothly switches off, relaxes, and attends to her children when she returns home after a working day—like Alicia Florrick in *The Good Wife* and other fictional characters—many of the women I interviewed recounted coming home after a long day's work exhausted and stressed. Paula, whom we met earlier, a former lawyer and nine-year stay-at-home mother of two, reflected:

> I would be really often in a foul mood when [laughs] . . . at the end of the day. Because I was just exhausted, you know, mentally exhausted. Yeah, it was . . . it was . . . I wasn't [pause] . . . I'm not a natural, kind of, um . . . I'm not [pause] . . . probably not as patient as I should be with young children . . . so I did find it, yeah, quite, um, [silence] wearing. It's very difficult, isn't it? Your feelings are so . . . my [pause] . . . it's so hard to sum it up . . . it's so, um . . .

The silences, stuttering, laughter, and incomplete sentences are tes-timony to Paula's struggle to articulate her feelings at the end of a long working day. These feelings derive not simply from exhaustion but from guilt. Paula feels inadequate, and implicitly judges herself against that "other woman" who, unlike her, is "a natural" and is capable of switch-ing off after a stressful day and attending to her children with patience and affection. Paula does not connect her feelings in a direct way to a particular media or cultural image. However, in my view, such troubling feelings, expressed by many of my interviewees, should be situated in rela-tion to the powerful fantasy nourished by popular representations and the proliferation of apps and platforms that exhort women to monitor and police their behavior, body, and feelings, in order to achieve the holy grail of work-life balance. Despite their astute recognition of the fragility and huge cost of trying to achieve a work-life balance, the women I inter-viewed clung to this ideal. Work-life balance served as what American fem-inist theorist Lauren Berlant would call a good-life fantasy, to which the women remained attached. It ignites a sense of possibility and continues to attract the women to desire it while, in fact, impeding their addressing the structural inequalities in their homes, as well as in their workplaces and society, which are obstructing the realization of their desire.[65]

COMING FULL CIRCLE: BACK TO DICHTER'S BALANCED WOMAN

Having "failed" to live up to the fantasy of the twenty-first century bal-anced woman à la Anne-Marie Slaughter and her counterparts, the women I interviewed seem to have become Ernest Dichter's ideal balanced woman. Less than a minute into my interview with Julie, a former publisher and a stay-at-home mother of two, she explained, "I have decided to have chil-dren, so I am going to care for them. I am going to be there for them. But then, that starts to affect you as a person, and the balance . . . you know, you need to have a balance because otherwise you're not the person that you need to be for them."

The balance Julie was once expected to strike between her work and family life, between the aspects of her private and public self, she now demands of herself to desire and achieve within the domestic sphere, for the benefit of her children (and her husband, as I show in chapter 4). Helen, a former accountant, let go of the work-life balance fantasy, concluding that "taking on a proper, serious, paid job alters that balance too much." However, like Julie, she reinstated the project of balance striking in her role as a stay-at-home mother. She proudly told me how she was balancing the "private" aspect of her self—full-time motherhood to two children—with the "public" aspect of her self—taking a part-time university course:

> I don't have to have everything dusted and put away, because I do have something slightly more important to do—studying. So that's nice. It would be awful if all I had to do when they were at school was to make hospital corners on beds. I'd hate that . . . and occasionally, if there's no milk for breakfast I don't have to feel terrible about it.

"How much aggression is involved in lining up life with fantasy?" Lauren Berlant poignantly asks in her seminal book *Cruel Optimism*.[66] The good life fantasy of work-life balance and the psychological obligation of women to be balanced repress and suppress contradictions, rather than making them an issue for society to address openly. The consequences of this aggression and the "choices" it has led women to make are the focus of chapters 3 and 4.

PART 2

Heading the Home

The Personal Consequences of Forced Choices

CHAPTER 3
Cupcake Mom/Family CEO

L ike many of the women I interviewed, Roberto's wife is a highly educated woman in her late thirties who left her job (as an accountant) after having a child. Both she and Roberto grew up in Latin America with stay-at-home mothers; "the social expectation during the 1970s," Roberto explained, was that "your husband will put you in a house and you look after the children." However, things have changed radically, he observed: "For our generation it wouldn't have been anything out of the norm for my wife to go back to work at the end of her maternity leave." Yet his wife—whose name Roberto mentioned not once during our interview—"chose" to go against that norm and look after the children and *not* return to work.[1] Even his five-year-old daughter, he told me with some sadness, "already recognized" that her mother was "out of the norm":

Her friends' moms would pick them up from school and they would be dressed in their various suits, whether they're working at the bank, or at some ministry, or they're teachers, police officers . . . And then her mom, you know . . . she doesn't have a suit or a uniform; there's nothing that distinguishes her from the others, I mean, the way the others are distinguished. So my daughter kept asking her mom, "What . . . what do you do? Why . . . why can't you do anything?" She recognizes that! My mom doesn't work, my mom doesn't do anything! And I think in her mind there's a diminished value to that.

How can Roberto and his wife make sense of what their child seems to struggle to understand? Why did Roberto's wife, whom Roberto told me went on maternity leave with the clear intention of going back to her workplace, quit her job and for the past five years choose to be outside paid employment? He tried to explain:

> From my point of view, it's her own choice. And I support whatever . . . whatever decision she made. I am okay with her staying with . . . with our daughter at home. I'm also okay with her going back to work like all working moms. So I told her, "You know, whatever you decide to do is . . . is . . . is really up to you." [pause] Her . . . her . . . her . . . um . . . her rationale for . . . for . . . uh . . . quitting her job was . . . she wanted to spend as much time as possible with . . . with the baby. She wanted to give, pretty much, all the attention she can give to . . . to . . . to . . . to . . . to the baby. [pause] That's . . . that's the way she . . . she . . . she, I guess, justified it to herself or, you know, rationalized it.

Struggling to give a coherent account and make sense of why his educated wife had become a stay-at-home mother, Roberto resorts to the notion of individual choice. He depicts his wife as a freely choosing individual independent of any pressures—crucially, any pressure from him. He's "okay" with whatever decision she makes; it's "really up to her." But then he pauses, as if not entirely convinced by his own explanation. He hesitates and stutters, trying to account for the rationale behind a decision that contradicts not just the dominant social norm, but also his and his wife's worldviews. Both, as he tells me later, are deeply concerned about equality; he takes huge pride in having studied household economics and gender, and in having awareness of "how gender power works." At the same time that Roberto clings to the idea of free choice to explain his wife's decision to leave paid employment to look after their child, he resorts to the contradictory idea of a woman's "natural calling" to raise her children, suggesting that the rationale for his wife's decision to quit her job was her desire to devote all her attention to the baby. However, he stumbles again, stammering and repeating the word "to" four times before completing his statement, which seems not to flow and sound completely right. After all, he points out later in the interview, the baby, who was the reason (supposedly) that his wife left her job, is now aged five and his wife remains unemployed. When Roberto finally completes his account, he pauses and then says that becoming a mother was how his wife "justified" her quitting to herself; this was how she "rationalized" it.

Indeed, for educated middle-class women, the choice to leave paid employment and become a stay-at-home mother requires intense and constant justification and rationalization, at least in the first years and, for many women, for many years beyond that as well. Betty Friedan's women were frustrated, bored, and desperate, but the feminine mystique justified, normalized, naturalized, and rationalized the subjectivity hailed by women's magazines, ads, and advice literature. They seemingly embodied the idealized feminine subject of their time, that of the happy housewife. By contrast, the women I interviewed know—as do their husbands and children—that they are, as Roberto described it, "out of the norm," that their choice of leaving paid employment to embrace full-time motherhood is non-normative. As we have seen in the previous chapters, the ideal feminine figure in the current cultural and political landscape is the confident, professional balanced woman who combines motherhood and career successfully. She recognizes the hurdles but perseveres in her quest to achieve a work-life balance, primarily by monitoring and modifying her thinking, feelings, and behavior. So what about the woman who supposedly makes the opposite choice? How do media and policy discourses construct her? And how do the real women behind these representations negotiate their identities in relation to these constructions? To address these questions, let us start by exploring contemporary cultural and policy depictions of women who left paid employment to look after their children. Against the landscape of these current narratives and images and the moral judgments they make about stay-at-home mothers, we will explore how the women in this study make sense of and negotiate their identities.

STAY-AT-HOME MOTHERS IN MEDIA AND POLICY DISCOURSE

A 2017 British Airways (BA) ad for European beach holidays shows a blonde, white woman and child, on matching beach towels on a peaceful and empty beach, playing a board game. Their backs are half turned to the camera, their gaze focused on the game. The apparel of the figures and the game they are playing connote that these are a middle-class mother and daughter, taking pleasure in each other's company and the tranquility that surrounds them. About three-quarters of the image is taken up by the wide blue sky, on which big white capitalized text occupying the entire length of the sky reads: "WHAT IF YOUR ONLY JOB WAS BEING A MUM?" The implication is, of course, that this is impossible. The woman in the image—possibly like most of BA's female customers—is a mother *and* a worker, who cannot afford to quit her paid job. However, the image, anchored by the suppositional question "what if," constructs the possibility of being *only* a mother who, crucially, is white and middle-class, as a compelling fantasy: a labor and stress-free occupation.

In contrast, a 2015 *New York Times* piece that generated heated debate in the newspaper's online comments section offered a very different depiction and moral judgment of middle-class stay-at-home mothers. The author, Wednesday Martin, described her move to the Upper East Side in New York and her discovery of "the women I came to call the Glam SAHMs, for glamorous stay-at-home-moms, of my new habitat."

> It was a shock to discover that the most elite stratum of all is a glittering, moneyed backwater. . . . The women I met, mainly at playgrounds, play groups and the nursery schools where I took my sons, were mostly 30-somethings with advanced degrees from prestigious universities and business schools. They were married to rich, powerful men, many of whom ran hedge or private equity funds; they often had three or four children under the age of 10; they lived west of Lexington Avenue, north of 63rd Street and south of 94th Street; and they did not work outside the home. . . . they exercised themselves to a razor's edge, wore expensive and exquisite outfits to school drop-off and looked a decade younger than they were. Many ran their homes (plural) like C.E.O.s.
>
> . . . There was the undeniable fact of their cloistering from men. There were alcohol-fueled girls' nights out, and women-only luncheons and trunk shows and "shopping for a cause" events. There were mommy coffees, and women-only dinners in lavish homes. There were even some girlfriend-only flyaway parties on private planes, where everyone packed and wore outfits the same color.[2]

The fantasy sold by the BA ad image of the mother on the beach, and Martin's sarcastic account of glamorous, lazy, bored, stay-at-home mothers capture the profoundly mixed and contradictory messages about (upper) middle-class stay-at-home mothers in contemporary cultural representations. On the one hand, as I will show, numerous fictional and factual images and stories in the media and policy idealize and valorize the middle-class, usually white, stay-at-home mother. On the other hand, middle-class stay-at-home mothers are constructed in many media and policy discourses as having wrongly and unfittingly chosen motherhood and domesticity over a career, and are frequently denigrated and ridiculed. They are represented as the stark opposite of the idealized "balanced woman" we explored in chapter 2. Let us unpack further the manifestation of this contradiction in cultural narratives that circulate in current media and policy discourse about middle-class stay-at-home mothers.

Idealized figures

The idealized figure of the middle-class stay-at-home mother emerged in American media during the late 1980s and early 1990s. American feminist journalist Susan Faludi called her "the New Traditionalist," the woman who has "freely" chosen to return to "traditional" lifestyle values of domesticity and feminine passivity. In her highly influential book *Backlash: The Undeclared War Against American Women*, Faludi shows how, as opposed to the superwoman who suffers from burnout and exhaustion as a result of struggling to combine motherhood and paid work, the New Traditionalist is exalted for "cocooning"—a recycled version of the Victorian fantasy of "the Angel in the House."[3] However, while subscribing to highly stereotypical, heteronormative notions of maternal femininities, these depictions of middle-class stay-at-home mothers in popular media and the press were "cleverly packaged in activist language, a strategy that simultaneously acknowledged women's desire for autonomy and co-opted it."[4] Rather than submissive housewife, the New Traditionalist was constructed as an independent thinker who had made an active positive choice.

This image of the stay-at-home mother was buttressed in the late 1980s by the heated discussion in American media of a *Harvard Business Review* article by business author and self-declared feminist Felice Schwartz.[5] Schwartz argued that women fall into one of two tiers: the career-primary tier, which includes women who prefer demanding, time-intensive career advancement models, and the career-and-family tier of women who prefer to raise families *and* have a career. Schwartz envisioned that women could switch between tiers, and intended that her classification and proposal should raise discussion of sexism and discrimination facing women executives. However, her proposal was taken up overwhelmingly by the media and by workplace policies to establish women in fixed positions. The *New York Times* dubbed the career-and-family tier the "mommy track," casting it against the "fast track," which referred to the career-primary tier.[6] In the mid-1990s, British sociologist Catherine Hakim's preference theory helped further these ideas. The theory relies on the (false) assumption that in places such as Britain and North America, women live in what Hakim calls "the new scenario,"[7] and enjoy genuine, unconstrained choices about how they wish to live their lives. Thus, some women (between 10 and 30 percent of the female population, according to Hakim) belong to the category the researcher terms "home-centered" (as distinct from "work-centered" or "adaptive"), referring to women who accept the traditional sexual division of labor and prefer not to be in paid work. Their choice to be homemakers, Hakim argued, is as valuable as being in paid work since they can "do as well from marriage careers as do men from employment careers."[8]

Notwithstanding criticisms of Hakim's and Schwartz's theories, and of the notion that women's different paid work and life trajectories are determined by fixed personal preferences and choices, the figure of the home-centered woman who chose motherhood over career to meet her preference has persisted. During the 2000s, the figure resurfaced in US and UK public discourse. A 2003 *New York Times Magazine* article garnered considerable attention for what it called the "opt-out revolution."[9] Sociologist Pamela Stone notes how the article

> distilled recurring themes in the media depiction: women, especially high-achieving, college-educated women, are choosing motherhood over careers, "rejecting the workplace" and the feminist vision of having it all, trading aspirations to professional success for the values and comfort of home and family, their actions representing not a passive acquiescence to traditional gender expectations but rather a proactive "opt-out revolution."[10]

In their analysis of US print media between 1998 and 2003, Pamela Stone and Arielle Kuperberg found that the portrayal of stay-at-home mothers adhered firmly to traditional and patriarchal notions of femininity. Most news articles were associated with traditional images of heterosexual, white, middle-class, married women. The focus was "almost exclusively on women as mothers rather than wives, and on family rather than work,"[11] and childcare was the most frequently mentioned activity. Women's decisions to "opt out" were framed almost always by the rhetoric of choice, "with virtually no mention of barriers, constraints, or lack of options."[12] The authors conclude that this portrayal signaled the emergence of "a new feminine mystique" in which "the decision to stay at home is distinguished from the old version by being couched in a discourse of choice" and female liberation.[13]

The media's valorization of the image of the middle-class stay-at-home mother as one of choice and female liberation was illustrated vividly in UK media coverage during the recession and post-recession period. A study conducted by Sara De Benedictis and myself of UK press coverage from 2008 to 2013 shows how even when women were those hit hardest by the financial crisis and austerity,[14] leaving the workplace and becoming stay-at-home mothers was presented overwhelmingly as a positive choice, motivated or justified by the woman's desire or interest in quitting her job or not entering paid employment.[15] For example, a feature in the *Sunday Times* magazine (January 10, 2010) recounted the personal stories of several women who had held senior positions in media companies and law firms and who were made redundant following the economic recession. The women's difficulties and anxieties were related, but the narrative was ultimately of a blessing in disguise which had allowed these former professional women to embrace—and even celebrate—their enforced new identity as stay-at-home mothers following the loss of their job. Ironically, even when the "choice" to leave paid employment was clearly forced on women as a result of redundancy, they were often depicted as individuals choosing to become stay-at-home mothers.[16] Furthermore, contrary to the expectation that middle-class stay-at-home mothers' choice would be derided for its (apparent) lack of contribution to the economy, we found that it was largely endorsed, including by the government. For example, the then UK Deputy Prime Minister Nick Clegg commended stay-at-home mothers' choice as "noble" and "admirable."[17] Concurrent with historical austerity discourses, such endorsements legitimize women's return to the domestic setting as rational and valuable.[18] They are part of what feminist media scholars Diane Negra and Yvonne Tasker describe as a nostalgic retreat to patterns that characterized postwar times—especially passive femininity and "maternal thrift."[19]

The idealization of women who "willingly" abandon their careers relies partly on the concurrent criticism and derision of working-class stay-at-home mothers. Unlike middle-class women's choice, which as we saw is frequently commended as noble and valuable, studies show how working-class poor women who look after their children full-time are consistently constructed as "abject" mothers who lead "inadequate," "mismanaged" lives.[20] Furthermore, presenting middle-class stay-at-homes in a positive light relies also on distancing them from domesticity and the derogatory connotations of housewifery. In the content analysis of UK newspaper coverage that Sara de Benedictis and I conducted, use of the term "housewife" was rare (1 percent in a 299 article sample).[21] Instead, popular press and popular culture frequently depict the middle-class stay-at-home mother as the "cupcake mom," focusing on her "intensive mothering" and "quality parenting," and the benefits for the women and their children.[22]

Popular culture has produced ongoing representations that romanticize and idealize the middle-class stay-at-home mother's maternal qualities. For example, cultural analyst Jo Littler shows how the "yummy mummy" functions in British celebrity guidebooks and "hen lit" novels as an aspirational figure whose maternity is fetishized and glorified, a construction that (not accidentally) coincides with the time when the state is withdrawing childcare provision, and lack of support in many workplaces for flexible and/or part-time working is widespread. The idealization of the yummy mummy, Littler argues, "obscures the effects of these policies as it renders looking after children a thoroughly private issue." It reduces mothering to an "individualized matter of 'psychological maturity' and 'personal choice' . . . occluding the questions of money and privilege."[23]

The positive construction of the yummy mummy and the cupcake mom is supported by the recurrent emphasis on the link between children's well-being, happiness, and success and their benefiting from full-time mothers ("proving" the negative impact of employed mothers on children's well-being and happiness). For instance, a longitudinal study reported in the UK *Daily Mail* newspaper, under the headline "Working Mothers Risk Damaging Their Child's Prospects,"[24] suggested that children of mothers who return to work after their babies are born are more likely to do worse at school, become unemployed, and suffer mental stress than youngsters whose mothers stay at home to bring them up. Even the gender equality champion Anne-Marie Slaughter who, as discussed in chapter 2, is a passionate advocate of women's participation and staying in the workforce, in recounting the motivations that led to her quitting her job, focused on the deterioration of her older son's behavior and his implied involvement in juvenile delinquency: "By eighth grade his behavior had escalated; he had been suspended from school and picked up by the local police. I received several urgent phone calls . . . that required me to drop what I was doing and take the first train back home."[25]

Exaltations of middle-class stay-at-home mothers also can be found in political and policy discourse. On the one hand, in the postindustrial economy, neoliberal governments forcefully encourage women to enter and to stay in the labor market.[26] Thus, it is generally women who are in the workforce, not those who leave it, whom government exalts. As I discuss in the next section, in the United States, President Barack Obama was notorious for criticizing stay-at-home mothers. On the other hand, different governments (and sometimes the same government) deliver contradictory messages. In his presidential campaign, for example, Donald Trump highlighted his childcare policy as one that "also supports mothers who choose to stay at home, and honors and recognizes their incredible contributions to their families and to our society."[27] Trump's proposed policy promised to allow families with a stay-at-home parent to be able to fully deduct the average cost of childcare from their taxes. During his campaign, Trump's daughter and advisor Ivanka tweeted that "being a stay-at-home mom is one of the most rewarding, yet challenging roles."[28]

In the United Kingdom, while government policies and discourses over the past three decades have been consistently critical of stay-at-home mothers, at the same time there has been a growing emphasis on "quality parenting," which has been implied to be primarily mothers' responsibility. For example, in his 2016 speech on life chances, UK Prime Minister David Cameron endorsed Amy Chua's 2011 bestselling memoir, *Battle Hymn of the Tiger Mother*, and expressed his desire to incorporate the key tenets of the tiger mother approach into social policy: "Work, try hard, believe you can succeed, get up and try again."[29] His statement was by no means praising stay-at-home mothers. However, in embracing tiger mothering (as did Conservative Member of Parliament [MP] Michael Gove shortly after the book's release),[30] which has been associated flagrantly with middle-class, pushy parenting geared toward cultivating children's tenacity, perseverance, dedication, commitment, and aspiration, Cameron reinforced the notion that it is the role of the mother (rather than that of both parents and the state) to provide children with quality parenting.

Denigrated figures

At the same time that middle-class stay-at-home mothers are idealized and praised in media and policy for their preference and choice of motherhood over career, they are frequently the object of critique, attack, and derision.[31] Some of these criticisms focus on the effect on children; for every report arguing that mothers in paid work have a negative impact on their children, another study is published suggesting that stay-at-home mothers' children are less happy and doing worse than those of mothers in paid employment. Other studies frequently reported in the press show that stay-at-home mothers are more likely to be depressed and to experience stress.[32]

Alongside these critiques, middle-class stay-at-home mothers are often disparaged and lampooned. Wednesday Martin's *New York Times* piece cited earlier echoes common stereotypical depictions of upper-middle-class and middle-class mothers not in paid employment: glamorous, living lavish lifestyles, lazy, bored, and, importantly, all this by their own free choice. Various memes[33] on social media platforms depict the "retro housewife" as precisely that. "I have so much housework, what movie should I watch?" reads a meme on Pinterest, with an image of a retro, bored housewife with lipstick and neat attire, suggesting she does not do any household chores. "Taking naps sounds so childish. I prefer to call them horizontal life pauses," reads another caption on a retro image of a white woman lying on her bed in a self-indulgent pose, wearing a floral gown.[34]

The image of the middle-class and upper-middle-class stay-at-home mother is reminiscent of the ridiculed "rich bitch" popularized by (especially American) television dramas such as *Desperate Housewives* and *Real Housewives*—a bourgeois, feminine mother who is ineffective, selfish, superficial, and pursues material gains single-mindedly.[35] However, distinct from the rich bitch, the middle-class, educated stay-at-home mother is *not* accused of ineffective mothering. Rather, she is constructed typically in relation to her "intensive parenting" in which she channels her skills, capital, and time. In the 2013 popular chick-lit novel *Bridget Jones: Mad About the Boy*, the postfeminist icon is in her early fifties, twenty years on from her girly singleton days. Bridget is now a widow and a stay-at-home mother of two small children, residing in a typical middle-class north London neighborhood. She continually judges her own "poor mothering" compared to Nicolette's, a caricature of the perfect hyper-aspirational intensive stay-at-home mother. Once a CEO of a large chain of health and fitness clubs, Nicolette is now "the Class Mother (perfect house, perfect husband, perfect children) . . . perfectly dressed and perfectly blow-dried with a perfect gigantic handbag."[36] She calls herself "CEO of [her] family," and describes her children as "the most important, complex, and thrilling product" she has ever developed.[37] Bridget Jones deprecates herself and her inadequate mothering, compared to Nicolette's and other mothering styles.[38] The effect, of course, is comic. Nicolette's "perfect" mothering is ridiculed and mocked; Bridget's mothering, we learn, is beset by frustrations, and is messy and imperfect, but healthy and ultimately happy.

The government is another prolific source of criticisms of stay-at-home mothers, especially through its championing of women's participation and staying in the workforce.[39] In his remarks on women and the economy on October 31, 2014, President Obama said, "Someone, usually mom, leaves the workplace to stay home with the kids, which then leaves her earning a lower wage for the rest of her life as a result. And that's not a choice we want Americans to make."[40] Unsurprisingly, Obama's comment sparked considerable anger among stay-at-home mothers, and a *Washington Post* headline responded to the President's remark with, "Why Is Obama Sticking It to Stay-at-Home Moms?"

Another way in which government constructs stay-at-home motherhood as an undesirable choice is through emphasis on the positive impact of nonmaternal childcare on child development and women's well-being and happiness. The rationale for UK national childcare strategies since the late 1990s under New Labour has presumed that "good quality day care in the earliest years has long-term benefits for children's social and intellectual development."[41] In 2013, the Coalition government's childcare policy further highlighted the importance of childcare for economic productivity, focusing on improving child development to enhance workforce skills and to exploit the full potential of the parental workforce. This agenda is part of broader neoliberal welfare and labor market policies of UK governments since New Labour, which strongly encouraged the rapid move of mothers out of the home and into the workplace once childbearing was over. While this agenda targets in particular lower-income families in order to reduce child poverty, the broader message is that an unreasonably long period out of the workplace is a burden on the taxpayer and comes at the expense of these women's long-term economic prospects.[42] This message gained additional force under the Coalition and Conservative governments' austerity programs during and after the financial recession (Conservative and Liberal Democrats coalition, 2010–2015; Conservative 2015–present). One of the Coalition's first acts was to freeze all Child Benefit and remove it completely from households with someone paying the higher rate of tax. Baby and pregnancy-related grants also were cut, and the child tax credits were reduced, particularly for middle-income households.[43] In 2015, Prime Minister David Cameron announced increased childcare entitlement—from fifteen free nursery hours per week for three- and four-year-olds to thirty hours. Echoing Obama's remarks, Cameron declared, "My message is clear—this Government is on the side of working people—helping them get on and supporting them at every stage of life."[44] In March 2017, on International Women's Day, Prime Minister Theresa May announced the allocation of a £5 million fund to help those returning to paid employment after long career breaks:

> While Returnships are open to both men and women, we should acknowledge that, more often than not, it is women who give up their careers to devote themselves to motherhood, only to find the route back into employment closed off—the doors shut to them. This isn't right, it isn't fair and it doesn't make economic sense. So I want to see this scheme extended to all levels of management and into industries where women are underrepresented.[45]

Though policy and political discourses tend to refer to parenting rather than mothering, as May's statement demonstrates, the message of returning people to paid employment is frequently directed at women and particularly mothers. As former director of the UK Family and Parenting Institute Katherine Rake noted in the early 2000s, for mothers who engage full time in unpaid caring work, these policies send out strong signals about the duration of such unpaid work that the government deems appropriate. The normative message emerging from government policy, Rake argues, is of institutionalizing paid work as the key route to citizenship—a message that sustains the longstanding undervaluing of unpaid caring work.[46] The former UK Chancellor of the Exchequer George Osborne repeatedly emphasized the urgency of increasing UK female employment, suggesting that women "who *want* to stay at home and look after their children" have made a personal "lifestyle choice."[47] Stay-at-home mothers would be excluded from receiving childcare support because they do not want to "work hard and get on," stated Prime Minister David Cameron's official spokesman in 2013.[48] In a briefing document accidentally released on the UK Treasury's website, officials said that families with one stay-at-home parent were less deserving of state help than families where both parents worked.[49]

Thus, stay-at-home mothers are cast in government policy discourse—as Roberto's five-year-old daughter already recognizes—as being "out of the norm," and crucially, by choice. It is therefore not surprising that, on numerous occasions, organizations and individual stay-at-home mothers have accused government policies, legacies, and discourses of systematically discriminating against, penalizing, patronizing, devaluing, and slurring stay-at-home mothers.[50] In particular, many argue that at the same time as the government introduces new policies aimed at driving mothers into the workforce, it is rapidly withdrawing its support from both families and people in employment. Social theorist Nancy Fraser observes a similar process under the globalizing financialized capitalism of the present era in the United States: state and corporate disinvestment from social welfare alongside aggressive recruitment of women into the paid workforce leading to care work being externalized to families and communities while diminishing their capacities to perform it.[51]

Hence, on the one hand, there is a strong expectation of intensive mothering, a withdrawal of the welfare state, and a crisis around work-life balance—processes that support acceptance and even valorization of middle-class women choosing to get off the treadmill and return home to devote themselves to full-time motherhood (especially when the husbands are making enough money for a family wage). On the other hand, in the post-industrial economy, governments and the media are advocating for and championing women who enter and stay in the labor market, but not those who leave it (though as we have seen, there is significant differentiation in how women of different classes are depicted in this context).[52] In twenty-first century Britain and the United States, abandoning years of education, training, and achievement is a deviant choice that does not make sense.

LIVED EXPERIENCE OF STAY-AT-HOME MOTHERHOOD

It is in the context of such contradictory and competing messages that circulate in contemporary public discourse that the women I met sought to make sense of their choices and identities. In accounting for their lives, the women frequently—and unprompted—positioned and defined themselves against popular images and stereotypes they perceived to be dominant images of stay-at-home mothers. The cupcake mom and the family CEO were potent points of reference to which the women related when defining who they were and, perhaps more significantly, who they were *not*. Interviewees felt they needed to continuously defend against perceptions of stay-at-home mothers as lazy and boring, a self-defense that frequently was linked to an apologetic admission of their socioeconomic privilege. "I am quite fortunate in many respects . . . [but] people think all we are doing is eating biscuits all day," said one woman. Another woman said, "I suppose I'm lucky because financially there's enough available. So, I do appreciate that . . . But then, you know, I'm not on Bond Street, walking up and down Bond Street, spending loads of money.[53] I'm not like some frivolous . . ." Yet another woman said furiously, "There is a perception stay-at-home moms get to put their feet up and watch television all day long, and give their kids chicken nuggets and chips every night . . . I've literally had people turning away from me and walking across the room, because they assume I've got nothing to say!"

The women I spoke to also defended themselves against the image of the idealized stay-at-home mother whose house is always spick and span, who bakes cakes, and who feels like a "natural" mother. For example, Susan, a forty-four-year-old mother of three girls, who had left her job as a medical doctor eleven years earlier, said, "I call myself a housewife, but I'm not . . . I'm not a particularly Mother Earth kind of person; you know, I don't find it that easy. Baking cakes is not my forte, really!" Similarly, Janet, a forty-three-year-old mother of two, who had left her job as an actress eleven years earlier, explained, "I don't feel like the most obviously maternal person, it was never what I saw for myself. I suppose I've not kind of grown into the thing that I've been waiting for."[54]

Voices of judgment

When I asked about the sources of these perceptions against which they felt they had to defend themselves, several women referred to the media (especially news and popular culture), but many cited the government. Dana, a former arts festivals manager and a mother of two, accused the UK government of persistent delegitimizing of stay-at-home mothers in order to serve its neoliberal ideology:

> There is this enormous experiment going on. The government really wants women to get back to work, because they really want us to engage in capitalism. And they just want us to buy products, so if people are working, they can buy things. And so, there's this mass social experiment going on, getting children into school at two years old, and pushing women to go to work.

Dana contended that anything that does not fit this model is totally devalued. Similarly, Christine, a forty-two-year-old mother of two, spoke angrily about government pressure to which she felt women were subjected:

> I do feel there's a lot of messages coming from government, especially in the last two or three years, that do not value that decision [to become a stay-at-home mother] at all. Things like the Shared Parental Leave bill,[55] encouraging moms to go back to work at six weeks, and fathers will carry on as normal . . . Somebody who chooses to spend time with their children is not valued at the moment, I don't think.
>
> There's such a strong message that you are not making a contribution. And that you are meant to work, if it's at all possible, you're meant to! You're meant to take advantage of childcare, you're meant to send your child or children to a childcare environment and you're meant to go back to work. If you don't do that, you're being a little bit uncooperative and a little bit unhelpful. You're not helping the economy, society at large, even if research might suggest that your children will benefit, we're not worried about that! You're not making a contribution!

These reactions to government discourse and policy are not mere detached intellectual analysis of politics and policy. They are emotional responses to what many of the women I interviewed experienced as oppressive demands and personal attacks precisely because their decision to leave paid employment and become stay-at-home mothers was *not* an entirely personal, free, and simple choice; yet this is how they feel it is construed by the government.

Rachel, a mother of three and a former senior accountant in a London-based global firm, whose husband is a partner in an accountancy firm, recounted how she used to be the ideal employee: "I was the person who didn't take maternity leave until two weeks before I was ready to drop, and everybody thought I was coming back in the office a couple of months after." Rachel carried on working after her first child was born, but like many of the women I interviewed, her and her husband's demanding long-hours work cultures were hostile toward family life. "I was thinking I ought to go back. It was all about *ought*, social pressure, feeling I ought to, absolutely," she explained. "Whose pressure?" I probed. Rachel replied:

> Um . . . I guess a lot of it is self-imposed. But you think, I've got a degree, I've got this far, I was a senior person, ah . . . How can I . . . you know . . . I shouldn't . . . ah, everything, you know, in the government was "Oh, you must go back to work!" It was all about getting women to go back to work. You must carry on working! And I was made to feel—definitely, I felt staying to look after the kids was a secondary thing. And I felt very guilty for wanting to do that . . . But ultimately, I thought, oh, sod it. I'm going to do it.

Note how Rachel moves from first identifying the pressure she experienced as internal and self-imposed, to locating it in the broad external environment—"everything"—then specifically in the government agenda, until she finally internalizes this message in her thinking and feeling: "I was *made to feel*—definitely, I *felt* staying [home] to look after the kids was a secondary thing. And I *felt very guilty* for wanting to do that." While Rachel decided to resist the pressure and just "sod it," it continued to insinuate itself into her psyche, and, like many of the other women I interviewed, she admitted to having constantly to defend against such judgments, and to justify her new "chosen" identity as a stay-at-home mother.

A second significant judgmental voice is that of the women's mothers, which the women felt often echoed the government's and media's criticism. Just over two-thirds of the women I interviewed talked about their mothers' disapproval of their daughter's choice to quit her job and embrace full-time motherhood. Marie, a former lawyer, whose mother was forced to give up her civil service job in the 1960s by the marriage bar that was in place in Ireland at the time, reflected with pause and pain:

> My mom didn't really sort of speak to me about it [her decision to quit her job] . . . She sort of brought us all up [Marie and her two sisters] to be financially independent and to have careers, and all of it was very, very, very, very important to her, maybe because it was something that she hadn't had, and also just that ability to do what you want, to have that freedom, to have a career.
>
> I guess because [sigh] [silence], because you [sigh] . . . I guess you feel that you're kind of [pause] . . . just letting womankind down a bit, you know, because we have moved on! And women have as much right to work as men, and should be able to work as much as men, and . . . and because I had studied hard and then I was . . . was . . . I thought I was okay at my job, you know, and I enjoyed it, and just having [a baby], I think . . . I think it is just . . . um . . . [pause] [eyes filled with tears] . . . not that you're throwing it away, but you know, you've worked very hard and, um, and just how you're going to be, I guess, perceived by other people and society as well. And just letting down the idea that if you are supposed to have it all, and you're supposed to be able to have kids and manage a successful career and . . . um . . . and I guess it is, you know, a feeling that I was letting my mom down a bit, you know, because I knew that she wouldn't be particularly happy about it.

Marie's account was particularly raw, but her experience was not atypical. It reveals the regret, guilt, and pain involved in her decision. Her disappointment and struggle to justify her choice are influenced profoundly by her mother's voice. Her mother, who had had no choice about giving up her career because of a discriminatory law, lamented this loss for the rest of her life and consequently reiterated to her three daughters how crucial it was to "have that freedom" that she did not have.

Yet perhaps even more agonizing were the voices and judgments of these women's husbands. This comes through very clearly in Laura's story, whose life trajectory I briefly introduced at the beginning of the book (see the introduction). To recap, Laura is a forty-three-year-old shy and soft-spoken mother of two children. She asked if we could meet in a café and not in her home where, over the past seven years, she has reinvented herself as a stay-at-home mother. Laura was brought up in a council house in the north of England by two working-class parents. Her parents wanted her to achieve more than they had done, and in the 1990s she went to study at the University of Oxford. After graduating Laura became a successful software programmer in a global firm—a job she did for nine years. She then married a floor trader and moved to London, and at the age of thirty-six, when she gave birth to their first child, left paid employment. She had never imagined herself as a career mother who "has a full-time nanny and juggles her job with small children." However, at the same time, she also did not imagine she would become a full-time stay-at-home mother.

Nevertheless, Laura stressed that she was content as a stay-at-home mother. "I don't particularly feel that I made a sacrifice in career terms . . . I'm not an aggressive career woman, but more of a nurturer," she explained. To justify her decision to give up career for motherhood, Laura drew on the popular construction of women as belonging to either the career-primary or home-centered type. The former she describes as the "aggressive career woman," an image consistent with many popular depictions of successful women in the workplace, while she sees herself as belonging to the latter—the "nurturer"—a construction that chimes with idealized depictions of stay-at-home mothers' maternal qualities and instincts. Crucially, this binary view was endorsed and encouraged by her husband: "My husband's mom went back to work when he was a very tiny baby, and he didn't like that, so he was quite keen for me to be at home, and has been supportive, very happy to be the breadwinner while I look after the children."

While Laura reiterated that her husband was fully supportive of her choice to quit her job and become a full-time mother, partway through our interview and in response to my question about her husband's job, Laura replied:

> He works in the City [the primary central business district of London]. It's very full-time . . . [He] never says, "What have you been doing all day, you lazy bitch?" [laugh] And I don't know why I even think, you know, so it's not him, it's me, anyway, so I do keep quite busy . . . I do seem to have

a need to justify my time and to make sure that everyone knows that I'm really busy, and that I don't just read magazines all day [laugh], which is really just answering the voice in my own head more than anything else, so I do keep myself quite busy with jobs.

. . . I think nobody really does think that I'm lazy, but I think that it's not right for a person to have nothing to do or I feel a voice in my head that tells me that, if I read a magazine in the daytime, or have a nap in the daytime, that that makes me a bad person . . .

The voice in Laura's head demands she justify her choice and the identity of stay-at-home mother she has assumed. Laura experiences this voice in her head as a totally private inner voice. Yet almost all the women I interviewed admitted to a similar inner voice of self-blame and guilt about being thought by others to be lazy and to have too much time on their hands—and this even while describing genuinely very busy schedules facilitating their families' lives, and as one woman put it "ensuring everybody has a good life."

Like Laura, the majority of the women I interviewed described their husbands as very supportive of their quitting their jobs and becoming stay-at-home mothers (an aspect we explore further in chapter 4). However, although considered supportive, both the women's and the men's accounts revealed that the husbands were simultaneously critical and often resentful of their wives' choices to stay at home to look after the children, though these feelings were rarely voiced openly. Rather, they were transferred and redirected into small comments of the kind Laura cited. The most striking element in Laura's account of the voice in her head is the imagined reproachful—even spiteful—comment from her husband: "What have you been doing all day, you lazy bitch?" Laura insisted that this was an imagined voice—that he had never actually said this. Nevertheless, it is a voice that penetrates her sense of self, causing her to think that she is a bad person.

The imagined voice of Laura's husband, who occupies a high-powered position in the financial sector, is vivid and was present in other guises in the lives of most of the women I interviewed. It reflects the voice of the productivity driven, long-hours work culture that they had left, but which their husbands still occupied. It is a voice rooted in a long history of undervaluing care work, which regards only very specific forms of labor as economically productive and valuable. This voice can be heard in numerous television dramas and films that glorify long hours working in demanding and competitive jobs and cast high-powered, successful lawyers, doctors, and politicians working around the clock as heroes and heroines. The current productivity culture, sociologist Judy Wajcman notes, valorizes being busy and having action-packed lives with commodified activities. Anything that strays away from this form of living is rendered unintelligible and is often delegitimized and denigrated.[56]

How can women defend themselves against these voices that threaten to take them over and diminish their sense of value and self-worth? How can they make sense of their choice when faced with their mothers' and husbands' judgments, which often echo or converge with the judgments of government and current culture? How can they justify and rationalize (as Roberto put it) their identity as former professional women turned into stay-at-home mothers in a cultural and political context in which their choices and roles are attacked and derided while simultaneously being idealized and praised? Simply refuting these voices and judgments is not an option, not least because the women often reminisce about their former identities and miss the pleasures, satisfactions, and value they derived from waged work.

For the 1950s able housewife, Friedan observed, "the only possible rationalization" was

> to convince herself—as the new mystique tries so hard to convince her—that the minute physical details of child care are indeed mystically creative; that her children will be tragically deprived if she is not there every minute; that the dinner she gives the boss's wife is as crucial to her husband's career as the case he fights in court or the problem he solves in the laboratory.[57]

However, the twenty-first century educated stay-at-home mother differs from her historical counterpart in at least three profound ways. First, she grew up in a radically different political and cultural climate that was fundamentally shaped by the political struggles of the 1970s, especially second wave feminism and the women's liberation movement, and exposed women's entrapment and subjugation by the feminine mystique. Second, unlike many of the housewives of the 1950s and 1960s, the stay-at-home mothers I interviewed had been in paid employment and had indeed made a choice—however constrained—to leave it. Third, as a consequence of the latter two aspects, the twenty-first century educated stay-at-home mother is extremely conscious of the price of being forced "to devote her every moment to the trivia of keeping house"[58]—the feminine mystique's diktat of her mother's generation. All of the women I interviewed stressed their dislike of domesticity. They did the bare minimum of household chores, and, for most cooking was, as former engineer Jenny described it, "absolutely functional" and something many declared they detested. They took no joy in washing and shopping; cleaning was "endless," "uninspiring," "mundane," and "boring."

Thus, for the twenty-first century educated stay-at-home mother, the main and sometimes only way to justify and rationalize her choice is to enroll in a new occupation: family CEO. While women frequently refuted the stereotype of the family CEO who runs the family as a small enterprise and buys into what Judith Warner calls the "perfect madness" of middle-class parenting, they described finding themselves assuming precisely this role.[59] The consequence of heading home was becoming head of the home.

Occupation: Family CEO[60]

I met Christine on a Monday afternoon in a backroom of a local North London community center. She sits there every Monday outside her children's two-hour Mandarin class. She texts me to say they're running late. When she arrives, she admonishes her ten-year-old son and seven-year-old daughter to get their notebooks and hurry into the classroom where the lesson has just started. "Phew, it's been hectic!" she sighs.

"Is that a typical day?" I asked. Christine replied, "Obviously, the kids are at school at ten to nine, and so before school, it's reading and breakfast and clothes and dashing around and finishing off homework." "And your partner?" I probed. He's a corporate lawyer, she explained, "working, not coming home, sleeping at the office, working, coming home, sleeping for two hours, going back." In the mornings "he's already gone to work. I think he has maybe done one [school] drop-off ever." "And when school finishes?" I asked. Christine replied, "Then, three o'clock, get ready to pick up the kids again and then come in here [the community center where the

Mandarin lesson is held], do a class here, then swimming lessons and more swimming lessons, play dates, violin lessons, and then homework."

How did Christine come to be entirely consumed by this hectic child-centered life? She qualified in 1997 as a primary school teacher, after which she started her nine-year teaching career in a London primary school. She became the school's deputy head teacher and assessment coordinator—two roles that substantially increased her responsibilities and workload as well as her satisfaction and financial reward. Like so many of the women I met, Christine was an ideal worker. A conscientious and devoted employee, she would unlock the school in the morning and normally would also lock up at six o'clock in the evening. "I was working sixty-five hours a week, and then [at the end of the day] I'd basically get home, eat, and carry on working for another three hours and go to bed."

So when Christine's first child was born in 2006, the decision to quit her job seemed obvious: "There was no way my husband could have shared the childcare . . . and so, that made the decision seem obvious . . . it almost didn't even require a conversation because it seemed so obvious. What would the alternative have been? A nanny that worked fourteen hours a day?!" Christine saw no alternative to fully withdrawing from the workplace; that her husband might make any adjustments to his job was not an option, partly because he earns more than her, but also because she accepted—if unwillingly—that she should be the "foundation parent."[61] However, while the decision to quit her career to look after the children seemed obvious, the new identity that this decision brought about was far from it:

> To just say, "I'm a stay-at-home mother," that is not respected, that is not valued . . . There's no value to it really . . . The assumption is that you're not contributing or you've wasted your education, or you're sponging, or you know . . . You cannot say, "I'm just a full-time mother," it is not valued. Especially when the children go back to school, then the absolute assumption is you have to be doing something. You're just constantly justifying your existence.

Christine has been seeking to find value and respect—words she used repeatedly—to justify her new "existence" as a full-time mother of two school-age children. She has found this value by translating her role of stay-at-home mother into a profession, a new career. "It's a little bit of an extension of what it was like when I was a deputy," she tells me. She has brought to this new role her professional knowledge and transformed herself from a senior manager at work to manager of the family. "I didn't want to get it wrong. I really felt a huge sense of responsibility, and you know, a huge vocation, partly because it falls on me, because my husband isn't around very much, and so what I do is a huge responsibility." If mothers who are in paid employment make a parenting mistake, she explained, it is forgiven "because they've got a lot on their plate, and they're juggling and it must be really hard." However, as a stay-at-home mother whose husband is practically absent during the week, Christine feels she "really [has] got to get the parenting right." "I feel like I've got to be a perfect mother. I'm not allowed to make mistakes, I'm not allowed to be selfish, I'm not allowed to be . . . if that makes sense? It probably doesn't . . ."

Striving to become the perfect, zero-errors mother was a theme running through all the women's accounts. Sociological and psychological accounts of the experience of modern motherhood suggest that this is characteristic of mothers' experience more broadly. In today's culture where motherhood is idealized and fetishized, mothers constantly are called upon to self-assess and measure themselves against some elevated benchmark of the perfect mother (a theme explored in chapter 4).[62] However, the simultaneous idealization and denigration of middle-class stay-at-home mothers seem to produce specific pressures and confusion. The struggle to make sense of an identity that is *entirely* reliant upon being a mother and which is the consequence of a forced choice has distinct implications and meanings. As Christine's rhetorical "if that makes sense?" question illustrates, she knows that the quest to be the perfect mother who never fails makes no sense. Yet she and every other woman I interviewed were deeply invested in trying to make sense of an identity that does not make sense.

To make sense of their new identities, to gain value and to be valued by others, the women I met have had to conduct what Paula described as "a radical rewrite" of the whole of their lives by becoming the managers of their families. Rather than being housewives who "bury themselves in dishpans"[63] like their mothers' generation, they have rechanneled their extensive skills and knowledge as former talented professionals into a new role. The 1950s and 1960s housewives were "restless in a life of baking, cooking, sewing, washing, and caring"[64] while the women I interviewed seemed to be restlessly occupied with different activities and responsibilities: ferrying children to and from numerous pre- and after-school activities, helping with homework, volunteering for child- and/or school related-activities such as helping with school performances, trips, and other educational activities, and acting as class parent representatives, school governors, accountants, arts directors, and legal advisers. And all this combined with managing domestic helpers and undertaking domestic do-it-yourself tasks plus the shopping, cooking, and washing.

Rachel, the stay-at-home mother and former senior accountant I cited earlier, described a typical day. As if acting out the frenzy of her daily life, she gave the following account, hardly pausing for breath:

Seven till half eight is packed lunches, breakfasts for the kids, I usually have to shop or a washing machine to put out or, you know, dull stuff but it's quite full-on, seven till 8:30 a.m., and my eldest is at secondary now so, one, she trots off to secondary, I walk the other two to school, and then I'll usually go for a run for an hour—that's my time. I do an hour, and then usually I've got—so, like, this morning I've just been working round till ten, I've been working for two hours on doing the accounts for the school, but it might be a school project, it might be something to do with the governors for school, it might be just admin—booking kids' courses and crap. At the moment it's budget time at school so there's an awful lot of, quite a lot of work I do at the moment, and then I will cook something for dinner, I'll do that during the day, make sure there's some food, and housework, dull stuff—probably half an hour, an hour of that.

[Sigh] It's making me sound really boring, doesn't it? But the day just goes. Only six hours and then, at 3:15 p.m., I'm back to school and, basically, between three and nine is my six hours of full-on, because my kids are at peak. They all do stuff so I'm taxiing a lot, doing a lot of homework, and music practice and juggling children being in different places, and reading and getting them to bed by nine, and nine o'clock, I'm free!

As this breathless extract testifies, Rachel is *not* a domestic goddess, nor is she (or the other women I met) a "desperate housewife" consumed with alacrity, as some popular images would suggest, by domesticity. The women's homes are clean and tidy—enabled by the substantial help of the paid domestic help they employ—but their primary focus is toward facilitating, coordinating, and monitoring their children's academic, social, and personal lives. The sociologist Annette Lareau calls it "concerted cultivation": a style of parenting performed by middle-class and upper-middle-class families, whose burden is borne mostly by mothers and is characterized by a hectic pace of activities organized and controlled by parents and their surrogates, geared toward cultivating the children's talents and stimulating their cognitive and social skills in a concerted fashion. Paula described the satisfaction and particularly the sense of control she derives from concerted cultivation, especially from dedicating herself to being involved in and closely managing and monitoring her ten- and twelve-year-old children's lives:

> I'm able to go in, I'm able to help with school trips and stuff like that and I quite enjoy being involved, knowing, you know . . . I really know what they're up to, I know what . . . I'm able to supervise homework and, I don't know, piano practice and all of that sort of thing so I'm . . . I suppose I feel like I'm on . . . I'm on top of things, whereas if I wasn't there I just wouldn't be as engaged, I suppose, with all of that stuff.

I heard similar explanations from many of the women I interviewed. The implication is that as the children grow up they need their mothers (no mention of fathers) more, not less: the immediate presence of the mother when the child leaves for and comes home from school is crucial for his or her emotional development. In primary and even more so in secondary school, children can drift socially, emotionally, and academically if their mothers are not around and "on top of things." My interviewees told me that in their former busy lives as professional women they had little sense of or involvement in their children's academic and social experiences, which now they have to the full. However, in the same breath Paula admitted that:

> It can go the other way, can't it? You can be probably too . . . slightly too engaged, I don't know . . . [inhales] I don't know if it helps them to stand on their own two feet if you're always there to remind them of everything. Kids whose moms aren't around as much probably have to be more self-motivated and self-reliant and that's probably a good thing for them. I'm sure it works both ways.

Women reflected on the possibly more negative consequences of their (over)involvement and presence in their children's live. Some cited reports they read or heard in the media and noted that their children were less independent, confident, secure, and outgoing than children whose parents were both in full-time paid employment. It is possible that these reflections are a result of the interview encounter: most women assumed I was a mother and knew I was in full-time employment. So, consciously or unconsciously, they may have qualified their observations about the impact of stay-at-home motherhood on children so as not to offend me. However, my interviewees frequently questioned the benefits and consequences of their decision, in their own heads. "Why am I busy booking kids' courses and crap?" Rachel, whom I cited earlier, asked. "It's making me sound really boring, doesn't it?"

Sara, a former senior financial director, offered an explanation:

> The moms around here, if somebody asks them what they do they'll say they're retired lawyers or they're retired management consultants . . . without actually just acknowledging that, actually, I stay at home and manage the family [laughter]. They're former accountants and lawyers and management consultants and City workers and doctors and, you know, people who have had quite high-powered, to some extent at least, or they were on the gravy train, jobs. So, they're very ambitious for their children there's a lot more competition than you'd imagine [laughter] amongst them . . .
>
> It feels like the Housewives of Crouch End,[65] you know, instead of the Housewives of Orange County, whatever it is! But that's what it's like. Because if you've worked in a high-pressured environment and you're trained and you're competent, then all that competition and energy doesn't go away. It just gets rechanneled and typically it's rechanneled into your kids and how well they do at various things and trying to find one thing they'll excel at and making sure that you are one step ahead of everybody else in terms of getting tutors or identifying issues or getting them to swimming galas or whatever. And the competition lives on, it's just in a totally different guise.

Sara provided an important insight into the personal and social consequences of women's heading home. The withdrawal of these women from the workplace was supposed to allow them to get off the treadmill, the oppressive toxic work cultures, and the Sisyphic quest to strike a felicitous work-family balance. Instead, in an effort to pass on their skills, ethos, and energy to their children, their skills and competitive energy have been rechanneled into the role of CEO of the family. As sociologist Annette Lareau notes, concerted cultivation is geared toward acquiring middle-class children with skills valuable for their future, skills needed to remain in the middle-class.[66] The women's heading of the home is focused on guaranteeing their children will be able to access positions that will allow them to preserve the privilege enjoyed by their parents, by instilling in them a competitive spirit geared toward fulfillment, achievement, self-realization, and success.

Sociologists Melissa Milkie and Catherine Warner describe this enactment of intensive mothering as "status safeguarding": mothers' vigilant labor to ensure a child's social and economic status in a competitive marketplace is sustained or improved. However, as their and other studies show, this intensive maternal labor is coupled with and produces high levels of anxiety, and "comes at a high cost to mothers' careers, physical and emotional health, and guilt."[67] Christine, the former deputy head teacher, reflected candidly on her anxious parenting. She related an incident concerning her son who, when doing homework, kept rubbing out his notes. She "got frustrated with him" and told him to stop rubbing them out. "Just put a line through them! In an exam situation, if you rub them out, you're wasting time!" she reprimanded. But her son insisted, "No, I really want to rub them out! I don't want them to be there, it's messy, I really want to rub them out!" "And so I was cross with him," she confessed, but immediately was overwhelmed with guilt and regret. "I feel like I'm *not* entitled to be cross. Because I removed all this stress. I'm not like a working mom, who is walking through the door at six o'clock at night, and who has so much on her shoulders. I cannot afford to be stressed!"

Rechanneling professional skills and workplace competitive energy into the children and living vicariously through them are enormously stressful for both mother and child.[68] Striving to be the perfect error-free mother is often unsettling rather than comic as portrayed in *Bridget Jones* and other popular representations. Those anxieties seem to be further exacerbated by mothers' fears that they may be unable to guarantee their children's future as (at least) middle-class adults. In the current economic climate, and in view of great uncertainty about the future of work, the idea of perpetual progress, that each generation should be better off than their parents, is being fundamentally challenged.[69] Some of the men and women interviewed remarked cynically that they were investing all this in their children so they could graduate from university, be unemployed, and come back to live at home.

Engaging in school-related activities such as fundraising, tutoring, and coaching school children, helping organize school performances (making professional costumes and stage settings, directing drama and music, etc.), advising on school budget or legal matters, seem to offer women a desirable balance; it allows them to "stretch their brain," and "do something creative," they told me. It helps to mitigate the isolation and loneliness that come with being a stay-at-home mother, especially of school-age children. Anne, a mother of three school-age children, confided that she had become depressed: "There is something really isolating . . . you can put on a face at the school gate and it's only for ten minutes and you go home and you shut those doors and you're there for the rest of the night and the day." Volunteering at several organizations related to her children's sports and school had helped her get out of the house and overcome her depression and isolation.

The scope of school-related volunteer roles seems ever-expanding, observed Jenny, a former engineer who runs computing after-school clubs for free, is chair of governors at her younger child's school, and chairs the finance committee in her older child's school. Local authorities' support has been cut dramatically, and schools rely increasingly on parents' expertise and skills. "In a nice middle-class area like ours," Jenny added, "schools are doing okay. There's usually an accountant and a lawyer somewhere, but if there isn't, you're totally screwed." Anne, who lives in another leafy, middle-class London neighborhood and is heavily involved in the parents' organization at her children's school, confirmed that. She told me proudly how in a meeting to discuss school funding cuts, the head teacher praised the parents' organization as the reason why the school was affluent. "And who makes up this organization? It's us! Stay-at-home mothers! That is our contribution to society!" Anne exclaimed. But while these unpaid, semi-public activities serve the schools' needs, help keep the women away from home and domestic chores, and provide them with some stimulation and satisfaction, they remain extensions of women's roles as mothers and family managers. They benefit the schools, the children, and the family, not the women as independent adults.[70] Crucially, as Arlie Hochschild noted, doing volunteer work offers women a private fantasy of a future public life, but does not interfere with their husbands' careers—a theme we develop in chapter 4.[71]

The women I interviewed seemingly "opted out" of what Rachel, whom I cited earlier, called "the enormous experiment of engaging in capitalism." Their choice to leave the workplace can be seen, as some of them suggested, as a resistance to neoliberal capitalism—to its exclusive valorization of the sphere of commodity production and the toxic competitive work cultures on which it depends. Their embrace of full-time motherhood can be understood as an attempt to shift priorities and to put care before competition. It is seemingly removed from the demands of advanced capitalism and the public sphere of work that they left, but which their government promotes and their husbands—mostly in high-powered, high-income jobs—occupy. Yet, as a consequence of *heading home*—a choice that was in part imposed by the pressures of advanced capitalism—women have become *heads of their home* who run their families as small enterprises, and endorse "intensive mothering"[72] as a means of trying to ensure the invincible middle-class future and security of their children. In rechanneling their professional skills and competitive spirit through their children, and taking on the role of family CEO, these women may be reproducing what many found so brutal in the workplace. They have reproduced neoliberalism in the sense that their children have become human capital—investing in them is a way of increasing good returns in the future.[73] In the words of Sara, the former senior financial director, "And the competition lives on, it's just in a totally different guise."

CHAPTER 4

Aberrant Mothers/Captive Wives

O stensibly, the stories of the women I interviewed are primarily mothers' accounts: motherhood was the primary cause of their decision to quit their jobs, and mother was the prime identity they consequently assumed. Yet behind the stories of motherhood lay subtle but profound accounts of wifehood. Women rarely spoke directly about their roles and identities as wives, but the choices they made, their life trajectories, and their everyday lives were profoundly shaped by wifehood. However, these modern, educated, and liberal women were intensely ambivalent about their roles and identities as wives. They and their husbands devised strategies to obscure the woman's wifehood and the conflicts involved in living an old, traditional, gendered split: the husband in the paid work and capital domain and the wife in the sphere of family and caring. This chapter is structured so as to illustrate this work of cover-up. It starts with the personal stories women tell themselves about their roles as mothers, and how they are propped by and in turn endorse popular constructions of motherhood. These personal and public stories of motherhood act as a mask that helps to conceal what is revealed in the second part of the chapter, namely the women's pivotal roles and identities as wives, and their deep ambivalence toward them.

Let me start with Tess's story, which offers a useful illustration of the ways in which the women's accounts, which draw on popular and policy narratives of motherhood, help hide their wifehood.

THE PERSONAL STORY OF MOTHERHOOD

At the beginning of our interview, Tess, a forty-nine-year-old former senior news producer and for the past six years stay-at-home mother of two, recounted:

> Already when I was eighteen, I was quite determined about what I wanted to do. I always thought I wanted to be a journalist . . . I've been single-minded that I wanted to have a career . . . That was my game plan! My game plan wasn't particularly to have children . . . I've kind of rejected that almost, not completely . . . I was in my twenties and thought, "Gosh, I'm not having children, that's going to disrupt my life!" And I was quite a feminist. I did feel women should work.

Tess's game plan was congruent with and arguably influenced by the dominant 1980s feminine ideal of the empowered, confident woman, who is determined to pursue a successful career (reminiscent of the character played by Melanie Griffith in the 1988 film *Working Girl*, or the lead female characters in the 1980 movie *Nine to Five* played by Jane Fonda, Lily Tomlin, and Dolly Parton). Tess was awarded a bachelor's degree in government and then received a year's training as a newspaper journalist, which was followed by appointment to her first job in a local newspaper in the south of England. Over the next few years, she moved between different local newspapers across England, gaining experience and further qualifications. In the early 1990s, she started her first job in television journalism for one of Britain's main television network companies. The job was intense and included many night shifts. Tess described it as "fun," a "great pleasure," and "fantastic"; it offered her "a huge variety" of experience as well as "huge freedom." She moved steadily up the career ladder and became a senior news producer. The organization she worked for was "very generous," and when her first child was born, she took a year's maternity leave. Two years later, after the birth of her second child, she took another twelve months' leave before returning to work for another three years, supported by a full-time paid nanny. However, when her older child started school at the age of nearly six and her younger child was three, she quit her job. Her workplace had offered a generous redundancy package which was "very alluring," Tess reflected. "It was a good time to go, a natural break for me."

But what made the break in Tess's successful, upward career seem natural? What made that moment a good time to go?

Before I got to ask these questions, Tess added important information about her decision to quit. She worked ten hours a day on top of which she had a daily hour commute to and from work. The children were young and "they wanted me," she explained. While her nanny "took the pressure off" for the first few years, once the children were at school, she felt acutely needed. Even today, she tells me, when both her children are at school, they want her to stay a full-time mother. "I think, I definitely think, I think they probably still want me now actually . . . They get upset when they hear me thinking of doing some job. What? What? You're going out to work? What about us?!" Thus, becoming a mother appears to be the major factor that led to Tess's momentous decision to quit her career, a decision helped by the generous payoff she received from her workplace.

On the mantelpiece in the room we are sitting is a photo of a family of four: Tess, two children, and a man, who I assume is their dad. I am struck that more than half an hour into the interview, Tess has not mentioned her partner. I am reluctant to ask about this in case it is a sensitive or painful topic. So I ask if I can take her back to the decision to quit her job. "You said the redundancy package was an important consideration," I comment. Tess responds:

> Yes, it was, it was. It wasn't, I mean it wasn't just about that . . . I was feeling like, um, I, I was a bit of a, you know, I'm a bit torn here . . . And, there were, there were other factors also as well. My husband is a lawyer. He works quite long hours. He's slightly younger and he wanted to follow his career and progress. And I could see that his career . . . I felt, was probably taking off . . . He wouldn't be a backup plan for me . . . [If the children are sick], there would be no way that my husband would say "Oh, it's all right, I'll take a day off work" [laughter]. For me that jarred, it really jarred. I couldn't foresee how I could [stay] in the workplace.

The decision to take a "natural break" is revealed as not so natural. Tess admits that the story of leaving a successful career solely because the children wanted her does not hold up. Motherhood and its incompatibility with her work were important but were only part of the reason why Tess left paid employment. Equally important was the prospect of her husband's career taking off and the demanding long hours it involved, which she knew would effectively make him an absent father and partner—that "jarred," as she put it, and brought her career to an end. The two-earner household could not cope with the pressures of both partners combining economic production and care, leading Tess to leave the workplace.

"But why was it *you* who left the workplace?" I ask, puzzled, especially since at the point of quitting her career, Tess was earning more than her husband. "When the children were sick," she explains, "it was me who always took time off, it wasn't my husband . . . I, funnily enough, I just thought it's me, it's me that has to, because I have to take care [of the children]. I'm the carer." Tess's use of "funnily enough" divulges her recognition that there is something that does not make complete sense about her "automatic" embrace of the role of the primary carer, which led her to give up her job. There is, she knows, nothing necessarily natural about quitting a successful and rewarding career to look after the children.

While most women who quit their jobs earn less than their husbands, in Tess's case (and those of some of the other interviewees) she earned more.[1] So the conventional wisdom that it does not make sense financially for the woman to stay in employment because of childcare costs did not hold. Tess's experience casts doubt also on the notion she so carefully crafted in the first part of our interview, that it was primarily motherhood that led her to leave the workplace. Her decision to leave her job to look after the children facilitated her husband not having to take time off, so he could continue his long working hours and develop his successful career. Thus, Tess's decision to quit a job she loved and enjoyed, and which she performed very well, was, it seems, as much about facilitating her husband's career as it was about her desire to spend more time with her children. It was a decision she made as a wife as much as a mother.

Similarly, Julie, a forty-two-year-old mother of two school-age children who quit a successful career in publishing, said:

> There are lots of amazing careers around here where women really do extraordinary things and, and with passion, [and] very positive ways of managing children! . . . There's a kind of conflict between wanting to be that working person, who's a good role model, who's, you know, um, who acts . . . and contributes to the family . . . um, and, um . . . I don't think that

goes away: wanting to feel that you're, that . . . that I'm contributing to the family in a different way . . . But if I make a decision to have children, then I see that as *my* responsibility to look after them . . . I have decided to have children, so I am going to care for them. I am going to be there for them.

Julie faced a conflict between wanting to be a good role model of a "working person" and feel she was contributing to the family financially, and wanting to look after her children because her husband "works all the hours that God sends." Like Tess, she struggles to suppress this conflict; even nine years after leaving her job, she confesses, it doesn't go away. Like Tess, Julie performs an emotional cover-up. The story of caring for the children being her sole responsibility helps her mute her envy of those women with "amazing careers," and her unrealized dream of being one of them.

For an emotional cover-up to work requires support and confirmation from sources outside the self. Successfully suppressing the crucial role of wifehood and its impact on women's lives and identities depends on a bigger story on which the women I interviewed drew, which helped obfuscate their compromise and conflict. Sociologist Arlie Hochschild describes this bigger story as a cultural cover-up. She discusses how in the 1980s, it was the image of the supermom—the imaginary woman who juggled family life and work and "was unusually efficient, organized, energetic, bright, and confident"[2]—which circulated in magazines, advice books, advertising, and on television. Hochschild argues that this image appealed to women in paid employment because it offered a cultural cover-up to accompany their emotional cover-up. It clothed their "compromise with an aura of inevitability," and obscured the strain couples faced to maintain a two-earner family, and their attempt to contain it.[3] In the second decade of the twenty-first century, contemporary cultural and policy representations continue to offer women a useful cover-up to cloak their emotional struggle. While the supermom image has not disappeared, other images have emerged, confirming to Tess, Julie, and many of the other women with whom I talked that their primary role is to look after their children. Public stories of motherhood, which I explore next, help the women I met hush the ambivalence and many of the contradictions in their roles as mothers and wives.

PUBLIC STORIES OF MOTHERHOOD

Contemporary culture is characterized by a "remarkable maternal visibility,"[4] where motherhood has never been "so visible, so talked about, so public."[5] Discussions about motherhood and representations of mothers proliferate in films, news, television, women's magazines, advertising, celebrity, guidebooks, social media, and literary fiction.[6] Despite important changes in representations of women in the media, research shows that women continue to be frequently depicted in caring roles, especially as mothers.[7] The sheer hypervisibility of mothers in contemporary media and culture compared to the much lower visibility of fathers (notwithstanding significant changes in the representation of men doing care work) works to naturalize and reinforce the association of women with childcare, and with caring more generally.

Not only is motherhood hypervisible, it also is couched overwhelmingly in terms of choice, and presented as free of overt patriarchal pressure and subjugation.[8] As discussed in chapter 3, stay-at-home mothers are consistently framed within a rhetoric of personal choice, with little mention of barriers, constraints, or regrets, even when their "choice" to become full-time carers is compelled, for example, by redundancy.[9] Furthermore, assumptions about good and bad mothering remain stubborn yardsticks against which women continuously are measured.[10] These have become pronounced during the recent period of austerity in Britain, with working-class mothers, and especially poor single mothers, repeatedly being demonized in political discourse and the press as contributing nothing to the economy, being incapable of governing themselves and their children in the "right" ways, and, thus, being responsible for making Britain a "broken society."[11] Against the poor, disenfranchised failing mother, the (upper) middle-class mother is frequently idealized as and scrutinized for providing "quality mothering," and acting responsibly. Politicians' wives, such as former First Lady Michelle Obama or Samantha Cameron, wife of former UK Prime Minister David Cameron, are typically held up as exemplary mothers, shown and said to be independent and modern women while also being great mothers.[12]

The increasing visibility of motherhood has reinvigorated the scrutiny and policing of mothers, documenting what mothers do and where and how they do it.[13] In the online sphere, mother-blaming and harsh judgments of mothers' parenting practices[14] have become common, accompanied by increasing pressure on parents, especially mothers, to project their family lives by sharing family snapshots via technology and social media platforms—a practice that has come to be known as "sharenting."[15] The 2016 Facebook Motherhood Challenge, which implored women to contribute by posting a series of photos that make them "happy to be a mother," and to tag other women whom they consider to be "great mothers," is one of many examples of the intensified scrutiny of mothering and the pressures exerted on mothers.[16]

Recent policy discourse and political rhetoric have fostered and, arguably, fueled the scrutiny and policing of mothering and mothers. Ostensibly, policy and political discourse sees mothers and fathers as synonymous and tends to refer to parenting rather than mothering. In the UK, after David Cameron became leader of the Conservative party in 2005, he consistently stressed a more inclusive view of the family structure, most notably in relation to homosexuality and people in civil partnerships.[17] As part of his broader program of modernizing and rebranding the Conservative party as more tolerant, inclusive, and in touch with contemporary society (a project of which his successor Theresa May has been a key supporter), Cameron's policy and discourse referred to the family as a whole and to the responsibility of *both* parents. For example, in his 2014 speech on families, Cameron emphasized the need to "support not just the mother and child, but the whole family,"[18] and in his 2016 speech on life chances, he referred to both "mums and dads [as] literally build(ing) babies' brains."[19] In this context, Cameron was cultivating his own image as a father and a family man.[20] In 2015, the Conservative government introduced a Shared Parental Leave system to enable mothers and fathers to share childcare during a child's first year—although to date, take-up by fathers has been astoundingly low.[21]

At the same time, in emphasizing the significance of good parenting for the child's development, in the same life chances speech Cameron spoke of the crucial role of "strengthening that lifelong emotional bond between mother and baby" and (as mentioned in chapter 3) referred to *Battle Hymn of the Tiger Mother*[22] as epitomizing an ideal parenting model. More broadly, UK government policy discourse persistently retains a traditional view of the family and conservative values concerning women's roles and responsibilities, even when—for the second time in its history—its leader is a woman.[23] UK government policy remains significantly compatible with the fundamental tenets of Thatcherism, which viewed strong families and (heterosexual and heteronormative) marriage as the bedrock of social cohesion and stability, and has designed policies geared toward the assertion of family responsibility. In Thatcherite welfare policy, while "expression of ideas about gendered family roles [was] more muted,"[24] the overwhelming aim was to retain the traditional family structure, roles, and responsibilities—the implication for women being that they could have "equality" so long as they continued, in practice, to care for the family.[25] Thus, while policy and political discourse communicates a veneer of equality, in practice it elides the enduring sexual and class politics that shape the experience of mothering.[26] Motherhood continues to be "sexed," with policies and political rhetoric reinforcing—albeit implicitly—the idea of women being the primary carers of the children.[27] Surrounded by such powerful and consistent messages about a woman's role and duty to be the foundation parent[28] and the good mother, it seems hardly surprising that the women I interviewed conceded that it was their primary (if not exclusive) role to raise their children—a view that, as various studies show, is stubbornly held by women and men more widely.[29]

Nevertheless, there have been some important changes in the representation of mothers and motherhood over the last two decades or so, related to broader social and political changes, including women's increased education and participation in the workforce, the influence of feminism, and the "queering" of motherhood.[30] Contemporary representations provide a more nuanced and complicated portraiture of motherhood from that which marked previous eras. More and more images deviate from the good mother/bad mother binary, destabilize taken for granted associations between biological sex and gender identity, and defy the "mommy myth," which has persistently governed the cultural landscape and reproduced a "highly romanticized and yet demanding view of motherhood in which the standards for success are impossible to meet."[31]

Television has been a key site for the production and circulation of more transgressive images of motherhood. Since the late 1980s and early 1990s, programs such as *Married with Children, Murphy Brown, Roseanne,* and *The Simpsons,*[32] to more recent shows, including *Big Little Lies, The Good Wife, Desperate Housewives, Weeds, Mad Men, Mom, Nurse Jackie, The Killing* (US), *The Replacement, Doctor Foster, Motherland* (UK), *Borgen,* and *Rita* (Denmark), have offered more complex depictions of ambiguous maternal figures. Feminist media researchers Suzanna Danuta Walters and Laura Harrison observe the emergence in American popular media of novel counter-images of "aberrant," "unapologetically non-normative" mothers, who resist male control and normative familialism.[33] Walters and Harrison argue that characters such as successful lawyer Alicia Florrick in *The Good Wife*,[34] frustrated housewife Betty Draper in *Mad Men*,[35] detective Sarah Linden in *The Killing*, and schoolteacher Rita in the internationally Netflix-distributed Danish drama *Rita*[36] ameliorate the inconsistency between "the public perception of ideal motherhood and the much more complicated (and often harsher) realities of everyday life."[37] Even the advertising industry, notorious for reproducing sexist stereotypes of femininity and conservative images of motherhood, in recent years has produced a growing number of non normative representations of motherhood, such as Fiat's "The Motherhood Feat" commercial, which pokes fun at the myth of the perfect, natural, happy mother, or Dove's 2017 #RealMoms campaign.[38]

The Internet, which has facilitated the intensification of scrutiny, judgment, and self-policing of mothers, simultaneously constitutes a key space for the articulation and expansion of more complex portrayals of motherhood. In recent years, there has been a proliferation of "mommy blogs," websites, and social media platforms that present nuanced and far more diverse stories and images of mothers. A study of the Sanctimommy Facebook community, for example, found that by mocking the self-righteousness often attributed to intensive mothering—in particular the ideas that mothers are naturally the most capable parent, and lavish enormous amounts of time and energy on their children—the social media platform provides a space for critiquing the oppressive ideals of motherhood and articulating alternative mothering practices.[39] Such platforms contribute to destabilizing and reframing the meanings of motherhood by highlighting that it is complicated, involving not just satisfaction and happiness, but also powerful emotions of frustration, disappointment, anger, and ingratitude.

The echoes of these more complex cultural scripts about motherhood reverberated in the accounts of the women I interviewed. The women took considerable pleasure in motherhood, and reflected on the satisfaction derived from their maternal roles. They relished being able to actively nurture their children, to be there for them at "any time they needed" rather than relying on paid carers. At the same time, they spoke, often quite openly, about the frustrations and difficulties motherhood involved. Almost all referred to the ingratitude and ungratifying aspects of motherhood, with some confiding painfully they felt taken for granted and invisible and, as some put it, always at the "bottom of the heap." The appearance of more complex, ambivalent, and "aberrant" maternal figures in the media, and the proliferation of mediated platforms giving voice to the mundane, messy realities and frustrations of motherhood, seem to have afforded the women I interviewed license and vocabulary to articulate their ambivalent experiences and complex feelings about mothering (indeed, some mentioned their participation in online platforms such as Mumsnet and Mothers at Home Matter).[40]

However, the intensified public visibility of motherhood and the emergence of non-normative maternal representations hide a constitutive aspect of women's lives. As the study by American sociologists Arielle Kuperberg and Pamela Stone (referred to in chapter 3) shows, a "new feminine mystique" has emerged in which "the role of mother has displaced that of wife."[41] Even a show like *The Good Wife*, which as its title suggests tackles the topic of wifehood head on, focuses considerably on the lead character's role as a mother and successful lawyer. Alicia Florrick's husband initially is in prison, and they live apart when he is released, so the show offers a very limited sense of wifehood as a lived reality. In the new feminine mystique, motherhood has ousted wifehood. This mystique helps the women and men I interviewed conceal the difficult compromises and ambivalence about the central role of wifehood in women's lives and its profound consequences for their identity.

PRIVATE STORIES OF WIFEHOOD

Disentangling the women's accounts of their identity as mothers from those of their roles as wives is tricky because the two are intertwined in their lives, and because the women are so deeply invested in suppressing the centrality of wifehood. They were very aware of the derogatory connotations of being a wife and continually distanced themselves from any notion that they might resemble the old-fashioned, traditional wives of their mothers' generation. Yet while wifehood was heavily veiled in these women's accounts, it was never completely buried.

Sara, a former financial director in a global American firm and stay-at-home mother of two, who is married to a high-flying banker, revealed the lurking wifehood in her story of a selfless mother's decision to quit her career:

> I did realize that what I was doing [working in a highly demanding long-hour job] was not helpful for the family, verging on destructive. It was quite selfish . . . a selfish choice to continue to work because the reason you're doing it is . . . it's providing *you* with what you need to live *your* life, and by that, with the structure, with the power, with the glory of doing what you're doing. It was satisfying *my* needs but it wasn't satisfying my children's needs or my husband's, for that matter. For two people to be going out and satisfying their needs if other people in their family are suffering, I need . . . mothers are supposed to be selfless, aren't they?
>
> But . . . but, gosh, you're writing all of this down, I'm wondering if I'm saying the wrong things!

Against the dominant expectation that mothers act selflessly, Sara constructs her self-realization through work as an indulgent and selfish act. She presents her choice to leave paid employment as a choice between two competing and incompatible commitments—to herself, and to her children. It is a choice between an identity as a worker *or* as a mother. However, hidden in her account is a third and significant commitment: to her husband. The job she performed, which she sees as "selfish," and which gave her "glory," "power," and "structure," failed to satisfy her children's needs *and* those of her husband. Beneath a genuine desire to satisfy her children's needs—a desire whose realization is enshrined in dominant representations—was the desire to satisfy her husband. However, unlike the sacrificial commitment to her children, which she discussed openly and proudly and supported by referring to the expectation that mothers should be selfless, satisfying her husband's needs was mentioned only briefly, almost in passing, and as interchangeable ("or my husband's") with satisfying her children's needs. Sara knows that admitting that her momentous decision to quit her job was made, at least partly, as a wife is "saying the wrong things." Admitting (as she does later) that she left that world behind her partly for her husband is incongruent with the dominant new feminine mystique in which she so much wants to believe.

For the majority of the women I interviewed, the consequence of the decision to quit their job was what they described as "falling into" an "old-fashioned" and "traditional" family setup. Many admitted that even before having children things were unequal in their marital lives: while both partners were in full employment, it was the women who managed the housework. In most cases, it was after the birth of the second child that the family system became unable to cope with the pressures of a two-earner household, and the woman "opted out" of the workplace and the family adopted a "traditional" "old-fashioned" setup. "I do the shopping, I do the cooking. It's fairly old-fashioned, I'm afraid," Dana said, taking frequent deep breaths. "We've fallen into very, sort of, traditional roles as a family, [deep breath] um, even though I'm not a very traditional sort of person," Paula explained apologetically. "Suddenly, we started taking on much more traditional gender roles," Jenny confided with uneasiness.

What does the "old-fashioned" family setup look like, and how does the gendered division shape women's lives and identities? And how does the current cultural imaginary, in particular the fetishization and idealization of motherhood, support the gendered split so as to obfuscate the centrality of wifehood in women's identities and the difficult feelings it entails?

Living the split

I asked the women and men I interviewed to describe the distribution of labor in their households. Women almost always responded with a smirk. For example, Helen, a former accountant whose success in her job earned her a distinguished performance prize, replied:

[Laughs] My husband works, works hard. He comes home. He picks up his iPad. He sits down. He turns on the television, and, um, that's, that's probably it! [laughs] Ah . . . I do all the paperwork. I pay all the bills. I organize the holidays. I do the schooling. I do . . . *So he doesn't really have to think, or be involved in anything other than his work . . .* So I've got that side of things. I've got to make sure that the house doesn't become a complete pit. I've got to do the shopping, the food shopping, um, and, ah, but I have fairly, fairly relaxed standards, should we say? [laughs]

Despite her "relaxed standards," Helen tries always to ensure "things are straightened" before her husband, a senior finance director of a large firm, comes home from work in the evening—a task that takes her an hour every day after she puts the children to bed. A year ago, to relieve the boredom and "keep her brain busy," Helen embarked on a master's degree. She used to read coursework in bed until one evening her husband said, "You know what I really hate? I hate lying in bed next to you and hearing you underlining things!" While the sound of underlining on pages might be irritating for someone trying to read peacefully in bed, arguably it was not just the sound that irritated Helen's husband. The sound of Helen underlining items in her textbooks was for him an unwelcome penetration of his wife's other life and identity outside her role of mother and wife. The public sphere of economic production, which he occupied exclusively, and the sphere of social reproduction, which she occupied exclusively, had to stay separate, so that, as Helen so directly put it, "he doesn't really have to think, or be involved in anything other than his work." What is so remarkable is that Helen did not feel able to stay working late in her study; her role as a wife meant she had to be in bed when her husband went to sleep at night.

The women I spoke to colluded, often unwittingly, in enabling an almost complete separation between their husband's role in the public sphere of work and their roles in the family sphere—a gendered division which, as historian Eli Zaretsky shows, is rooted historically in institutional forms of capitalism and patriarchy.[42] Tess, the former news producer and a stay-at-home mother of two whose account I introduced earlier, said pensively, taking frequent breaths, pausing and laughing:

> My husband doesn't get home until 8:30 p.m., so I'm not expecting him to do anything. Quite honestly, it's all over by then, you know [laughs]. He doesn't do household chores actually; I don't think I've seen him pick up a hoover in ages! [laughs] . . .
>
> In the weekend—I do, um, I will, kind of, do most . . . well, I will do the cooking, and, you know, family meals and stuff. [indrawn breath] Shopping if it needs be, those little bits and pieces. Other than that he will probably take them out to play some cricket, um . . . The cricket season for them starts very soon, but he, he will [pause] . . . certainly go out and just take them for a practice session if it's a nice day. [indrawn breath] But other than that, I would say . . . he's not particularly hands-on with them.

Actually . . . [pause] . . . he doesn't really do much homework with them. His element of homework is "go, you go and do it by yourself," you know [laughs], it's like "come to me if you've got a problem." But he's not . . . I just don't think he's that way inclined. I wonder if that is an element of . . . [indrawn breath] . . . he's been so much in the workplace, so long [pause]. He's sort of switched off from those sort of things really [pause]. And maybe I've given him that choice as well, you know. As an element of [indrawn breath], I've sort of, um . . . taken that role over a bit, because I do actually think sometimes [laughs], I'd rather have it done properly than not [laughs], not done very well, and it's a big mess. But, you know, there is a make-a-rod-for-your-own-back to a certain extent if you do that.

Tess's account highlights sharply how she abandoned the possibility of challenging inequality in favor of compromise, and how, as a consequence, the old separation between the sphere of economic production (stubbornly associated with men) and the sphere of social reproduction (cast as a feminine sphere of care) is being reproduced in her family's everyday lives. Tess's comment that her husband has "been so much in the workplace, so long" can be read as a historical statement: men have been in the sphere of economic production for so long, switched off from the family. "Men switch off when they finish work on Friday and tend to think: that's it! Leisure time now! That's my time!" Tess added later, taking a deep indrawn breath and bursting into laughter. She is one of many women who, as the British sociologist Rosemary Crompton noted, withdrew the idea of debating inequality in the household with their husbands in favor of personalizing the problem and its solutions—finding ways to manage the household and caring responsibilities almost exclusively on their own.[43] Women like Tess have colluded in this arrangement, in the past as housewives, now as CEOs of their family and as wives. In so doing, they have made a rod not only for their own backs but for society at large. "Maybe I'm just a bit too easy on him," Tess confessed, restlessly clicking her tongue.

Money

Money is a key marker of the separation between the sphere of economy/work/men and the sphere of family/care/women. Couples' arrangements in relation to money differed: some women had joint bank accounts with their husbands, while others also had their own separate accounts. Husbands always had their own separate accounts. A couple of women had only their personal account and depended on the husbands transferring money to it. One of these was Anne. She was brought up in a working-class family in the north of England and was financially independent from an early age and never asked her parents for money. She reflected, "I find it difficult . . . because I've always been really independent and I've always had my own money whereas now if I need something I have to go to my husband and say, 'I've run out of money this month and I have to do this.'" Having to ask her husband for money infantilizes and discomfits Anne.

Other women—even those with joint accounts—reflected on the infantilizing effect of being financially dependent on their husbands. Julie, for example, whose experience was mentioned earlier in the chapter, described her irritation because her two children "are always asking for money from Daddy" and think that she asks for money from Daddy too, like they do. The former marketing manager Louise described how when her daughter was five, she engaged in a shopping role-play with play money. "Do you know where money comes from?" Louise asked her daughter. "Yes, I do!" her daughter replied assertively. "It comes from Daddy!" "The fact that she thought that money came from her daddy was a slap to her mommy," Louise confessed somberly.

However, some women appeared untroubled by their dependence on their husband's income and the money-related arrangements that acted as reminders of their dependence. Rachel, a former accountant and mother of three who has been out of the workplace for ten years, said that despite the fact she and her husband did not have a joint bank account, her husband was "completely unquestioning" and she "never felt beholden." However, even women like Rachel admitted having at least some fleeting thoughts about what financial dependence means. Almost all the women stressed that although theoretically they had the freedom to spend the money their husbands gave them how they wanted, they were "sensible," "reasonable," "stingy," and "cautious," especially about buying things for themselves. On the other hand, many women said that their husbands were "generous," had "expensive taste," and were happy to spend a lot of money both on their own hobbies and gadgets and on holidays and going to restaurants, theaters, and such with their wives. By internalizing a sense

of self-control and self-responsibility (like teenagers praised for han-
dling their pocket money in a sensible manner), and by self-policing their
spending, the women further cemented the split between their husbands'
world of capital and their world of care, and consolidated their identities
as wives in the very traditional sense. As the feminist social theorist Nancy
Fraser astutely observes, in a world where money is the primary medium
of power, those who do unpaid work "are structurally subordinate to those
who earn cash wages, even as their work supplies a necessary precondition
for wage labour—and even as it also becomes saturated with and mystified
by new, domestic ideals of femininity."[44]

Spatial segregation

The split between the husband's sphere of the economy and the wife's
sphere of the family was shaped significantly and maintained by spatial
separation. The husbands normally left home very early in the day and
returned late in the evening; many were away overnight during the week
on business trips, while, as Anne put it, for the women the home was
their workplace. The introduction and implementation of flex policies in
many workplaces, which seek to challenge "presentism" and allow workers to work from wherever they want, have been heralded as carrying
huge promise for breaking down the gendered split. By enabling men and
women to work from home, so the argument goes, partners can share the
housework and childcare more equally. However, while some of the men I
interviewed and the husbands of the women I spoke to worked part of the
time from home, they still worked long hours and could scarcely contribute to childcare and housework. Roberto admitted that:

> A lot of the housework, the chores in the home, still fall on my wife,
> because even though I am home, I'm sitting behind a desk and a computer.
> And I really can't get up and go because it's . . . you know . . . you can't
> focus like that! So, while I'm conscious of . . . of the need to, you know,
> to share the burden of the household, it's not . . . it doesn't come, you
> know, naturally.

Another woman told me that her husband sticks a "Do Not Disturb" note
on his home office to prevent his children (and her) from interrupting him

while he's working from home. The failure of the promise of greater gender equality by working from home was comically exposed by a March 2017 *BBC World News* interview that went viral. In the video, professor of international relations Robert Kelly, a white middle-aged man, is seen sitting at a desk in his home study, responding to the interviewer's questions on the impeachment of the South Korean president. Unexpectedly, his four-year-old daughter opens the door behind him and strolls into the room toward her father, swinging her arms cheerfully. Kelly notices her entry, but continues to look at the screen while trying to push her behind him out of the way. A couple of seconds later her baby brother bursts in, wheeling along in a baby rambler, followed soon after by Kelly's South Korean wife (a stay-at-home mother whom many social media users mistook for the nanny),[45] who throws herself bodily around the room in an effort to capture both of her mischievous children, then bent double as she drags them out. This hilarious clip revealed (among other things) how men's smooth and uninterrupted home working is dependent, at least in part, on their wives keeping the children out of sight, and keeping their husband's home work space safely separated from the rest of the home and its labor.[46]

A remarkable example of the way in which the women I met help to maintain the spatial separation, and how in turn, this maintains their roles as wives and keeps them "in their place," came up in Anne's interview. Anne's husband works as an information technology consultant in the City. He leaves the home early, normally returning from the office around 9 p.m. Therefore, he rarely drops the children at school or contributes to their care during the week. However, once a week he works from home. He is an avid squash player, and on the day of his weekly squash match he needs to be at the squash court near their home at 6 p.m. I was interested to know whether on the day Anne's husband worked from home he contributed to the childcare and/or housework. I asked Anne whether she found his presence at home on these days made a difference. She replied:

> Oh, yes! I tend to have to get out of the house because he needs to work. We have three kids and we don't have an allocated area for him to work. So he works in the kitchen . . . He had to work from home on Monday because of the tube [London Underground] strike and I was trying to cook. It was 10 a.m. and he said, "How much longer are you going to be because you're making too much noise?" I said I don't know, and he said,

"I have to rejig my whole day, so when you know when you'll finish cooking, can you tell me, because you're disturbing my work!" [scowling and
laughing] The irony! [she added sarcastically]

For the irony not to implode and lay bare Anne's submission to her husband's control, and for women to cope with the huge compromises and difficult feelings their collusion with their husbands generate, they and their
husbands devise strategies, language, and programs that conceal the crucial role of women as wives, and mute the conflicts they face in living the
gendered split between capital and care, work and life, economy and family.
As explored in the next section, this ongoing emotional cover-up work corresponds to and draws upon the cultural cover-up offered by contemporary
representations, discourses, and imaginaries of gender, work and family.

COVER-UP STRATEGIES: FAMILY MYTHS, TALES, AND PROGRAMS

Essentialist discourses of natural gender difference

One way that the women and men I interviewed justified and, in turn, reinforced the gendered separation of spheres was by drawing on notions of
essentialist "natural" gender difference. Explaining why it is she rather
than her husband (who is largely absent during the week) who helps the
children with homework on the weekend, Simone said, "He can switch
off his head really easily whereas I'm a worrier person." Similarly, Tim
explained his blasé attitude to his teenage daughter's behavior compared
to his wife's by their essentially different approaches. Yet he did not see
how this difference might be a product of the division of labor between
them rather than nature. "My wife and I approach it slightly differently,
because I suppose I invest less of my own sense of self-worth and self-
actualization in my success in getting my daughter to do things. I just
accept that she's who she is, and this is the way it is, and some of the things
I'd like to get done won't get done."

Unlike Tim, Helen's husband gets grumpy easily, she tells me, whereas
she is calmer and complains less. This is why, she explains, in addition
to mothering the children and running the house during the week, it is
she who does all the ferrying of the children to their weekend activities.

Because of the "personality" differences between Helen and her husband, she says "it is easier, to be honest, to get in the car and do it myself than to ask him to do it."

Descriptions of the woman's and man's opposing qualities varied among interviewees; for example, Simone described herself as a worrier versus her "switched off" husband, while Helen described herself as calm and getting on with things compared to her grumpy husband. However, the binary structure was repeated in almost all accounts, and was used to depict the wife's and the husband's psychological traits as if they belonged to two distinct, non-overlapping groups. In explaining their experiences in these terms, women and men drew on widespread essentialist ideas of sexual difference, and especially the notion of sexual difference as a psychological matter—an idea famously popularized in the 1990s by John Gray's bestseller *Men Are from Mars, Women Are from Venus*[47] and extended more recently in popular appropriations of evolutionary psychology that explain sexual difference as natural and unavoidable.[48]

Naturalizing the sexual differences between them helped the women and men I interviewed to explain and justify their choices as being the result of unambiguous givens which they cannot change and for which they have no direct responsibility. Thus, for example, the women I interviewed were mostly the parent who helped the children with their homework during the week *and* over the weekend because they were "switched on" and "hands-on," unlike their "laid back" and "switched off" husbands.[49] At the same time, such comments were suffused with ambivalence. "I don't think that's necessarily sexist to say there are differences between men and women . . . you have some variances, you know, variations and some people who maybe fit more into a different mold," Charlotte said, as if to qualify her description of the "natural" differences between her husband and her. The women and men I interviewed were well aware of the old-fashioned (as many put it) and sexist current of such notions and discourses of sexual differences, yet these ideas helped them justify their choices and freeze in place existing inequalities.[50]

The egalitarian ideal

Curiously, essentialist notions of women's and husbands' "natural" psychological differences were often articulated alongside descriptions of the couples' relationships as egalitarian partnerships. The women and men I interviewed described divisions of labor where the husband was largely absent during the week and often was too tired to contribute to childcare at the weekend, as "absolutely fair," "equal partnerships." They drew on a liberal-individualist and gender-egalitarian imaginary which posits the family "as a kind of unit or team, a partnership of equals," even when, as Angela McRobbie notes, "this means a stay-home Mum and full-time working father."[51] For example, Rachel, mother of three and a former senior accountant, left her job soon after her second child was born, which coincided with her husband's promotion to a partner in the same firm. Rachel's mother worked in the 1960s as a nurse, but on becoming a mother was "made to stop working because of that generation," a decision she "really begrudged;" she had had to "fight very hard to go back to work." Thus, when Rachel quit her career, her mother was terribly upset. "But when she later saw that actually we're a team and we're an equal partnership, and it works," Rachel recounts, her mother accepted her daughter's resignation from paid employment. Rachel used the egalitarian myth to convince her mother, and arguably herself, that her "equal partnership" with her husband works, that her experience was significantly different from her mother's.

Rachel confides that her "having a good job was quite a kudos" for her husband. "He liked saying, 'My wife was this high-powered whatever in the City.'" Showing off his former high-flying professional wife in public—like the Victorians used to display the wives they possessed in public functions—is part of the cover-up story the couple helps sustain. It signals that Rachel was not the traditionalist, old-fashioned housewife subjugated to patriarchal dominance (like her mother), but rather an independent woman who had fulfilled her professional ambitions and had made the free choice to be a full-time mother. However, that her husband finds her former professional background gives him "kudos," and that he shows her off to project his own worth, reveals the deeply unequal power relationship that the couple works so hard to cloak. Clinging to the ideal of the egalitarian couple allows Rachel and her husband to appear as a liberal, progressive couple, while simultaneously preserving inequality and patriarchal privilege that are predicated on Rachel's uneasy embrace of wifehood. "We *present* as a team to the kids," admitted Janet, the former actress who reminisced about her former self as an independent woman with a professional career, and reflected on the deep imbalances in her marriage. Similarly, Roberto told me,

"It's important to *give my wife the feeling* that 'you are also in charge,' that 'you are also in control.'" Sustaining the equal partnership myth involves a constant and conscious act of presentation and performance.

The men and women I interviewed seem to produce a discourse that Margaret Wetherell, Hilda Stiven, and Jonathan Potter call "unequal egalitarianism."[52] In their late 1980s study of students' views of the status of employment opportunities for women, the researchers found that respondents drew concurrently on two kinds of talk. One was around practical considerations, which were presented in essentialist terms, explaining inequality between men and women in the workplace as based on constructed natural sexual differences. The other was a form of talk endorsing the general liberal values of egalitarianism, individual freedom of choice, and equally shared responsibilities. Participants combined the two ideological forms, producing what Wetherell and her colleagues describe as a *de jure/de facto* discourse: they perpetuated patriarchal privilege and the status quo while continuing to present themselves in positive liberal terms.[53] Thus, the practice effectively undercuts the ideal, but repeating the ideal allowed participants to present themselves positively and buy into a particular kind of liberalism.

Peter's account illustrates how the competing tropes of essentialist differences on the one hand and equal relationships on the other co-occur in his justification of his and his wife's choices. Peter is in his mid-forties and is a senior director at a global technology firm, dad to two school-age children, and husband to a stay-at-home mother. He is one of the "diversity champions" in his organization, known for advocating gender diversity and committed, as he put it, to "stamping out gender bias." He describes the division of labor in his household:

We have divided up the labor in my house, such that my wife buys most of the food, she cooks most of the food, right? I do all of the maintenance work around the home and the garden. I do all of the sporting events with the kids at the weekend, she does all the ones in the week. That works for us. It feels balanced. I have tried to do the shopping, particularly when at some point my wife went back to work. I took on the shopping as one of the balancing activities. Everyone got fed [laughs] but it wasn't ideal. She's just better at it! Equally, I'm a lot better at cutting the grass. The stripes would not be straight if she cut the grass [laughs].

The family setup that Peter describes is unquestionably more even than that reported by most of the women I interviewed. However, even this model—which Peter takes pride in as balanced, fair, and based on his and his wife's different "natural" skills and strengths—is deeply uneven. Although he does a proportion of the cooking, his wife also cooks. On the other hand, shopping, which has to be done regularly, is mostly his wife's responsibility, while mowing the lawn, which is his exclusive responsibility, is an every-couple-of-weeks activity. The labor involved in children's sporting activities over the weekend cannot be compared to the labor involved in caring for the children throughout the week *and* during those weekend activities—his wife's responsibility. Peter endorses the egalitarian and meritocratic imaginary which posits that each partner does what he or she supposedly is best at, and the rhetoric of teamwork and balance which he imports from the workplace—"that works for us," "it feels balanced." The egalitarian imaginary helps to obscure the fundamental power imbalance that derives from the sheer fact that Peter is a senior accomplished professional in the sphere of economic production, and his wife is a former professional who now fully occupies the undervalued and unpaid sphere of social reproduction and care, as a mother and wife.

The essentialist/egalitarian story functions as what Arlie Hochschild calls a family myth: a jointly devised story the couple repeatedly tells themselves and believes in because it helps them avoid conflict.[54] It covers up the deeply unequal context for the woman's "choice" to give up her career, in which they continue to live. As Tanya's observation reveals, keeping the façade of equality ensures that pent-up feelings are hushed, otherwise difficult (and in some women's cases, explosive) discussions about marriage might erupt. "Simon and I have quite an equal relationship," Tanya said. "If he ever dared stop me doing something, I'd say, 'Do you know I gave up my career for you and I'm entitled to half your money!' . . . Yeah, we'd never get there!"

However, from time to time, the cover-up momentarily breaks down, exposing the fundamental mismatch between the egalitarian ideal and the unequal lived reality. Liz, a former academic who is married to a lawyer and quit her career eight years earlier after the birth of her first child, related a small incident that briefly disrupted the family myth of egalitarianism. Her 9-year-old son brought home a questionnaire from school asking how much he helped around the house. He ticked off "I do lots of shopping,

I do lots of cleaning the bathroom." Irritated, Liz challenged him: "This doesn't seem to be correct! I don't think you do a lot of this stuff!" Her son insisted he did. At this point, Liz's husband intervened, saying, "No, he really comes shopping with me quite a lot when I go shopping." "But I go shopping three times a week, and you guys are never there!" Liz replied crossly. Liz's fury triggered her exposure of the carefully constructed family myth of the egalitarian couple. However, such momentary challenges to the myth rarely affect the status quo. What is more, as her account hints, Liz's anger is aimed at her son's rather than her husband's failure to share the load. Ultimately, she suppresses the contradiction that surfaced during this incident. "There you go," she concludes with laughter, "different perspectives on who is doing how much!"

Rejecting housewifery

Central to crafting and sustaining the family myth of an egalitarian relationship are women's consistent efforts to distance themselves from housewifery and domesticity. As discussed in chapter 3, unlike the captive housewives of their mothers' generation who "bur[ied] themselves in dishpans"[55]—an image popularized by contemporary representations of 1960s women such as Betty Draper in *Mad Men* and popular memes of retro housewives[56]—the women I spoke to were emphatic that they were *not* housewives. All stressed how much they detested domesticity and kept their performance of household chores to the bare minimum, aided by paid domestic workers. The husbands, for their part, normally encouraged their wives to delegate as many of their domestic duties as possible to paid helpers.

The women I met used two key strategies to distance themselves from housewifery, both crucially enabled by their financial privilege. Yet these very strategies that helped them avoid becoming *housewives* sustained and reinforced their identities as *wives*. The first was replacing traditional housewifery with "creative" activities related to the house. Over two-thirds of the women I interviewed engaged extensively in planning, managing, and sometimes partly executing home building and decorating jobs. In contrast to the derided housewifery responsibilities, such as cleaning and cooking, DIY-related activities were described as "projects" in which women took great pride and from which they derived substantial satisfaction. As I entered the home of Charlotte, a former lawyer with a successful lawyer husband, she proudly showed me the outcomes of design and decoration jobs she had undertaken in the previous two years. Later in the interview, she recounted in painstaking detail the various jobs she did in "project managing" the rebuilding of the house. "Every single thing you see in this house, every single single single thing in this house I had to take a decision on! Everything!" she exclaimed with satisfaction and a proud sense of achievement.

The second strategy employed by some women was enrolling in some form of advanced study. Several had decided to study for a master's degree either through online distant learning or on a part-time basis, three had pursued a PhD, and others had taken short courses in adult education institutions in London. Studying enabled them to "use their brain," as they frequently put it, and crucially, it allowed them to establish themselves as more than just housewives, especially since it involved physically and mentally leaving the sphere of the home and its extensions: the school, shops, and children's extracurricular activities venues. One example is Helen, the forty-five-year-old former senior accountant and mother to two children aged six and ten, whose husband is finance director of a large company. Aware of the risk of falling into the perfect-housewife trap—"to have to have everything dusted and put away" and "make hospital corners on beds"—two years ago she started studying for a master's degree, but did it slowly, module by module, so she could drop the children off and pick them up from school every day. This enabled her not only to fill the hours the children were at school but also (and crucially) "It's enough of an excuse to allow me to be a terrible housewife!" as she said frivolously. But the "self-indulgent" time she spent at university while her children were at school and her husband was at work had to be covered up: "I was having this lovely time going to several lectures a week and my kids didn't even know. My husband didn't even know. Totally unimpacted by it, and I did that for two years, and it was fabulous."

To be able to escape housewifery Helen has to be sure her husband is "totally unimpacted" by her business. She needs to cover up her other engagements from her children and from him. From time to time, her husband would come home after a long day at work "not realizing that anything's been done and making comments like 'Ah, so who have you had coffee with today?'" Such sarcastic comments, which were described repeatedly by other women, disclose small bursts of anger and resentment, alluding to the huge burden and personal cost borne by the men as sole breadwinners. However, like most of the other women who gave examples of similar comments from their husbands, Helen too avoids confrontation or engagement in a serious discussion about them. "We try not to have this conversation!" she says with self-irony. Other women described similar occasional sarcastic comments from their husbands: "How was your holiday today, have you enjoyed it?" Sharon's husband occasionally teases her when he gets back from work, "Oh, you've had a busy day organizing all the stuff, was it hard today?" Tanya's husband makes similar cynical comments from time to time. "But, you know, he's winding me up. I know he's not serious," Tanya assures herself. Other women I spoke to at times felt offended by such comments, but rather than challenging them would seemingly ignore the "joke." Leaving their husband's lives "totally unimpacted" as Helen put it and maintaining the split requires them to get the joke and avoid difficult conversations. It rests on jokes and silences that enable the diffusion of friction or conflict as the basis for a smooth operation of family life. As Helen reflected (and note the repetition of the word "he"): "I'm quite good at organizing things, so one of things that happened, *almost without talking about it with my husband*, is that he, he, he, he has his career, and his job, but I do everything else."

Gratefulness and good fortune

All the women I interviewed described themselves as fortunate to have such supportive husbands (strikingly, none of the men I interviewed described their wives in this way). This was often tied to a sense of luck deriving from their financial privilege; their husbands' high earnings afforded them the choice to quit their careers. In her study of highly educated American women who quit their careers, sociologist Pamela Stone recorded similar gratitude among women toward their husbands for enabling them to choose to leave their jobs and stay at home.[57] However, in my study, I found that women's sense of good fortune and indebtedness played an important role in suppressing the complicated and often difficult feelings stemming from the women's ambivalence about their choice and its consequences for their identity, specifically as wives.

Katie, a former accountant at a London-based global financial firm and a stay-at-home mother of two children, whose husband is an insurance broker at the firm that once employed her, commented:

> I'm lucky to have a wonderful, understanding husband. He'd have said, "You know, whatever you want to do, we will work it out so that we can, we can" . . . But he did say to me, "I'm so glad you didn't go back to work, I don't know how we would have all coped, with both of us being out at work! It would have been . . . life would have been so difficult!"

Yet Katie's sense of luck and gratitude to her supportive husband hides difficult feelings about the choice she made and its consequences for her identity. This is illustrated in the following quote, in which Katie's voice oscillates seamlessly between "I" (*italicized*) and "we" (underlined). Her husband's voice, mediated through her voice (in **bold**), interrupts and reconstructs her account, and then collapses back into the joint voice of "we" (all emphases are mine):

> *I* really enjoyed my job . . . It was good, it was fulfilling, *I* really enjoyed it . . . **My husband would say, 'You can say that now when you look on it with rose tinted spectacles, but it was long hours.'** There was travel . . . *I* used to come home at midnight sometimes in tears . . . *I* went on maternity leave and *I* think *I* fully intended to go back to work, but *I* suddenly realized that that might not be the best thing for us . . . When it actually came to it, *I*, umm, we realized that having . . . once you get over the shock of having a baby and how it changes your life which you never realize beforehand [laughter, imitating her own voice cynically]: 'That's fine, *I'll* be able to go back to work, it would be lovely!' we realized that it wasn't going to work. So, **my husband is away a lot** overseas on business and *I* think we just made the decision. *I* mean, my husband said, **'If you really, really, really want to go back to work, of course we'll work a way out to do it, but you know, then if you just think that maybe it's a good idea just to leave, then, you know that would be absolutely brilliant.'** In fact, *I* think **he** probably **preferred** that *I* didn't go back to work because **he had enough** people who worked for him and with him who did the part-time thing and **he just saw** how difficult it was . . . So *I* made the decision, it was really difficult actually, *I* had a sort

of emotional, psychological trauma over it because you leave your life behind.

Katie's husband reminds her how difficult, stressful, and unrewarding this pre-stay-at-home-motherhood life was. He constructs the possibility of her returning to paid employment as almost obscene; she can make the choice to return to her job, but she must "really, really, really" want it, and contrasts it to the "absolutely brilliant" alternative of leaving paid employment and becoming a stay-at-home mother, thus reproducing the male breadwinner/female carer model. And while Katie concludes with a statement that confirms her decision as a personal choice—"*I made the decision*"—her voice collapses into that of her husband, exposing the hidden gendered power dynamics of marriage which, in significant ways, shaped this choice. Behind Katie's sense of luck lurk ambivalence and painful feelings about her decision to leave her job and the "emotional and psychological trauma" she had suffered as a consequence.[58]

Bolstering their sense of luck and gratitude, these women repeatedly praise their husbands' contribution to housework and childcare. The comment of Dana, a former arts festivals manager and mother of two, was typical:

> We've got quite an old-fashioned setup, although he would do, so, yeah, I would do, tend to do the children more, I don't do cleaning work, I have a cleaner, who comes in. But yeah, I do the shopping, I do the cooking. But equally, if I, if he, it's fairly traditional, but if he came in, and I said, "I haven't had time to cook, can you cook?" he'd cook. So, it's, you know, we really get on well, like that. He would do, he does all the DIY in the house. You know, he would do all the decorating.
>
> I know other moms who are stay-at-home, and they're decorating, and they're doing this.

Dana starts her account intending to describe her husband's contribution—"although *he* would do"—but segues into detailing her *own* workload. To ease the difficult recognition of the unequal distribution of labor between her and her husband, Dana employs two tools. The first is an example of an exception to the norm: the occasional times when her husband cooks. Referring to the exception helps Dana construct the unequal setup—which she admits she is part of and has actively sustained—as ostensibly less rigid than it seems, the gendered split between her husband and her as supposedly malleable. The second tool is what Arlie Hochschild calls "the going rate," to indicate the market value of a man's behavior or attitude. Comparing her husband to the going rate of other women's husbands, Dana feels lucky: unlike those husbands, hers does all the decorating jobs. Hochschild found that the going rate was a tool that both men and women exploited in the marital struggle, but which was advantageous mainly to the male side, becoming the "cultural foundation of the judgment about how rare and desirable a man was."[59]

Cultural representations are a prolific source for benchmarking the going rate of husbands. Despite important changes in the representation of men's involvement in housework and childcare, this involvement is still too often depicted as something special, deserving commendation[60]— which is precisely what the women I spoke to frequently awarded. An outdoor ad for Nestlé's popsicles (mentioned in chapter 2) is illustrative: showing a man in a superhero costume playing with his young child, the ad calls on men to "become a superdad" by purchasing the popsicles and engaging in an imaginary role-play with their children. By contrast, mothers playing with their children are nothing special in current representations, and certainly not something that would merit a "supermom" badge. Buying them sugary ice-lollies might even be grounds to accuse them of bad mothering!

Similar to what Hochschild describes in her study in relation to the activities men undertook, such as walking the dog, grilling fish, and baking bread, in my study women fetishized cooking as a single act that symbolized their husbands' entire sharing of the labor in the home. Unlike their own "basic," "boring," "for-survival" cooking, women praised their husbands' cooking as "gourmet" and "indulging." For instance, Julie, a mother of two and a former publisher whose husband "works all the hours that God sends," observed: "When my husband comes home, he's great with the kids. He comes and reads to them and, um, then he'll get downstairs and do his emails. He's definitely there whenever he can be. Because he can't do the boring housework, you know. He would. He's a great cook, you know, actually he's a great wasted cook [laughter]."

"So, on weekends, would he normally cook?" I asked. "Very occasionally," Julie replied. "He's mostly much too tired [giggle]. It would be nice and he would like to do it. But, you know, he's got work to do at the week-ends as well, so . . ." Thus, Julie applauded her husband for the great cook-ing he could *potentially* do, rather than the cooking he actually does. The ideal image of her husband's cooking is confronted by the lived reality of him having to work at the weekend. Recognizing the tension between the ideal and the real, Julie giggles, and defends her husband's failure to meet the desired image by depicting him as a helpless captive of his job.[61] Here again, the numerous films, television shows, and media stories depict-ing men as helpless slaves of greedy capitalist organizations (think, for instance, of Jordan Belfort in the film *The Wolf of Wall Street*) provide a use-ful common sense for women to draw on, to construct their husband as one of these men. Of course, the men to whom these women are married work around the clock, in highly demanding and pressurized jobs. How-ever, it is the notion that the men had no agency whatsoever to change these conditions that women used to help preserve the enduring inequal-ity in their marital and family lives, and which kept them in their place as wives. The possibility that *they* might be tired at the weekend, having mothered the household and managed family life throughout the week, was rarely enunciated.

Notably, the few men I interviewed did not present themselves as hap-less victims of their professions. Tim spoke of the technology business he owned and ran as his "other baby"; Roberto stressed how much he enjoys his job despite its pressures and demands; Peter took pride in his fulfill-ing role in the firm for which he worked. However, like their wives, they praised themselves against the going rate. For example, Tim takes pride in prioritizing his life and his family over work compared to some fathers he knows "who never see the kids, are up at sparrow fart, back at midnight, and they're working like crazy." Yet the sexual division of labor between his wife and him was still profoundly unequal. He works long hours in a genuinely hard and stressful job, but one that is valued and paid, and considered *real* work. His wife's work, by contrast—taking the kids to and collecting them from school daily, doing the food shopping, driving them to and from their after-school activities, and cooking the family meals—is invisible, unpaid, and unvalued. "I will then get back about 6:30 p.m., at which point the kids are fed and had their bath, so there's not much for me to do," Tim admitted. Yet the low going rate of the totally absent fathers put him in a positive light and ensures the status quo remains undisrupted.

SELF, LESS

Pamela Stone describes a sense of invisibility, of being devalued, and of lacking a sense of self-worth in the former high-flyer women she interviewed, similar to what the women I interviewed expressed. Stone argues that for the women she interviewed loss of professional identity was the most prevalent and pressing problem as they transitioned to becoming stay-at-home mothers.[62] However, for the women in my study, the overridingly prevalent (although largely hidden) problem seemed somewhat different from, and more radical than, mere loss of professional identity. The deeper and more profound problem they faced was the waning of their identity and seamless collusion into wifehood, at a time when individual identity is fundamentally reliant on the world of paid work, and when care work and other reproductive work are continuously devalued.[63]

As I have shown in several instances in this chapter, the voices of the women I interviewed frequently commingled with their husbands'. At its most profound level, this was manifest in women's pleasures, imaginations, and desires. Anne, for instance, said:

> One of the things I love about being a stay-at-home mom is that I can shop well and eat well . . . I love that. My husband got home last night and said, "Oh! I can smell chili! That's my favorite." That is wonderful! That he came home from a really long hard day's work and that makes me feel good. I know it wouldn't make every woman feel like that but for me . . . I feel I'm fulfilling a role. That is my role. It's about quality of life.

Anne may sound like a submissive wife, but she prides herself on being an independent, empowered woman. When I asked Katie how she imagined her life when the children were grown up she replied by referring almost exclusively to *her husband's* future: "I imagine my husband retired, and both of us doing our own interests . . . I'd want my husband just to be relaxing and playing golf and doing things that he . . . he's not far off for retiring. He wants to teach. He would love to teach history, so I just think it would be great. That's how I see our lives." While it is easy to regard such comments as vindication of these women's passive submission to their husbands and adherence to the stereotype of the retro housewife, the story that emerges from their accounts presents a far more complex and ambivalent picture.

Women's "falling into an old-fashioned setup," which implies embracing wifehood, was a consequence, at least partly, of colluding with two key tenets of the heteronormative cultural story of motherhood: mothers ought to be the primary carers, and mothers are supposed to be selfless. Although cultural representations of motherhood are evidently more diverse than in the past, in allowing nonheteronormative maternal figures and the expression of feelings and experiences previously tabooed, mothers and motherhood continue to preoccupy and dominate popular imagination. Heterosexual marriage, so policy and media tell us, is the backbone of a healthy society, and caring is primarily a woman's role. Yet wifehood is an unpopular and invisible identity: women's primary roles in the twenty-first century are workers and mothers, not wives. "Aberrant mothers" who are "unabashedly sexual and refreshingly professional," whose "relationship to both work and family is rich and deep"[64] are celebrated; "good wives" are denigrated. Those messages and representations offer a cultural cover-up that dovetails with and supports the emotional cover-up of the women I met. They help mute the contradictions and weather the ambivalence and difficult feelings emerging as a consequence of their reinvention as wives and mothers.

The women I met no longer suffer like the housewives of their mothers' generation from what doctors in the 1950s and 1960s called "the housewife's syndrome" or "the housewife's blight."[65] However, they continue to be entrapped in—and help to renew, sustain, and expand—the split between the home and personal life on the one hand, and the economy and production on the other. By colluding in this gendered split, and its deep and inseparable links to patriarchy and heteronormativity, these women have precipitated the waning of their own identities. Obeying the demand to be selfless mothers, and the unspoken demand to be selfless wives, they have allowed their self to become less.

Despite the strategies of denying and suppressing wifehood that they and their husbands devise, many of the women I met know that they have inadvertently colluded with and deferred their identities to their husbands. Tess, whose account was explored in detail in this chapter, captured this difficult knowledge when describing the weekend family supper routine:

I'm thinking . . . when I'm putting out food on the table, I put the boys down first, then my husband, then me. And I'm thinking it's wrong, isn't

it? So I'd, I'd evidently think of myself as being the, the person at . . . I'm
not terribly, terribly, terribly upset about that, don't get me wrong . . . But
it's just something I have noticed, you know.

Maybe I should be more upset about it, I don't know.

Do you have to listen back to this? [laughter] There's quite a lot in
there, isn't there?

Tess's painful quote summarizes the tension I described throughout the
chapter. She has assumed the role of the selfless mother and selfless wife.
However, while the former is legitimized and encouraged by societal and
cultural scripts (though it produces ambivalent and difficult feelings), she
wrestles with the latter: the admission that she serves her husband's needs
before her own. "Do you have to listen back to this?" she says, embarrassed. She knows she "should be more upset about it" yet the only way to
weather the difficult feelings such admission generates is to avoid becoming "terribly, terribly, terribly upset about that"—that is, to disavow anger,
and use the cultural story of motherhood to cover up her ambivalence
about wifehood.

PART 3

Heading Where?

Curbed Desires

CHAPTER 5

The Mompreneur/Inarticulate Desire

"**H**ow do you imagine yourself when the kids are grown?" I asked the women toward the end of our interviews. The question was met almost always with long silences, pauses, and hesitation. Women expressed a desire to return to paid work, but struggled to imagine and articulate it in concrete terms. They have processed the "easy route out" of staying out of paid work, and rejected it. They genuinely wanted to cease to occupy the role of stay-at-home mother and yearned to return to some form of creative and rewarding paid work. One woman told me that even after eleven years outside paid employment she craves to go back to some form of paid work. "At times, I think: oh God, give me a job!" she bellowed. Yet the women I interviewed were unable to see what such future work might look like, and what person they might become in that fuzzy future. How is it that women who participated actively in the workforce and whose identities were inseparable from their working lives go blank when it comes to imagining their future selves in the context of paid work? If they desire so clearly to return to some form of paid work, why do they struggle to articulate the substance of such work? To address these questions let us start by looking at an instance of this struggle.

OPAQUE FUTURES OF WORK AND SELF

Marie, who is in her early forties, is a former solicitor and a mother of two, married to Jack, who is also a solicitor. Both Marie's and Jack's parents live abroad, which leaves them with no local family support. Marie left paid employment with a heavy heart. Her mother had instilled in her a strong belief in the importance of being financially independent and pursuing a professional career as the basis for "being free." Identifying herself as a feminist, Marie speaks in the first part of the interview with agonizing clarity about the decision to quit her job and its consequences for her identity and for her family. But then her narrative breaks down. "You sort of become more of a housewife, as opposed to staying at home to look after the children," she recounts in a mix of tears and laughter which disclose her sadness about the decision to quit, and her discomfiture in the new role of housewife. She avoids using the word "housewife" again, replacing it with silences and the abstract "that": "I'm struggling with the concept of being a . . . [silence] I don't . . . [silence] I just think that . . . I just don't think that . . . *that* would be enough for me. I think I would need to do something." I asked Marie what that "something" might be. In stark contradiction to her eloquent account of her decision to leave her job, during the first hour and a half of our interview, Marie's response was inarticulate and confused, laced with hesitations and pauses:

> I don't know . . . [pause] I mean I might do something different. I haven't really thought enough about it at the moment . . . But [pause] . . . um . . . [pause] yes, I mean, it's still an option for me to go back to the job that I was doing. Well, I mean . . . I guess I'd have to . . . [pause] Yes. I mean I guess I would have to . . . um, I guess I would have to . . . [pause] um, I would have to do some catching up, but [pause] . . . um, but it wouldn't . . . it wouldn't be a bar to me.
>
> So certainly it is an option. But I think I just [pause] . . . I would have to do something more. I couldn't [pause] . . . I couldn't just stay at home and not have children to look after, if you know what I mean . . . during the day. I think I would [pause] . . . Um, it just would be a bit odd sitting here nine to three. I mean at home there's only so much cleaning, and I don't take that much enjoyment out of that. I mean it's nice when it's all . . . when your house is nice and clean, but actually doing it, no, it's not.

Um, I don't know. I just think that I would want to do more with my life than that [wipes off her tears].

Marie's stammered and incoherent account of what she might do in the future contrasts with her acute conviction that she does not want to stay in her current role of stay-at-home mother. She yearns "to do more with her life" than sitting at home "nine to three," and cleaning. She momentarily entertains returning to her former job as a solicitor in the City, and attempts desperately to capture the promise held by this possibility— "certainly it is an option," she asserts. However, Marie knows this is not a real alternative; the very conditions of her husband's job and her former work were what decided her to leave. They both worked as solicitors in leading law firms, jobs that involved long hours, frequent late nights, attending evening and weekend events, extensive travel, and being on call outside formal office hours. Tears run down Marie's cheeks; she searches anxiously, but fails to find the resources for hope.

The similarity between Marie's account and the accounts of the housewives Betty Friedan interviewed in the 1960s is arresting. Friedan's women had a "vague undefined wish for 'something more' than washing dishes, ironing, punishing and praising the children."[1] The solution of the feminine mystique to that undefined desire for "something more" was realizing their potential as mothers and wives and removing any barriers to those roles. "In the women's magazines," Friedan observed, it was "solved either by dyeing one's hair blonde or by having another baby."[2] However, in the second decade of the twenty-first century, the solutions on offer for women like Marie are different. And it is in the context of those solutions, or new "mystiques" that are proposed by and perpetuated in the media and policy, that we can start understanding Marie's struggle.

THE NEW MYSTIQUE OF THE GIG ECONOMY AND THE MOMPRENEUR

Contemporary constructions of work have their origins, at least partly, in the 1980s, when entrepreneurialism became marked as an ideal work form, heralding the shift away from traditional jobs for life to more flexible types of work. In promoting the spirit of enterprise, the neoliberal policies being implemented in industrialized countries at that time—notoriously under

Ronald Reagan in the United States and Margaret Thatcher in the United Kingdom—sought to attenuate the harmful effects of the huge unemployment which erupted as the result of massive overcapacity and the failure of many businesses.[3] "Entrepreneurship and self-employment were promoted as a route out of dependency and unemployment for the individual, and as a means of creating economic regeneration for the nation."[4] The entrepreneur was cast as a heroic figure able to revive wilting economies and marked by the capacity to take risks.[5]

In the UK and US media and policy spheres, women have been positioned as ideal subjects to benefit from (and in turn, drive) the shift from traditional jobs to flexible entrepreneurial work. A memorable celebration of women's entrepreneurialism appeared in the popular 1987 Hollywood film *Baby Boom*. The film follows the character of J. C. Wiatt (played by Diane Keaton), a highly driven career woman who works as a senior management consultant in Manhattan and progresses in her career until becoming the adoptive parent of the baby of her deceased cousin. Having to cope with a chaotic little baby who was forced upon her turns Wiatt's life upside down. As Margaret Tally observes in her analysis of the film:

> Though played for laughs, it soon becomes clear that Keaton's character cannot maintain what is portrayed as a dysfunctional, typical 80-hour workweek for an active career woman with the arrival of a new baby. Keaton's character soon jettisons the dysfunctionality of the frenetic work world and learns the joys, with a series of comic mishaps, of new motherhood.[6]

However, J. C. Wiatt does not resort to becoming a full-time mother; the gourmet food she prepares for her adopted daughter sparks the idea for a new business. Wiatt becomes a successful maternal entrepreneur, or "mompreneur": "a mother who establishes her own business from the kitchen table whilst her children crawl beneath it."[7]

Janet Newman's analysis of the pages of advice manuals from the 1980s describes a similar construction, which celebrates the entrepreneurial woman as someone who can succeed and can find her own niche in the world of work, provided she possesses "enough self-reliance, financial nous, competitive spirit and the determination to overcome the barriers" she may encounter on the way.[8] This image of the mompreneur, notes cultural analyst Jo Littler, tries to reconfigure the relationship between economic production and reproduction in a different way from the notion promoted by the "career woman" figure. The mompreneur image attempts to bring work from the masculinized public sphere into the space of the home, a reconfiguration that is seen as automatically empowering.[9]

Constructions of the maternal entrepreneur in the 1980s, Littler observes, were closely connected to the ideological onslaught of Thatcherism (and Reaganism) on social welfare, and its endorsement of free market enterprise. It is in the context of the state's ongoing withdrawal of and demonization of collective childcare provision (e.g., day care nurseries) that started in the 1980s, and became pronounced following the 2008 financial crisis and ensuing recession, that the figure of the mompreneur (or mumpreneur in the United Kingdom) "is frequently packaged as an enticing meritocratic solution which offers a promise of resolving problems of restrictive work and expensive childcare whilst also providing glamour and personal fulfilment."[10]

Over the past decades, the mompreneur has received growing media visibility and cultural presence, evident in a plethora of dedicated websites, specialized conferences, guidebooks, popular fiction, "momoirs," and the rising number of Google hits recorded on the term.[11] In these outlets the figure is often cast as a woman who has moved from traditional employment to owning and operating a new venture that fits better with her role of mother.[12] Policy discourses and initiatives show a parallel emphasis on and push for women's and specifically mothers' entrepreneurialism. For example, in 2005, the UK government created the Women's Enterprise Task Force to encourage female and especially mothers' enterprise.[13] This was followed by several more initiatives such as Prowess, set up to increase women's confidence and networking skills,[14] and Start-Up Britain. In 2012, in a speech about Start-Up Britain, Prime Minister David Cameron referred to the benefits deriving from women's enterprise, using the example of the Body Shop founder Anita Roddick, who started her business from her kitchen.[15] Finding the "missing million" female entrepreneurs was central to the Cameron government's Women and the Economy Action Plan. In 2014, it launched the "Business Is Great" website offering advice to women on entrepreneurialism, and announced its £1 million Women and Broadband Challenge Fund as part of the government's superfast broadband rollout, to encourage women-led businesses to compete for funding to create online businesses.[16]

Similarly, US government policy documents and initiatives construct female entrepreneurship as crucial for economic growth, and as a way for women to achieve a work-life balance and fulfill their aspirations. In February 2017, President Donald Trump and Canadian Prime Minister Justin Trudeau announced the creation of the US-Canada Council for Advancement of Women Entrepreneurs and Business Leaders. A White House press release stated that "President Trump wants to pave the way for women to bring their unique perspectives and strengths to the business world, and to harness the full potential of female entrepreneurs in our economy to make America great again."[17] In this context, Ivanka Trump, daughter of and advisor to the US president, has risen as a central figure representing and spearheading female entrepreneurship. In her 2017 book, *Women Who Work: Rewriting the Rules for Success*, Ivanka Trump relates her positive experience as a female entrepreneur who created a successful apparel and accessory business (strikingly, overlooking the access to capital and resources she enjoyed and which many women looking to start their own businesses do not possess), and prides herself on successfully combining launching and managing this business with being a mother and wife. Capitalizing on her success, and further consolidating her image as champion of women's empowerment, during the July 2017 G20 summit, Ivanka Trump rolled out the Women Entrepreneurs Finance Initiative (We-Fi), a World Bank fund focused on promoting women's entrepreneurship in developing countries.

Both media and policy representations construct mompreneurship as encompassing several features. First, it is constructed as the solution to the problem of combining work and childcare.[18] Littler argues that in various popular texts, mompreneurship is presented as a meritocratic solution to an array of problems exacerbated by the recession and, especially, expenditure on childcare, and the gendered inequalities and inflexibilities of much paid work. However, at the same time as mompreneurs are being heralded by media and governments, they are being devalued. Management scholar Kate Lewis notes how "public portrayals of female entrepreneurs depict them as less professional, successful and purposeful than their male counterparts."[19] Lewis shows in her analysis of media stories how women's businesses are often framed as small stable firms that are inferior to men's businesses in both their practices and performance. The former are based around skills regarded traditionally as female, and are undertaken in domestic settings and as a means of forging a link between a nurturing role and economic agency.

A second characteristic of the mompreneur figure is that she is self-employed. Her popularity is situated in the context of the increase since the 2008 recession in the number of self-employed workers; she has come to represent and, in turn, legitimize the current push for self-employment.[20] Investigating discourses of entrepreneurialism and contemporary creative work, Stephanie Taylor notes that since 2011, unemployed people in the United Kingdom are able to apply for the New Enterprise Allowance "in an expectation that the imagined inactivity of the unemployed person will be transformed into the commendable activity of the entrepreneur."[21] Specifically, there has been an increasing focus on self-employment and entrepreneurialism in the creative sectors, often exemplified by digital micro-businesses. These types of work are often presented in the media and in government communications as autonomous, flexible, and free from sociocultural barriers. For instance, an *Independent* article explaining the dramatic 36 percent increase between 2008 and 2015 in the number of freelancers in the United Kingdom, and the even more dramatic 115 percent rise in fields such as media freelancing, cites Chris Bryce, CEO of the Association of Independent Professionals and the Self-Employed (IPSE), which supports freelancers and contractors in the United Kingdom:

> There are a lot of benefits to working for yourself; from dictating your own working hours, to negotiating your own rates, to being your own boss. . . . Most importantly we see that those who are self-employed are able to create their own work/life balance, one which best suits them. . . . We have also seen a huge rise in the number of freelancing mothers—an increase of 70 percent over the last five years. . . . It is clear that freelancing can provide an adaptable lifestyle that full-time employment can't.[22]

Bryce's comment is characteristic of the way that self-employment, especially in the context of the gig economy or on-demand economy, is often couched in terms of the promise of individual control, freedom, independence, agency, self-fulfillment, and self-realization, as alternatives to the shackles of the Fordist nine-to-five working day, with mothers often imagined as the key beneficiaries of that promise. "Gigging reflects the endlessly personalizable values of our own era," *New Yorker* columnist Nathan Heller observed.[23]

At the same time, recent discussions of the gig economy and what President Barack Obama described in his 2017 farewell address as "the relentless price of automation"[24] increasingly highlight the risks and negative consequences wrought by the removal of the securities and benefits afforded by more traditional office-based jobs. Yet even many of those more critical discussions about the future of work continue (if inadvertently) to perpetuate the association of self-employment with flexibility, freedom, and control, especially in relation to mothers. Consider, for example, a *Guardian* article spotlighting the precariousness and insecurity involved in being a self-employed entrepreneur, and the growing evidence of the huge costs borne especially by low-status workers in the on-demand economy. The article discusses lack of employee benefits and rights such as holiday, sick, and maternity pay, unfair treatment in the context of financial products such as loans, mortgages, and insurance, impossibility for budding entrepreneurs to secure funding from banks and loan agencies due to lack of credit history and/or assets, inability to enforce debt management on clients who do not pay, and enormous difficulties for small businesses to break through due to stringent contract conditions, lengthy forms, or long payment schedules.[25] However, the image (figure 5.1) accompanying the article is in complete disjuncture with the text: a white mother in a white sweater is sitting calmly at her neat home desk with a laptop, a book, and a coffee mug on it. She is checking her smartphone with one hand, while cradling her contented baby with the other. The picture tells a very different story from the text: mompreneurship, it tells the reader, is the ideal solution to combining work and childcare, providing you (the white middle-class mom) control, flexibility, and satisfaction in the comfort of your home. The woman's white sweater, the baby's white bodysuit, the white chest of drawers in the background, and the neat setting connote order, balance, and tranquility, hiding the messy, often chaotic and stressful experience of caring full-time for a newborn, let alone combining it with paid work. The image obscures what every parent knows all too well: that doing paid work in a serious and successful manner while caring full-time for a young baby is practically impossible.[i]

As manifest in this image, a third aspect of the mompreneur is home working, which is prevalent among the self-employed. Research shows that

FIGURE 5.1 The mompreneur, "What Entrepreneurs Want from the 'Self-employment Revolution,'" *Guardian*, October 6, 2016. *Image courtesy of Alamy*

many home workers see the boundaries of work and home being increasingly blurred. They work longer hours than their employed counterparts,[26] experience isolation,[27] and are demanded to exhibit what scholars Lisa Adkins and Maryanne Dever describe as constant "work-readiness"—the post-Fordist economy requirement for continuous working or preparedness for work, which overrides any boundaries between workers' lives and work, and legitimizes the continuing removal of state support for these individuals.[28] However, these aspects seem largely to be absent from representations of home working. Rather, working from home is depicted in overwhelmingly positive terms as a convenient solution suited particularly to women's unequal burden of childcare. "Want more women working in tech?" reads a headline in the technology magazine *Wired*. "Let Them Stay at Home!"[29] In her analysis of the depiction of female workers in mainstream information and communication technology (ICT) advertising, Melissa Gregg demonstrates how popular culture and government policy converge in promoting working from home as an ideal arrangement for mothers, perpetuating the false assumption that it is possible to take care of small children and work at the same time. In so doing, Gregg argues, policy and media messages reinscribe women's "natural preference" for flexible labor and working from home because their (constructed) primary role is caregiver.[30]

This myth has become so commonsensical in current discussions on women, family, and work that, despite the majority of women in industrialized countries working outside the home, the stereotypical image of the home-working mompreneur is highly visible and popular. A Time.com report (May 6, 2016) is illustrative. The headline reads "Moms in the Midwest Are More Likely to Work Outside the Home Than Anywhere Else in the US." The article discusses the possible reasons for the higher rates of mothers' participation in the workforce in this US region, highlighting benefits offered to mothers by companies, especially in Minnesota, and the smaller wage gap in some Midwest states compared to national figures. Yet curiously, the article is accompanied by a stock photo of a young, beautiful, African American woman in a white t-shirt seated at her home desk, talking on the phone and gazing at her laptop, with a baby on her lap.[31] The meaning conveyed by the text clearly contradicts the meaning conveyed by the photo; the former stresses women's participation in the workforce *outside* the home, the latter reinforces the myth of women as natural and ideal entrepreneurial *home* workers, who simultaneously and seamlessly care for their children.

THE ELECTIVE AFFINITY OF WOMEN AND THE GIG ECONOMY

In this context, the gig economy, sharing economy, or on-demand economy is cast in various instances as the ideal platform for women's and specifically the mompreneur's self-realization and success. While some recent policy and media reports discuss the precariousness, vulnerability, and inequalities of labor in the gig economy, much of the discussion is overwhelmingly utopian, casting the sharing economy as an imperative that produces and sustains a new employment paradigm and "democratizes capitalism," as put by Chris Lehane, a former strategist in Bill Clinton's administration and at the time of writing this book Airbnb's head of global policy and public affairs.[32] Digital earnings platforms are argued to offer important benefits, including the freedom and flexibility to work at a time and place of one's choosing and the ability to turn a hobby or pastime into a source of income.³³ Surveys suggest that these supposed benefits are currently enjoyed by more men than women. In the United Kingdom, male workers are estimated to outnumber women by roughly two to one,³⁴ while reports on the US gig economy suggest a more even split, although still populated more by men.³⁵ However, certain segments of the gig economy, including professional freelance, direct selling, and service platforms, are found to be more densely populated by female gig workers, with some suggesting that women are outpacing men.³⁶ Social media platforms, valorized as springboards to successful and rewarding careers in the gig economy,³⁷ are particularly associated with women; a study by Pew Research Center found that women are much more likely to utilize social media when selling items online.³⁸

Women are increasingly called upon as the ideal workers of the gig economy: news media and online sites frequently position the gig economy as the future of women's work, as the UK and US workforce shifts to even more freelance and contractual work. "The face of 'gig' work is increasingly female—and empowered," reads a typical report in *USA Today*.³⁹ Such enthusiastic accounts frequently present the gig economy as offering a desirable form of work in order to balance and overcome the inequalities that women, especially mothers, face in the job market.⁴⁰ Female entrepreneurship in the on-demand economy is recurrently represented as a positive alternative to careers within male dominated corporations, offering opportunities for flexibility, creativity, and self-fulfillment.⁴¹

Etsy, the e-commerce website for handmade, vintage, and unique factory-manufactured items, has been paradigmatic of this framing, placing women at the forefront of the exciting possibilities offered by the digital economy. Valued in 2016 at a phenomenal $3.3 billion,⁴² the craft website has been heralded as an ideal platform for women to realize their entrepreneurial spirit (described by one book as "Etsy-preneurship") and associated with a vision of gender utopia in the digital economy.⁴³ The online sphere is replete with stories of women—almost always mothers—turned successful Etsy shop owners. For example, the blog "How I (Successfully!) Started an Etsy Store" describes Etsy as "ground zero for aspiring entrepreneurs," encouraging women to realize their dream of "hanging out their shingle on Etsy," and calling for them to be inspired by other women shop owners "who turned their passion projects into profits."⁴⁴ Such stories frequently frame becoming an Etsy entrepreneur as the realization of the "balanced woman" ideal (which we discussed in chapter 2). For instance, a seller of handmade home decorations recounts on her website how through her business she has learned "that balance is everything," and how she is able to successfully combine running a business with "maintaining a tidy home, cooking for my family and spending quality time with them."[45]

Women's self-branding plays a constitutive role in the construction and success of Etsy and similar craft, fashion, and beauty sites and blogs.[46] Analyses of these websites show how the stories posted by Etsy and eBay shop owners, fashion bloggers, and the like, and the inclusion of their children in their personalized stories, stress the value of being able to work from home while children are young—"a crafty way to 'have it all.'"[47] Women's self-representations on these sites stress glamorous lives and cast their commerce as "passionate shopping,"[48] masking the labor, self-discipline, and capital needed to realize such visions.[49] The discourse of "passionate work," Angela McRobbie argues, represents a shift to post-Fordist modes of working, in which emotional and immaterial labor are fundamental yet invisible and unrecognized.[50] In their study of fashion bloggers, Brooke Erin Duffy and Emily Hund note that passion functions to downplay the bloggers' entrepreneurial labor, (re)creating the idea that "individual success [is] obtained through inner self-discovery,"[51] and thus placing blame on individuals, asserting that if you are not successful in the shifting terrain of precarious work then this is because you lack passion.[52] This aspirational labor in the digital economy, Duffy contends, "has romanticized work in a moment when its conditions and affordances are ever more precarious, unstable, flexible—and unromantic."[53] Similarly, Elizabeth Nathanson's analysis of online fashion blogs in the context of the recession suggests that women's blogging "illustrate[s] a fantasy of self-determination and future prosperity through fashion," which maintains consumerism as a crucial component of femininity and reifies the idea that success is achievable regardless of structural constraints.[54]

Not only is women's success in the digital economy constructed as uncurbed by structural constraints, in some recent discussions it is presented as a way to crack those structural constraints, and particularly the workplace's structured incapacity to accommodate caring responsibilities. Anne-Marie Slaughter's bestselling book *Unfinished Business* is exemplary of this view. The American foreign policy expert recognizes criticisms of the on-demand economy—especially those popularized by cases such as Uber, related to employees' below-minimum wage and lack of benefits and protection. Nevertheless, she underscores the gig economy's "enormous promise," especially for women.[55] She writes:

> The on-demand economy offers the prospect of far more flexible, self-scheduled work hours. It points to the end of the office as we know it, the place you must go to earn a living. That is exactly what many workers who are trying to fit their work and their caregiving responsibilities together need.
>
> Moving up the income sale, the on-demand economy is likely to be a godsend for professionals who are also caregivers. Lawyers, business executives, bankers, doctors, and many other professional women could continue to advance their careers or at least stay in the game while being the kind of parent they want to be.[56]

Yet Slaughter's eager account hides the prospect that rather than breaking down the rigid male-dominated structures of previous models of work and realizing the gig economy's many promises, in this much-hyped economy many (if not the majority of) women will manage at best merely to "stay in the game," and arguably, many will not enjoy even that.

Google's Campus for Moms, rolled out in several cities around the world, including London, where it was launched in 2013 and endorsed by the then UK Minister for Women Nicky Morgan, neatly epitomizes the utopian gender vision of the digital economy. Parents (the clear majority of whom are mothers, as suggested by the name Campus for Moms)[57] enroll in a variety of venture capitalist- and investor-led lessons on marketing, branding, and fund seeking, which they can attend with their children. The concept, which has spread to other international Google sites, has been hailed as one of the tech industry's flagships, inspiring other firms to "revolutionise childcare."[58] An *Evening Standard* article praising Google's Campus for Moms under the headline "Bringing Up Baby (While Launching an Online Empire)" nods at the feminist politics of this initiative, suggesting that "while there are still pockets of male-dominated tech firms, many start-up founders are now thirtysomething parents with a child-friendly culture in mind."[59] Instead of the stereotypical middle-class white mother sitting at her home desk in front of a laptop and holding her baby, the image accompanying this article is of a hipster-mom (supposedly) in the Google's Campus for Moms in Shoreditch, a trendy London neighborhood (figure 5.2). It portrays a young, dark-haired, tattooed woman with a blonde-streaked pony tail, wearing a striped skirt, a sleeveless shirt, and trendy-looking glasses, gazing at a laptop screen and holding a baby on her lap. She clearly is not attending to the child, yet the child, clad in a trendy romper, is calm and contented, creating the illusion that he is being cared for.

Childcare in this image is constructed as a negligible task that can be simply and easily combined with creative and satisfying paid work, an insidious fantasy that reinscribes women's primary roles as caregivers. What the image fundamentally fails to show is that women should be released from childcare in order to pursue meaningful paid work. While the woman in the image notably is different from the stereotypical mom-preneur, like the latter, it too mystifies the fraudulent offer of the digital economy's new employment paradigm for women's self-realization, empowerment, and gender equality. The article ends with an exemplar

FIGURE 5.2 Mother and baby in Google's Campus for Moms, "Bringing up Baby (while Launching an Online Empire)," *Evening Standard*, October 20, 2016. *Image courtesy of Getty Images*

figure embodying the myth of the successful mompreneur in the gig economy. It relates the story of Sarah Wood, founder of the video ad tech company Unruly, which was bought in 2015 by News Corp for £114 million, who
on the day she met with Rupert Murdoch to announce the deal brought
her sick son into the office.

Such contemporary representations of the mompreneur, argues Taylor,
constitute a "new mystique," continuous with the feminine mystique of
the 1960s when small-scale, home-based entrepreneurial projects such
as crafting confined women to the home and prevented their capacity
to grow as part of society.[60] "The new mystique attached to working for
yourself is part of a process of exclusion by which increasing numbers of
workers . . . are encouraged to accept a marginalized position in the neolib
eral economy," Taylor writes.[61]

If the pillars of this new mystique are the figure of the mompreneur and
enthusiastic constructions of the gig economy, how and to what extent do
they shape the imaginations, desires, and dreams of the women I interviewed? How can we make sense of the struggle that opened this chapter—
women wrestling to imagine and articulate their dreams of future paid
work in concrete terms—against the imaginary that current representations of the mompreneur and the gig economy furnish and propel?

INARTICULATE DESIRES

It is remarkable how closely the accounts of the women I interviewed of their
imagined futures resonate with the promises offered by the mompreneur
and gig economy imaginary. Most interviewees described their desire to do
more with their lives in terms of running their own successful businesses
from home, in a harmonious balance with their caring responsibilities. They
pictured their desired future self as working on a small scale, mostly alone
and from home, motivated by the hope of self-development, self-realization,
satisfaction, pride, and freedom from the strictures of full-time work in an
office, rewarded by a steady income and stimulating employment.[62]

Katie, a former accountant and a stay-at-home mother of two children
for the past six years, exclaimed, "It's time for me to move on! . . . I would
have quite liked to have started my own business doing something." However, on being asked what kind of business she would like to start, Katie was

unable to specify a particular type or area of her future dream business. Nor could she describe the nature of the work she desired: "I'd love to set up my own business, but I just haven't got any ideas." The only accounts she and most other interviewees seemed able to give of their imagined future were vague descriptions that subscribed to the terms and conditions of the mompreneur fantasy and the gig economy: self-employment, control, flexibility, self-fulfillment, passion, and satisfaction. Katie explains, "Well, being self-employed, you know, just basically working for myself, I think, you know . . . just, basically being self-employed, being able to dictate my own hours and my own workload and being satisfied with what I'm doing. Being proud of what I'm doing."

Similarly, Julie, who nine years earlier had quit her job as senior publisher, said, "If I can develop myself, I quite like the idea of working independently as well as being outside of an organization." However, the notions of self-development and self-determination were detached from any concrete view of a specific type of professional area or skill. In fact, it is precisely the vague and undefined character of the self-employed entrepreneur that seemed so seductive and served as an imaginary basket into which the women threw their self-realization and self-determination fantasies. The account of Dana, a former arts festivals director and a stay-at-home mother of two for the past ten years, sheds some light on how the fuzziness of future work is justified by the promise of self-development:

> *Me:* How do you imagine yourself when the kids are grown?
> *Dana:* Mmm . . . I think about that quite a lot. I think that's what I'm thinking about a lot, at the moment. Um . . . and I would say, I haven't really got a clear plan, or idea, but that's, I am thinking about that a lot, I'm sort of thinking, you know, by the time my [younger] son is sixteen, you know, it'll be another ten years, so he's six at the moment. You know, that's a long time not to have any plans in place. *But I don't think people work like that anymore.* You know, *we're just constantly developing ourselves, aren't we? It's just, society has changed.* So, I think I've got to try and find some sort of niche, for myself, that I feel comfortable with, whatever that may be. . . . But, to come to a bit more peace, I think. I wouldn't say I'm really not at peace, but I've not quite found it.

Me: So what would this niche be about?

Dana: I just don't know.

Me: You don't know?

Dana: I don't know. I really, really don't know. I think, you know, lots of,
   I don't know.

Dana's total lack of clarity about what she might do in the future might seem surprising, especially given that both her children were already school age at the time of the interview. She recognizes that "not having any plans in place" is not an acceptable approach, and thus, to justify her complete vagueness about the future she draws on two prevalent discourses. The first is the therapeutic discourse of self-development. Dana situates her lack of any concrete plans within the broader idea that "we're constantly developing ourselves." The therapeutic discourse posits a self that is continuously preoccupied with its emotional development and growth. As sociologist Anthony Giddens noted, the self becomes a reflexive project that individuals have continuously to work on, transform, and improve.[63] While this narrative makes individuals responsible for their psychic well-being, sociologist Eva Illouz observes that "it exonerates the person from the moral weight of being at fault for living an unsatisfactory life."[64] Thus, on the one hand, the therapeutic narrative of self-development and self-transformation locates responsibility for emotional and psychic well-being in the self: Dana is pursuing an ongoing quest to "find some sort of niche" where she can feel "comfortable" and "at peace." On the other hand, the same narrative releases her from any sense of moral culpability: being out of the workplace for the past ten years and having no idea of what she might want to do in the future is cast as part of an ongoing process of self-development.

The therapeutic notion of self-development dovetails in Dana's account with a second set of discourses about the gig economy and the future of work. Dana's vision of what she might do in the future is divorced from any institutional market context—the very premise of the gig economy. She intends to find a "niche"—an entirely spectral construction of the field of work she might pursue. This language of the on-demand economy supports a fantasy of a future boundaryless career, which, unlike her previous career, would afford her huge flexibility and opportunities for self-fulfillment and self-development. The notion that people no longer "work like that anymore"—that is, in structured, office-based jobs and in stable, defined, professional domains requiring specific skills—nourishes the fantasy and releases Dana of the need to actively look for concrete prospective jobs.

A similar fantasy of self-employment as affording flexibility, satisfaction, and freedom animates Rachel's account. Ten years earlier, Rachel had quit her job as senior accountant in a highly demanding environment. She excitedly cited a report she had heard on the radio that the jobs that provide the greatest satisfaction are those of self-employed workers:

> I don't think I could be employed, only self-employed. . . . I can't imagine I could be in the inflexibility of working for a company anymore. I can imagine working for myself and being paid but not being employed. I think the inflexibility would drive me nuts. That's why I like the freedom, actually—the freedom. There was a . . . [sigh] oh, God, what was on the radio this morning? Oh, it was—there was a . . . I don't know if you heard the radio this morning. Someone's released a survey about which jobs give you the best job satisfaction. So it's, obviously, a big report came out this morning. They were debating it, and it basically turned out that— it was basically the jobs that gave you the most flexibility and control over your life were the ones that made people the happiest. People like farmers, um, vicars, ah, personal trainers. It was all people who could work for themselves, and I think that would be a very key area. I couldn't be in the confines of being employed, but I've been my own boss for so long, I would hate to be at someone else's beck and call now. It'd have to be on my terms.

Rachel's account, like Dana's, reveals a fundamental uncertainty about any concrete possibility of future engagement in the world of paid work, which is underpinned by a strong conviction of the incapacity of traditional forms of work to provide the flexibility, happiness, and control she aspires. The imaginary of the boundaryless gig economy and self-employment as its paradigmatic form of work offer a supposed route for realizing these qualities and meanings that cannot be found in "the confines of being employed."

In particular, it is working from home that was cast by the women I interviewed as taking control of one's life, and as a way to reconfigure their relation to work. Paula, a former lawyer, regretted having taken her mother's advice that "law is a really good job for a woman," and fantasized about the fact she could have "done something from home":

> I wish I had done . . . yes, I wish I . . . could do something flexibly from home that would've felt like the best thing for me. So something like . . . If I'd been a, a graphic designer or something like that and able to just work from home, um . . . I mean, you know, graphic design is just a . . . just one example of something which . . . I know some people who do that and manage to fit it in and they still work really hard but it's working from home and they can fit it around things. I mean, that's just one example but, I mean, it could've been lots of other things. I mean, it could've been going into . . . going into publishing or something. I've got another friend who does do copyediting, sort of, in publishing so she works from home as well. She moans about her job all the time but to me it looks like an ideal job because it's . . . I think it's interesting, it's creative and it's . . . she does a couple of hours' work a day from home; that seems perfect to me. So, yeah, I would've . . . I wish I'd . . .

Like other women's accounts, Paula's description of her desired work is rather vague, lacks specificity or clarity, and is punctuated by pauses and hesitations. However, the one thing she *is* clear about is the *location* of her desired work: home. She ignores her friend's "moaning" about the conditions of her job, which contradicts the fantasy of home working as liberating, and insists that it "looks ideal."

"The picture of the happy housewife doing creative work at home—painting, sculpting, writing—is one of the semi-delusions of the feminine mystique," wrote Betty Friedan.[65] More than half a century later, the picture of working from home in its updated version of engaging in a gig economy–related activity such as graphic design or selling crafts online, continues to have considerable purchase on women's imaginations and psyches.

It is notable how thoughts about the future among so many of the women I interviewed were confined to the home. The paradox for many of these women is that home is the location where they experience dependence and difficult inequality in their daily lives as stay-at-home mothers, and where they suffer loneliness and isolation (feelings that several of them confided). Staying at home has weakened their capacity to socialize, and crucially, to de-individualize and de-privatize both their pleasures and struggles. Yet when it comes to their imagined future lives as mompreneurs, all the inequalities and feelings of isolation associated with the home seem to be silenced. Mompreneurship naturalizes the home as the locus of unequal labor; the home is recast—in both the women's accounts and media and policy discourse—as an as an almost magical space; an ideal location for middle-class, creative labor. The women envisage themselves as self-employed flexible home workers who participate in the digital economy, and enjoy control, freedom, and independence in the very space where daily they are reminded of their dependence on their husbands (an issue explored in chapter 4). They appropriate the imaginary of working from home as a healthy, sane, and balanced alternative to their *former* careers within male-dominated corporations, but crucially, also, as an alternative to their *present* careers as stay-at-home mothers within unequal marital relationships.

Coupled with the promises of home working is the prospect of participating in the on-demand digital economy. "Something to do with data analysis would be interesting and quite exciting," said Liz, a former academic and a stay-at-home mother of two. Katie, a former accountant and a stay-at-home mother of two, exclaimed, "I just want to do courses and just get myself out there! I want to do desktop publishing [or] . . . doing sort of newsletter design . . . I want to do a course that's like a social media course, 'How you can use social media to boost your business' and things like that."

However, getting "out there" is conditioned on a crucial caveat: "It would have to work around the kids"—a phrase that was repeatedly used by women when describing the terms and conditions of their hypothetical future imagined jobs. "It would have to be something between nine and three, that I could do from home and [that] pays lots of money," Katie declared with a huge laugh. Katie genuinely desires something different in the future (she repeatedly used the phrases "I want" and "I'd like to"). She wants to follow the mompreneur's successful path and start her own business, but is aware of what stands in the way to realizing it. "We're all looking for that elusive job that we can do between nine and three and pays lots of money. If you find out what is, let me know!" she admitted with laughter that masked her pain. "I mean it's not much to ask . . . it's got to be out there somewhere?" she said with yet another loud laugh.

Rather than looking *in there*, into the unequal conditions that sustain their roles as primary (if not exclusive) caregivers and home managers, these women look *out there*, for some kind of external force that will remove the inequalities and allow their desires to be unleashed and realized. For the past eleven years, every year between September and December, Janet had sought that external force, searching on websites such as Mumsnet for entrepreneurial projects that would give her "that perfect elusive part-time job that would fulfill your dreams, pay a fortune, and fit in with your kids." Like Katie, Janet recognizes that the idea of becoming a mompreneur to solve the problem of combining work and childcare is a fantasy she cannot realize within the unequal conditions of her life; she is the foundation parent[66] who almost always will have to be there for her children before and after nursery and school. Nevertheless, Janet clings to the fantasy and its promise.

Thus, the imaginary of the home working, self-employed mompreneur who participates in the exhilarating digital on-demand economy seems simultaneously to unleash and re-contain women's desire. It feeds their dreams of doing more and getting themselves out there—developing and fulfilling themselves through creative, stimulating, rewarding, and well-paid work—while simultaneously reminding them of the "mom" in mompreneur. The notion of the mompreneur avoids any questioning of why caregiving continues to be assumed to be the primary responsibility of women, and offers instead a fantasy that melds work in both the private and public sphere into a new configuration tailored to women.[67]

It is perhaps unsurprising that the husbands of the women I interviewed embraced the idea of mompreneurship and the promise of the digital gig economy. Many of the women said their husbands (echoing the husbands of some of Friedan's interviewees)[68] encouraged them to "work out" what they were "passionate about" and "really wanted" to do in the future, and that they could do from home, and that would "fit around the kids." Tim, whose wife had quit her career as an art curator nine years earlier, is an impassioned enthusiast of the on-demand economy and the enormous promise it carries for gender equality:

> The sort of reshaping of the digital economy and the fact that I could do what I do and be female and have children and it would have very little impact because I make my own working time and I control the business,

and if I say to people we're going to have the meeting at my local café, or we're going to do it by Skype, or you're going to ask me by email, that's what will happen, right? So if I can do that, other people can do that, you know, and as work changes so that it becomes outcome-driven, project-driven, rather than attendance-driven, and it becomes digitally interme-diated rather than physically intermediated, all of this stuff recedes a bit.

Which is why you're seeing the tech industry, particularly the social media end, has so many more senior female execs because their work-ing model is much more family friendly, intrinsically is much more life friendly, they don't have a work-life separation, they have a kind of ménage, and that works much better. So you've got, you know, Sheryl Sandberg and you've got, what's her name, ah, ah, ah, the Yahoo woman? Melissa Myers! People like that are making a very good fit of acting as models for a new employment paradigm. . . . Whereas in the more con-ventional industries it's still, being a female banker is still stupid, being a female lawyer is still stupid because of the way these people choose to run their businesses, as if it was still the nineteenth century.

This "new employment paradigm" in which women work from home *and* continue to be the primary caregivers, Tim regards as the route to a utopian vision he describes later in the interview as "beyond gender politics." The inequality once experienced within the office in "stupid" rigid jobs and professions, such as banking or law, seemingly is resolved by the emergence of women's flexible, "digitally intermediated," home-based jobs. Ironically, the role model women he sees as epitomizing this new paradigm of work, of the ilk of Sheryl Sandberg and Melissa Myers, work in highly demanding long-hours jobs which are deeply incompatible with family life (as discussed in chapter 2). Most strikingly, Tim—who asked that we meet in his office rather than his home—sees no role for himself or men more generally in bringing to fruition this utopian vision. From the outset he frames his account from the point of view solely of the woman: "I could do what I do *and be female* and have children." The possibility that one could be a male who pursues a successful job and looks after his children is excluded from this vision. As Littler observes, "We do not hear of 'dadpreneurs' mixing their family life with domestic-based entrepreneurial activity. The masculinity of the entrepreneur is the unnamed norm."[69]

As we have seen so far, the stay-at-home mothers' inarticulate desires to return to some form of paid work echo the popular figure of the mompreneur or digital housewife, and are fueled by the on-demand gig economy's promise of flexible self-scheduled work hours. The mother with young children who runs her own successful business from home supposedly presents a felicitous balance between caring responsibilities and paid employment, and celebrates the melding of women's entrepreneurial spirits and maternal roles. However, against the compelling fantasy that representations of this figure stimulate, those educated stay-at-home mothers I interviewed seemed unable to articulate the substance of their future dreams, let alone what needs to happen for them to be realized. Current research indicates that this struggle is characteristic of the contemporary landscape of work and employment more broadly; it is part of what Stephanie Taylor and Susan Luckman describe as the "the new normal of working lives."[70] For example, in her study of cultural and creative workers, Rosalind Gill found that they switched between optimistic and pessimistic accounts and could not articulate their imagined futures. Similarly, in Julie Wilson and Emily Chivers Yochim's research on *Mothering through Precarity*, American work-at-home mothers yearned for different worlds "yet were often unable to sense or think them."[71]

Occasionally, however, this difficult struggle to imagine one's future exposes—albeit momentarily and never fully—the cracks in the imaginary of the mompreneur and the future of work, and unveils the limits of utopian visions of gender equality in the digital economy.

CALLING THE MOMPRENEUR'S AND THE GIG ECONOMY'S BLUFF

Like most of the women I interviewed, Laura expressed a strong desire to return to some form of paid employment. She too had an extremely vague sense of the type of employment she might undertake in the future and exactly when she might do so. However, unlike the other women, Laura admitted to failing to see herself occupying the image of the mompreneur:

I find myself really lacking in any great ambition. It would be nice if I kind of, couldn't wait for the children to be gone to school, so that I could start my novel or open the café I've always wanted to open, but there's nothing in particular that I want to do, and I'm not really very much of an entrepreneur. So I will probably just look for a part-time job. And so what my life looks like when they're [the children] gone completely, depends on what that route is going to be. I don't really know . . . I probably could get a part-time role in the sort of area I worked in before. I don't have a burning need to retrain as a chef or an interior decorator, so I probably will just go back into it.

Me: Would you have liked to do something like retraining as an interior designer?

Laura: No! [laughs] But a lot of people view this as an opportunity: "I want to be a homeopath," "I want to be an interior designer," and they go and do a course. I can't think of anything in particular. I wish I could, because I would quite like to start something and I don't think there's any point in just picking something out of a hat. So, I'll probably go back to what I was doing before. Just a bit up in the air, my mind at the moment.

In her candid and self-reflexive response, Laura exposes the prevalent dreams of women around her—the dream jobs that cultural representations construct and propel, but that she had failed or refused to own. She is ambivalent about the mompreneur and the typical paths to its realization—writing a novel, opening a café, retraining as a homeopath, chef, or interior designer (many of which were mentioned in my interviews with other women as future aspirations). While Laura avoids directly criticizing the image of the mompreneur or the women who desire it, she scoffs at the possibility that she might become one. Her tone discloses cynicism about the construction of the mompreneur as having "great ambition" (which she admits to lacking), and the gig-economy rhetoric of a burning need and passion to retrain in one of the popular mompreneur flex jobs. She reflects on the common view of these jobs as opportunity, but alludes to their arbitrariness and superficiality: "I don't think there's any point in just picking something out of a hat."

At the same time, Laura wrestles with the inability to fit her dreams into the popular mompreneur mold and the gig economy's passionate work model. "It would be nice," she says, if she had that "burning need." "I wish I could think of anything in particular that I want to be."

Compared to the great ambition type of jobs to which other women aspire, but which, however, lack any institutional context, returning on a part-time basis to her former paid work appears like an unattractive default, an unambitious and unappealing option. Paradoxically, this is perhaps a much more viable and secure employment prospect than any of the entrepreneurial jobs the women I interviewed desire, but it is one that mostly is ousted from the imaginary of the future of work in a digital age and the gig economy.

Interviewees scarcely, if ever, referred to the risks involved in the imagined self-employed life they envisioned for themselves. They saw themselves as resilient individuals able to withstand the risks of this type of precarious employment. I asked what would happen if they got divorced, or if the husband was made redundant. "I would figure it out" or "work something out" was a common reply. Helen, a former accountant and a mother of two told me, "I would then go back to work, of course, and I know that I could pay my way. I could probably talk my way into a reasonably paid job without too much difficulty." The fact that many of the women were in their mid-forties and if they were ever to return to full-time paid work it would likely be in their fifties following a decade or more out of the job market was not seen as a barrier. The story of fictional characters like Alicia Florrick in the series *The Good Wife*, who re-enters the workplace after thirteen years as a stay-at-home mother and smoothly re-embarks on a demanding career, seems to have been inserted powerfully in these women's psyches; like Alicia, if need be, they could seamlessly reinvent themselves and adapt to the new conditions.

However, the accounts of two of the women I interviewed cast critical doubt on this narrative and offered a radically different vision of their future selves. The first was of Geraldine, a former lawyer and a stay-at-home mother for the past thirteen years (just like Alicia Florrick!), who had graduated in law (just like Alicia Florrick) in the 1990s from the prestigious University of Cambridge. She qualified and worked for a few years as a barrister, but disliked performing in court and retrained as a solicitor. As a newly qualified solicitor in her mid-twenties and following fierce competition with highly talented candidates, Geraldine was appointed legal manager of one of the UK's leading hospitals. However, she lasted only a few weeks in what she described as a "full-on heavy-duty job." Soon after starting the job, she became pregnant. "The job involved an hour and a half's commute across town every day, every day, and I was vomiting on every tube platform." With the strong and explicit encouragement of her husband (also a solicitor), a few weeks into her new job she quit, though "never wanting to quit forever."

When Geraldine left employment to look after their children, her husband seemed supportive; her becoming a stay-at-home mother suited his demanding career and the family's needs. However, twelve years later they divorced. Faced with a radically new reality, and loss of financial dependence on her husband's income, Geraldine was forced to look for a job. She was looking for "*not* just a part-time job that would fit around the children, but more of a career job . . . A fairly *comprehensive* work." In contrast to the boundaryless, flexible amateurish character of the mompreneur types of job that "fit around the kids," and (supposedly) award women a sense of freedom and satisfaction, Geraldine was seeking a "comprehensive job" that would give her a steady income and financial security. However, her quest for such a job was "not just from a financial point of view," she told me. It was also "from a *respect* point of view . . . wanting and feeling like I needed to have my own world again." Rather than freedom and flexibility (promised by the mompreneur), Geraldine wanted to have control over her life and to be recognized. Even were her circumstances such that she could afford financially to engage in a part-time, home-based, mompreneurial job, she told me, that would not allow her to regain her "own world again" or the connection to the world around her and, crucially, the respect she felt she had lost—of her ex-husband, her children, and society.

The mompreneur option fails to offer Geraldine what Betty Friedan over fifty years ago asserted was "the way out of the trap for a woman": "a job that she can take seriously as part of a life plan, work in which she can grow as part of society."[72] For the most part, mompreneurs are amateurs, not professionals, and "it is the jump from amateur to professional that is often the hardest for a woman on her way out of the trap."[73] Unlike the conviction held by most women that they would "figure it out" and manage were they to have to return to full-time paid employment, Geraldine is finding that after so many years outside the labor market returning to work and reinventing herself are extremely difficult. "If things don't go to plan and you have to get back into the job market," she said in a shaky voice, her eyes brimming with tears, "what am I doing?! You know, thirteen, fourteen years out, hasn't left me in a very strong position."

The second story is of forty-seven-year-old Emily. The daughter of a successful businessman and a stay-at-home mother, Emily was a stellar student and was awarded prestigious scholarships to pursue a bachelor's degree in history and then a highly competitive international Master's in Business Administration (MBA) program in North America. She embarked on an extremely successful career in sales and marketing in a global firm, "smashing all sales figures," later becoming COO at a technology firm. In her late thirties, she married an accountant who at the time earned half what she was being paid. Following her husband's relocation to another country, Emily left her workplace. In the country to which they moved, she got pregnant and for the next nine years was a stay-at-home mother. She recalls, "The way I imagined it would be that I put my weight behind trying to turbo charge my husband's career and that he would be made a partner. But I really underestimated how much I was defined by work and how much I loved work." When she left the workplace, Emily tells me, she just assumed that if she wanted to return, "there would be no problem . . . hard work and effort—I'd get there!" However, similar to Geraldine, the fantasy burst: when Emily wanted to return to paid employment there was an economic recession, her marriage broke down, and she found herself divorced, unemployed, and the sole carer of her nine-year-old son.

Buoyed by alluring accounts of the gig economy's great possibilities, Emily and four partners established a start-up company about which she was extremely passionate and enthusiastic. "I took equity and took very little money because you hope that if you can, you know, get this start-up airborne you're going to make a lot of money!" she recalls. However, the start-up ultimately failed and now, Emily confesses tearfully:

> Well, I've no financial stability. I've no financial security. I spent my inheritance and my savings . . . My son, he'll say that he's going to spend his pocket money in case we need it for food or electricity or whatever like that . . . So I have a couple of choices. I either go: "Okay, I'm going to work part-time in Marks and Spencer [department store] if I'm lucky and get through and always live in a rented accommodation and that, or else I'm going to knuckle down and move heaven and earth to get my career. But I have to say, it all really caught up on me. It just . . . I went through a couple of weeks . . . it was really, really black and I just thought, you know, how am I going to, you know, how am I going to get through?

Emily insisted throughout the interview that she did not want her experience "to sound too negative," while Geraldine described her position as "quite an extreme." However, their experiences are far from rare. Divorce is far from uncommon (estimated at 42 percent in the United Kingdom and 50 percent in the United States), and although the gig economy is growing, so are the failure rates of start-up businesses and gigs. Geraldine's and Emily's accounts painfully expose the fragility of the fantasy of women returning to paid employment after a prolonged break and being able to almost magically reinvent themselves as mompreneurs and enjoy control, freedom, flexibility, and self-fulfillment in the on-demand economy. It is a fantasy of finding individualized solutions to structural problems, offering a ready-made script that enables women to deny the deep contradictions between their desire—getting themselves "out there"—and the conditions that stand in the way of its realization and keep them in the home to look after their children. As Littler observes, mompreneurialism rarely disrupts androcentrism by encouraging men to get more involved with childcare.[74] Rather, it continues to position mothers as the primary childcarers who are simultaneously seeking to render their home-based state economically productive. It reinforces the idea that women somehow should "work it out" and manage both spheres, a pattern which, as the next chapter shows, the women I interviewed genuinely want to disrupt but feel they have little, if any, capacity to do so.

CHAPTER 6
Inevitable Change/Invisible Chains

DESIRING CHANGE WITHOUT A SENSE OF AGENCY

As we saw in chapter 5, almost all of the women I interviewed wanted to return to some form of paid employment to give them the sense of meaning and purpose they lacked: "something for myself," "to keep my brain active," to "get my own world back." Yet interviewees spoke not only about their desire to make changes to their personal lives but also—and passionately—about the need for societal change. They spoke about the impact of neoliberal, toxic work cultures on their decision to quit their jobs, and on women in the workplace more broadly. They criticized their husbands' absence from the home and over-presence at work, and expressed their deep frustration with and anger about the unequal distribution of labor at home, and the oppressive cultural messages about women's roles as mothers and carers. They wanted workplace conditions and cultures to change in fundamental ways; they hoped the gender pay gap would disappear; they spoke ardently about the need to challenge gender stereotypes and defy societal norms. Notably, a quarter of the women I interviewed accused their former employers of sexual discrimination and had challenged them (often legally) on issues such as pay, maternity rights, and unequal treatment related to childcare.

Maggie was one such woman. A former journalist and for the past eleven years a stay-at-home mother of four, she grew up in the south of England with a builder father and a mother who worked as a telephone exchange operator. "My mom had to work. I've always seen her working hard with four children. She was absent in the evenings," Maggie recalls. Her upbringing cultivated in Maggie a strong working ethic. "I always had this idea that women should work," she said. "If you'd said to me when I was at university, that 'actually, you'll be a full-time mother,' I would have been quite shocked!"

Maggie's social consciousness had been fundamentally shaped by her parents' influence but also, and importantly, by the cultural and political climate in which she came of age. "You see," she added, "having grown up with feminism . . . It was the era of Greenham Common . . . Doc Martens–wearing women and the miners' strike . . . lots of discussions about feminism. What it means to be a woman . . . Fighting for equal pay . . . and self-esteem." "It wasn't a particularly radical era," she added, laughing, but the ideas that circulated in the United Kingdom in the early 1980s—especially feminist protest such as the Greenham Common[1] and working-class protests such as the miners' strike[2] that were extensively reported in the media, shaped her social consciousness in significant ways.

Maggie was the first in her family to pursue higher education. On graduating, she became a journalist, but after her second child was born she quit her job. Like many of the other women interviewees, Maggie's husband's demanding job and her long-hours job were wholly inconsistent with family life. Throughout the interview Maggie expressed frustration and anger—often with marked sarcasm—about the unequal labor women carry out and the unequal distribution of labor she experienced in her everyday life. She was particularly forceful about the gender pay gap from which she had suffered and which she had challenged at her last job.

However, notwithstanding Maggie's frustrations, regrets, and anger, and despite her genuine desire for personal *and* societal change, she had limited sense of her own agency in making this change happen. When her husband was made redundant, it was "a window of opportunity" for her; the possibility that she might go back to some form of paid employment excited her. "It would have been great to have had him at the helm of the family and the household!" she exclaimed. However, the window closed a few weeks later when her husband found a new job. "We should have had the conversation then," Maggie said ruefully. She did not initiate a conversation about her desires and needs, and the change she yearned for remained mere fantasy. "If my husband could work, say, three-and-a-half days a week and I could work the rest that would be ideal! But that won't happen unless there was some sort of national directive that the working week is shortened or split." The option that her husband would reduce his working hours to contribute to childcare and housework so that she could return to paid employment was cast by Maggie as unattainable. For her, a national directive to reduce the working week was a fantastical, almost magical solution.

Like Maggie, other women I interviewed thought government should bring about the change they desired, but failed to imagine themselves in any role that might help to realize such change in their private lives and/or at a societal level. Other interviewees pointed to the women "trailblazers" driving gender equality. For example, Anne spoke passionately about women's equality in the workplace, saying:

> I feel that women are still prejudiced against when it comes to the workplace, when it comes to the jobs that are available for them, job sharing . . . There are some women out there who are trying, certainly higher up, to break down those barriers, for example going out and having job interviews together and proving they can do it . . . Hopefully by the time my daughter gets older . . . it is changing, there are certainly more opportunities, but I don't think there's any less prejudice . . .

I asked Anne, "So where would change come from?" She replied, "From these women who are trailblazers, who are trying from the top down to prove that as a CFO (chief financial officer) that role can be two part-time women. The more women who can go and have the balls to do it—senior women who can prove they can share jobs!" "And do you expect we will see men sharing jobs as well?" I asked. "Wouldn't that be lovely!" Anne sighed with a sneer.

When Anne quit her job, she won a court case against her employer, who refused her request to move to part-time work after the birth of her first child. Yet, eleven years on, Anne has no sense of her capacity to fight inequality. She looks to those "trailblazer" women "who have the balls" to break down the barriers and shape a different future for her daughter, but she does not look to herself or her husband. Her cynical response to my question about men sharing jobs ("Wouldn't that be lovely!") reveals her bitter acceptance of the endurance of patriarchal structures, as if they were fixed, unchallengeable, and inescapable. The revolution, according to Anne, will be when women at the top will be able to share jobs and combine them with their caring roles, while men continue to hold full-time power positions, relieved of any meaningful caring responsibilities.

American researcher Mary Douglas Vavrus wrote of women like Anne and Maggie that they are "smart, talented, ambitious, well-educated women, who, if they chose to do so, could start an economic revolution, by, for example, forcing GDP [gross domestic product] calculations to include the labor of the 'Economic Woman' . . . these women could alter radically [the] system that de-values mothering labor."[3] Yet, after years as full-time mothers outside the sphere of paid work, these highly talented women do not feel they have the capacity to enact change in their own lives, let alone in bigger societal structures.[4] How can we make sense of this paradox? If they yearn so deeply for change for themselves and future generations and, if in the past, they had exercised their agency to challenge inequality, why do women like Maggie and Anne see no role for themselves in effecting it?

Let me begin to address these questions by looking at Charlotte's story, which illustrates how genuinely difficult it is to propel such change, even when one truly craves it and takes active steps to achieve it. Charlotte had quit her job as a lawyer ten years earlier to become the full-time mother of three children, all now in secondary school. Her husband is a high-flying lawyer, and his contribution to childcare and the running of the household is extremely limited. Charlotte is proud and happy she had been there for her children on a full-time basis, which, she believes, had benefited her children enormously, especially compared to the children of mothers in paid work. Two years ago, when her children became more independent, Charlotte began contemplating a return to some form of paid employment that would give her a sense of purpose. "I'm now in the situation where I'm 46, I feel very capable, I feel capable, very capable. If you gave me something to do I think I could turn my mind to it and do it and learn pretty quickly!" she said with deep conviction.

The previous year, Charlotte had applied for a senior job in a high-profile international non-governmental organization (NGO). Prior to this she had completed a master's degree which put her in excellent stead for this job; she felt confident and well able to perform it. Although she had been outside the workforce for ten years, Charlotte was shortlisted for an interview. She became very excited about the possibility that she might be appointed, but when informed about the date of the interview she discovered it clashed with an already booked family holiday. She told the NGO about this and said she could only do the interview over Skype. However, on the day of her interview, the Skype did not work and she did a phone interview, and "so obviously," she explained, "I didn't get the job."

Why didn't Charlotte feel able to ask her husband, whom she describes as "very hands-on" and "very supportive," to take the children on holiday so that she could attend the interview for the dream job for which she had studied and was well qualified to perform? Why did her husband not make the offer so she could attend the interview? Why did so many of the women I met choose, like Charlotte, to draw a veil over their desires and avoid rocking the boat?

Janet, a forty-three-year-old mother who had quit working as an actress eleven years earlier and who yearned to return to some form of paid employment, offered an explanation:

> That's part of the deal. You leave work and you go back into an environment and it's sort of done for you . . . the children will be older and the structure has kept you in your world. I have to kind of throw the table over and go: Mom wants a job! [laughter] You know, you can't all just depend on me anymore. Mom wants a job! [laughter]
>
> . . . I'm a great one for the status quo, you know, it's all working for the family, let's just leave it!

Janet's insightful observation—suffused with self-irony and laughter, which helps to mask the deep pain engendered by her admission—suggests that what robbed her of her agency was her constant succumbing to the structure of the family. The family structure relies entirely on her as primary carer and manager of the household—a role that, notwithstanding important changes in public perceptions, is associated stubbornly with women and is profoundly devalued. Undermining the status quo that Janet admits she helps sustain and oil demands a serious rethinking of the whole structure on which her family depends, and the deeply unequal division of roles, labor, and spheres. It demands defiance of the norms that women like Janet have respected for many years. It is a daunting task that requires courage. To use Janet's words, it requires these women to break out of the psychological structure that has "kept them in their world" and kept their husbands in the public world of economic production, "unimpacted" (as another woman put it)[5] and unchallenged.

Liz offered insight into a further obstacle that stands in the way of some women's capacity to effect the change they desire, namely financial comfort and security:

> Sometimes you make a choice, just based on 51 percent of you wants one thing and 49 percent of you wants the other thing. You go with the 51 percent and there you go . . . slight regret, because you think, well . . . and [pause], so you can't have everything, can you? . . . And my husband's work was terrible. And I was thinking, "Well, what if I absolutely put my foot down and said, you have to change your job?" That might not have been possible, and we wouldn't have had the house we live in. You know, we were aware that rent and mortgages are incredibly expensive, so that's sort of like . . . it's a bad thing, it's terrible I gave up my job, but what can you do? [sigh]

Liz traded an important part of her identity for financial comfort. She entertained the possibility of putting her foot down, but the "we" of the family overrode her: note the switch from "what if *I* absolutely put my foot down" to "*we* wouldn't have had the house *we* live in." She knows that giving up her job was a "bad" and "terrible" decision, but it is too painful an admission to live with. So she weighs it against giving up living in a house, and constructs quitting her job as more logical and safer than giving up living in a house that is both mortgage and rent free—a rare prospect for the majority of people living in the United Kingdom. "But what can you do?" she sighs fatalistically, casting the choice to give up a substantial part of her identity as inevitable.

The women's choice not to rock either their personal or the societal boat seems surprisingly incongruent with current cultural and political narratives that exhort women to lean in, to sit at the table and take charge. Charlotte's effective withdrawal from the opportunity to get the job she so much wanted, Janet's prioritization of her family over her own desires ("Mom wants a job!"), and Liz's fatalism—"but what can you do?"—seem at odds with the dominant narratives of popular feminism that celebrates women's confidence, empowerment, and agency.

POPULAR AND NEOLIBERAL FEMINISM:
EMPOWERMENT AND AGENCY

Feminist media scholar Sarah Banet-Weiser argues that recent years have seen remarkable intensified media circulation of what she calls "popular feminism."[6] She explains that feminism is popular in two senses. First, it circulates in various media channels and outlets on social media platforms and, as such, is highly visible and widely accessible. In this context, sexism has resurfaced noticeably in public discourse to become a key term again, thanks to, among others, campaigns such as the Everyday Sexism Project, Hollaback, #MeToo, and #TimesUp,[7] and discussions of gender inequality that suffuse the mediated public sphere. "On any given day," feminist critic Rosalind Gill observes, "in the UK at least, there will be news stories about instances of sexual harassment, inequalities in pay, the gender make-up of company boards or political parties, the sexualized treatment of female celebrities and the 'confidence gap' between girls and boys."[8] Second, Banet-Weiser writes, feminism is popular in the sense of being liked and admired: "No longer confounded by the postfeminist silence and rejection of feminist politics, a version of feminist subjectivity has become norma- tive if not trendy, assuming a place of heightened visibility" in contempo- rary public discourse.[9] This kind of "liked" feminism is governed by the concept of empowerment and its key cultural tropes of confidence, agency, self-esteem, and rights.[10]

Spearheading the popular feminism trend are high-powered women such as Facebook's COO Sheryl Sandberg, foreign policy expert and presi- dent and CEO of the think tank New America Anne-Marie Slaughter, and more recently the daughter of and advisor to the US president, Ivanka Trump, who lays out her "feminist" agenda in her 2017 book *Women Who Work: Rewriting the Rules for Success*. Notwithstanding the differences between their accounts, these women promote a predominantly individu- alistic notion of female agency, calling on women in the workplace to "lean in," to assert their positions, and to make themselves noticeable, to "forge a path through the obstacles, and achieve their full potential,"[11] (Sandberg) to "take charge"[12] (Slaughter), "dream big," "make your mark," and "stake your claim" (Ivanka Trump).[13]

In the wake of the heightened visibility of such high-powered women— those "trailblazer women" that Anne and other women I interviewed looked up to—and in the context of feminism's resurgence and the circulation of numerous exhortations to women to empower themselves, my interviewees' lack of agency appears puzzling. These are educated women who are exposed to contemporary messages about women's and girls' empowerment, confidence, and self-esteem, through popular feminist television (several interviewees mentioned shows such as *The Good Wife*, *Orange Is the New Black*, *Grace and Frankie*, and *Homeland*), women's magazines, newspapers, radio programs, and social media. Can it be that the "magnet" of these current popular narratives—to borrow Richard Sennett and Jonathan Cobb's metaphor, which I cited in the book's introduction— failed completely to enter the women's imaginations and to shape their experiences?[14]

The answer lies partly in the critique of popular feminism and what feminist scholar Catherine Rottenberg describes as the rise of neoliberal feminism. Rottenberg and others such as Banet-Weiser and Gill observe that concomitant with its revival, feminism is being reformulated in radically different terms. Circulating in contemporary self-help and guide books, films, television shows, and apps, and on social media, emergent forms of popular feminism have shifted from notions of equality, social justice, liberation, and solidarity that propelled previous feminist movements, to focusing on women's individual empowerment, confidence, resilience, and entrepreneurial spirit. Many of the examples of media and policy representations and discourses discussed in previous chapters belong to this recent variant of feminism: exhortations to women's self-confidence and celebration of women leaning in (chapter 1), idealizations of the balanced woman who strikes the felicitous work-life equilibrium (chapter 2), depictions of women as freely choosing, empowered, maternal figures (chapters 3 and 4), and the emphasis in media and policy on women's entrepreneurial spirits and empowerment in the gig economy (chapter 5). In place of critique of the structural conditions that underpin and perpetuate gender inequality, many of these current "feminist" messages demand a transformation almost exclusively within women's psyches, with the capitalist and patriarchal structures and material realities conditioning these psyches remaining largely unchanged.[15]

It is true that some enunciations of popular feminism and some high-powered women who publicly espouse feminism acknowledge the existence of larger structural inequalities. For example, in her popular feminist manifesto *Lean In*, Sandberg identifies structural issues such as childcare costs, pay gap, and gender stereotypes that need to be tackled. On Mother's Day 2017, the social media giant's COO called for a higher minimum wage, paid family leave, and affordable childcare in the United States.[16] Anne-Marie Slaughter, for her part, insists that it is not enough to tell women they need ambition, confidence, and a partner willing to share domestic duties, and calls for a national policy that values care.[17] Ivanka Trump has presented herself as championing families, especially working mothers, and in May 2017 proposed a $25 billion federal paid leave program that would provide both mothers and fathers—adoptive and biological— with leave that would be financed by the government (possibly through a tax increase).[18] And with the ongoing fallout following the exposé in late 2017 of Harvey Weinstein's sexual abuse of multiple women, discussions inspired by #MeToo have made broad reference to structural and societal issues in addressing sexual harassment and sexism in the workplace and in society more generally.

However, many of these contemporary so-called feminist accounts and comments are underpinned by the notion that challenging structural inequalities is daunting, too big, and thus an unrealistic or even an impossible mission. Instead, they often promote the importance of making small changes through intense self-work and self-policing, promising that this self-work will lead to empowerment and self-transformation. As Rosalind Gill and I argue, they "propose a 'feminist' program in which women positively and constructively develop strategies to change themselves *within* the existing capitalist and corporate realities they face," because changing those very realities is cast as impossible.[19] For instance, in the *New York Times* bestseller *The Confidence Code* (mentioned in chapter 1), the exhortation to women to become confident as a route to achieving equality in the workplace and other domains is predicated partly on the "pragmatic" view that masculine domination and gender inequality are virtually impossible to challenge at the structural level. "The reality looks foreboding,"[20] write the American journalists Katty Kay and Claire Shipman;[21] blaming external obstacles is "easy but misguided."[22] Rather, since the realities and the environment cannot be changed, Kay and Shipman call their female readers to recognize "the things we do to ourselves" and, through a series of behavioral steps and self-monitoring, to transform their selves, consequently avoiding any serious critique of structural inequalities.

Indeed, a central emphasis in representations that circulate in the media and in workplace and government policy on gender equality is women's need to overcome their inner obstacles and "self-inflicted" wounds, which prevent their becoming confident, empowered, and successful. One of the most popular theses explaining what stops women from achieving top positions and succeeding in the workplace is the impostor syndrome. "Despite being high achievers, even experts in the field, women can't seem to shake the sense that it is only a matter of time until they are found out for who they really are—impostors with limited skills or abilities," Sandberg writes in *Lean In*.[23] The psychological concept is used frequently in policy discussions on gender equality in the workplace and in programs designed to help women tackle and overcome their feelings of being a fraud.[24] In the media, many famous actresses, including Emma Watson and Kate Winslet, and the poet and civil rights activist Maya Angelou have confessed to having dealt with this syndrome. This has become such a prevalent explanation that *Huffington Post* journalist Samantha Simmonds suggested that the decision of Britain's Prime Minister Theresa May to call a snap general election in June 2017 was the result of that inherent defect "every successful woman I've ever met or interviewed suffers from—imposter syndrome." Simmonds ponders, "Maybe she just didn't feel good enough to be Prime Minister—didn't feel like she'd earned it or that people believed in her, and by going to the country she could finally put those self-doubts to rest"[25] (though the putative strategy to gain confidence of course backfired as the Conservative party lost its majority in these elections).

Thus, while contemporary messages of women's self-empowerment enthusiastically endorse and promote individual-based changes as the solution to social change and gender equality, they reinforce a sense of fatalism about the very possibility to effect any larger, structural change. They tell us that things are not fine, but simultaneously reinforce that "that's how it is" and, thus, the main if not the only barriers that can be defied are those within the self. The French sociologists Luc Boltanski and Eve Chiapello describe this sense of dominant fatalism as vital to the moral justification of capitalism. They highlight the role of cultural representations in perpetuating a sense of fatalism and in waning critique of capitalism:

> If, contrary to prognoses regularly heralding its collapse, capitalism has not only survived, but ceaselessly extended its empire, it is because it could rely on a number of shared representations—capable of guiding action—and justifications, which present it as an acceptable and even desirable order of things: the only possible order, or the best of all possible orders.[26]

Various self-help and guide books, films, popular shows, and social media texts and apps (examples of which we have looked at in previous chapters) seem to do precisely that, namely promote small changes as feasible and desirable *within* the current order, which, they imply, is the only possible order. They urge women to change their own thinking, feeling, and behavior through self-work—a project that is constructed as not only achievable and rewarding but also one that ultimately will lead to a bigger change. As social psychologist Amy Cuddy concludes in the hugely popular TED talk where she lays out her theory of power posing, whose key beneficiaries are women, "Tiny tweaks can lead to big changes."

Furthermore, the big change that purportedly will materialize from the tiny tweaks—that is, realizing gender equality in public and private life—is constructed as inevitable, almost natural, an organic change that slowly and steadily will happen. This construction was vividly exemplified in 2016 in the World Economic Forum's ninth Global Gender Gap Report, which found that economic disparity between women and men around the world was increasing even though the gap was closing on other measures such as education. Headlines related to the report's finding read: "Gender Pay Gap Could Take 170 Years to Close" (*Guardian*); [27] "WEF: Gender Wage Gap Will Not Close for 170 Years" (*Al Jazeera*);[28] "Women Won't Earn as Much as Men for 170 Years" (*NBC News*);[29] "Gender Equality Will Happen—but Not Until 2095" (*Telegraph*).[30] Arguably, the intention of the report and its coverage was to call for urgent action to close the gender equality gap. However, the scientific factual language and the assertion that the gender pay will not close within a timescale of almost two centuries resemble reporting on a natural phenomenon that scientists observe but have no control over. It constructs the closing of the gender pay gap as an organic process that advances at a glacial pace and will naturally reach the desired goal in 170 years.

This narrative is bolstered by repeated comparisons between the current state of gender equality in liberal democratic industrialized countries and conditions in the past. This historical comparison works to reduce discontent about and critique of the present; after all, it implies, things are so much better than they used to be. Change in this narrative is presented as one-directional, progressive, and steady, as if things can only get better, and a trajectory of continued equalization is taken for granted, as if there were no possibility of progress stalling or of retrenchment. This construction was frequently evident in the policy and corporate gender diversity-related events I have attended over the years. In many of these events, calls for the need to change workplace conditions and challenge norms and cultures that perpetuate gender equality would be "balanced" by reassuring stories of "how much has changed."

One such story came from the head of diversity and inclusion in a leading global firm at a symposium in which I participated in 2016. Asked by the panel's chair to describe the gender equality challenges in his organization, the director recounted an amusing personal anecdote: "When my kids were small, we had a cat, and I turned out to be very allergic to cats. I said to my daughter, who was four at the time, either I have to go or the cat has to go. And she said, 'Well, Daddy, you're not here very often!'" The speaker paused for the audience laughter, and added, "[Fortunately] the world's changed a lot since, that was about twenty years ago!"

The humorous story works to "prove" that the world has changed dramatically and gender equality has been achieved at home. The director later admitted some enduring gender equality challenges in his organization; however, his opening cat story implied that however serious those current challenges might be, ultimately, they too will inevitably be overcome. Rather than dwelling on the obstacles that need to be overcome, this speaker and other panelists highlighted an optimistic story of positive progressive change. In a similar vein, in a preparatory meeting for another event on gender equality in the workplace in which I took part, the organizers—five women involved in promoting diversity and equality in their organizations—stressed the importance of framing the event as hopeful and highlighting positive change. "We should avoid using words such as 'barriers' and 'obstacles' in the title, to not put people off," they said. "We should emphasize that things are changing in the right direction, although there is still some work to be done."

This emphasis is consistent with contemporary representations that communicate a positive sentiment of women's empowerment, confidence, and resilience. Inspired by and building on positive psychology, the "happiness industry,"[31] and new age/self-help discourses that promote enduringly feminine ideas of serenity, inner calm, warmth, happiness, success, and positive energy,[32] countless messages addressed to women today favor positive affect and outlaw "negative" feelings, specifically anger, indignation, and complaint. Anne-Marie Slaughter's interventions in the debate on gender equality neatly exemplify and, in turn, reinforce this trend. As Catherine Rottenberg notes, Slaughter's entire program for gender equality, which she laid out in her much-cited essay "Why Women Still Can't Have It All" and later developed into the book *Unfinished Business*, is predicated on the quest of the white, middle-class woman to find "happiness through a balancing act, which itself becomes the sign of women's progress."[33] The emphasis on positive attitude and energy is manifest also in exhortations to professional nonwhite women, as illustrated, for example, by the website of the US Black Career Women's Network, which is "dedicated to the professional growth of African-American women" and defines the "black career woman" as "a black woman who is confident and tenacious," who notwithstanding the challenges she faces, "continues to uphold a positive attitude and image, build a network, pursue professional development, education, and mentoring to accomplish her goals."[34] Similar positive calls—in ads, social media, women's magazines, self-help books, apps, and other media—are disseminated through the multiplication of "inspirational" aphorisms coaxing women to love and celebrate their self-image: "Identify your passions and create a life you'll love" (chapter 1 in Ivanka Trump's *Women Who Work*), "Believe in yourself or nobody else will," and so on.[35]

The celebration and favoring of positive affect and positive mental attitude, and the concurrent disavowal of negative feeling and thinking are intimately linked to the turn to the "here and now" in neoliberal feminist discourses, exemplified by numerous self-help texts, blogs, and messages that cajole women to "be present in the moment." For example, in *Women Who Work*, Ivanka Trump urges women to "nimbly seize the moment"[36] instead of struggling with the futile effort to achieve a work-life balance.[37] Similarly, writing on the *Leaders & Daughters* advice website, senior vice president for retail at Apple and former CEO of Burberry Angela Ahrendts urges her daughters to "always be present." Analyzing two well-trafficked "mommy blogs" of American women who gave up successful professional careers in the corporate fast track, Catherine Rottenberg shows how the women bloggers repeatedly express their desire to savor the moment, be present, and live each moment fully and meaningfully, a desire that is inextricably linked to broader contemporary discourses of happiness and balance. Rottenberg argues that "living in the here and now institutes an affective investment in the status quo" and, thus, the turn to the here and now both undercuts the possibility of imagining an alternative horizon and undermines all efforts to make concrete demands aimed at creating a more egalitarian society.[38]

Even voices critical of popular feminism and its celebration of women's empowerment often imply a narrative of progress and seeming inevitable change. For example, writing in the *Guardian* (May 10, 2017), Rachel Aroseti lampoons "the meaningless offshoot of feminism" manifest in the "splurge of feminist-minded TV" such as Netflix's *Girlboss*. She criticizes *Girlboss* for recommending young women should "ape the behaviour of men, never complain about inequality and become active participants in their own objectification." Yet, notwithstanding her critique of the show and its empowerment-style feminism, Aroseti ends on an optimistic note, not much different from that of the director cited above. In taking us back "to the dark days of 2006," she writes, the show "remind[s] us how good we (usually) have it now."[39]

The notion that things are so much better today and that progress is inevitable and natural, and the focus on the here and now, are tied to and, in turn, work to reinforce a call for women to be patient. In corporate and political discourse about gender diversity in the workplace, there is an emphasis that gender diversity (let alone equality) takes time and requires patience. For example, the chairman and CEO of a medical equipment company cited in a McKinsey & Company report on female leadership in the workplace explains, "It takes time and commitment to get it right."[40] A more provocative iteration of the same idea comes from the internationally renowned Spanish-Swiss architect Santiago Calatrava. In February 2017, commenting on the results of the Women in Architecture survey, which showed gender discrimination was rife in architecture, Calatrava urged female architects to "just wait a second" for pay equality.[41] Similarly, remarking on the stark lack of judicial diversity in the United Kingdom, the well-established judge Lord Jonathan Sumption said:

> We are simply deluding ourselves if we try to pretend that selection from that pool on merit alone will produce a fully diverse, or even a reasonably diverse judiciary quickly . . . In this area, as in life generally, we just cannot have everything that we want. We have to make choices and to accept impure compromises. We may even have to learn patience.[42]

ENTERING WOMEN'S IMAGINATIONS: THE MAGNET OF NEOLIBERAL FEMINISM

Situated in relation to these discourses, the accounts of the women I interviewed seem less perplexing. Their psyches, hopes, and beliefs seem to have been shaped, if subtly (but insidiously), by current dominant narratives about gender equality and change, and by enunciations of neoliberal feminism. Liz's conclusion "but what can you do?" and Janet's defeatist acceptance that the status quo will not change, echo the fatalist sentiment in current discourse about the impossibility of challenging larger structural conditions of inequality. Anne's hollow hope that somehow things inevitably and naturally will change—which, as we will see in the following discussion, was repeatedly expressed by other interviewees— bear the imprint of the contemporary narrative of a seemingly organic, inevitable progressive process of gender equalization. Maggie's and other women's failure to see their own roles and agency in effecting the change they desire corresponds with the notion perpetuated in many current popular texts that challenging inequalities is too daunting a project. The women I interviewed seem to have followed Lord Sumption's advice and learned patience.

The imprint of dominant discourses of gender equality and especially neoliberal feminism is perhaps most profoundly evident in the hopes many of these women expressed about their children's futures, and in the messages they convey to their children about their futures. Almost all the interviewees, unprompted, expressed their deep hope that their children would live in a fairer, gender-equal world. The women with daughters especially stressed their hope that their daughters would be treated equally and would not have to experience the discrimination, unequal conditions, and sexist perceptions many felt that they had suffered.

Louise, the former marketing director we met in chapter 1, who experienced unequal treatment at her workplace and challenged her former employer about sexual discrimination, said:

> I really genuinely believe that . . . I'm sure my daughter's generation will be different, there will be some questions. Well, I hope . . . I hope the scenery will be kind of different by then. I really hope . . . I know that nothing actually has changed dramatically, but I can't bear to think there's not going to be some kind of breakthrough in gender equality by the time my daughter comes into work! I can't bear to think it won't be! There's such a noise about equal opportunities and flexi-working!

Underlying Louise's hope is a deep anxiety that the desired change of scenery will not be realized. She moves from the affirmative "I genuinely believe" and "I'm sure" to a hesitant "I hope," which she repeats three times, ending with an admission that she knows "that nothing actually has changed dramatically." She knows that alongside the "noise about equal opportunities" sexism is rampant: Louise makes various references to stories she has read and witnessed of women being discriminated against at work, of mothers being sneered at by the head teacher of her daughter's school, of everyday sexism, and of young girls—including her own daughter, who thinks that "money comes from Daddy"—being pigeonholed in conservative gender roles.[43] Nevertheless, by clinging on to the "noise about equal opportunities and flexi-working"—the noise of popular feminism and government and workplace rhetoric about progressive change toward gender equality—Louise denies that her daughter will face an unequal reality similar to (or worse than) the one she faced. However, when probed about the sources from which the change she was so convinced would happen by the time her daughter enters the workplace, will come, Louise replied:

> Well, I don't know. Well, I guess, I . . . I just, there are chinks of light when for example in Sweden you've got, they're about to start reducing

the working week, for men and women and there are paternity laws . . .
I think these glints of light will come through . . . and as soon as
people . . . they're proven to work, then there will be pressure on other
European countries at least to also implement them. So I think we're
looking for leaders in . . . to show that it can be done. And then the pressure will mount.

. . . I suppose it's the old curmudgeonly people at the top who've got
an idea of how things work and . . . and if you put a little bit more effort
to coordinate, a little bit more time or you know, just kind of do it! So
somebody will do it and then everybody will realize that actually that's
the way it has to be done.

There is a striking paradox in Louise's account, which resonates in those
of other women. On the one hand, she is genuinely discontented with the
status quo—she repeats with sincerity that she cannot bear to think that
there will be no fundamental social change. Louise identifies as a feminist.
She cares and is passionate about women's equality in the workplace and
other domains; she was tearful when speaking about her daughter's future
as a young woman. On the other hand, when it came to identifying responsibility for making the changes she so passionately desires, her account is
fuzzy and does not include herself. Reverberating the wider public narratives of gender equality progress, she describes the "glints of light" and
the mounting pressure as if they were natural processes whose occurrence
was inexorable. She looks to Sweden—a country several interviewees pictured as a gender equality utopia, and concludes with a diffused and vague
sense of responsibility that "somebody will do it and then everybody will
realize that actually that's the way it has to be done." The noise about gender equality allows Louise to suppress her anxiety about the persistence of
inequality and feeds her fuzzy hope for a slow, supposedly organic inevitable progress.

Jenny's hopes for her daughter also draw on contemporary narratives
related to gender equality and, particularly, popular/neoliberal feminism's
celebration of individualized empowerment, self-actualization, and fulfillment. Jenny is a forty-eight-year-old stay-at-home mother to a thirteen-
year-old daughter and a ten-year-old son, and is married to a white English
man who works as a senior lawyer in the City. She was brought up by a civil
servant father and a mother who had been a teacher, who, when Jenny

was born, left paid employment to look after her three children. As a girl, Jenny told me, she was "quite political." In secondary school she founded the black women's student society and later, in university, was involved in black feminist activism. She dreamed of becoming an engineer, but was told by everyone that she would never achieve this because she was a girl. In the interview for a university scholarship she was asked if her father was an engineer or whether she had a brother who was an engineer; her answer to both was no. But Jenny was resolute and in the 1990s graduated with a degree in engineering.

Following graduation, in her early twenties, Jenny started working as a software engineer in a telecommunications company, an environment she found demanding (it included a lot of travel), but, in her words, "exciting," "liberal," and "accommodating." She progressed in her career and after nine years, when her first child was born, on the advice of a female colleague, moved to part-time working. For several years, this arrangement worked, but when the company was taken over by a global firm, the working conditions and atmosphere worsened quite dramatically, and Jenny decided to take voluntary redundancy. Following that, she worked in several organizations on a part-time basis, but three years ago quit completely. She had been very unhappy in her last workplace—the work was not stimulating, the pay was poor, and she was on a temporary contract with no job security. Her husband worked long hours and during the week was largely absent from home. During that same period, her daughter was being bullied at school. Jenny realized that she and her husband were so busy that they had "totally taken their eye off the ball." "That just highlighted I needed to be around more," she explained, "and I took a little bit of time off and then it just stretched out and . . ."—so, for the past three years, Jenny had been a full-time stay-at-home mother.

Jenny is anything but the stereotypical cupcake mom or new traditionalist: she detests baking and cooking and finds being at home alien to her identity. She reflected with irritation on how, since she left her job, she and her husband had taken on more traditional gender roles and commented with frustration that "This isn't us, this is not us, you know! . . . That wasn't us. We, we *share* the roles!" Jenny concluded our interview in deep sadness: "My sixteen-year-old feminist self would be horrified seeing me not having a kind of role outside of the home."

Thirty-two years on from her sixteen-year-old feminist self, Jenny seems to have embraced a rather different version of feminism, which she imparts to her daughter:

> Sometimes it feels like feminism is kind of dead. But you know, in a funny way I think it's so much more ingrained in our children. You know, what a ridiculous suggestion that you can't do something because you're a girl or you're not going to be as good at it! I've definitely made my daughter conscious [of feminism]. I've said, "You know, sometimes you just have to push yourself forward." We've always encouraged her to think about subjects that we think she's good at, to be able to see herself as good at math . . . Yeah, so we have talked about that in relation to studying and work. [I tell her]: "You can do this! You could do that!"

The woman who in the 1980s founded the black girls' society at her school and became an activist during her university days, the woman who in the face of doubters became an engineer, and who then was harmed by neoliberal work cultures and gender inequality in the home, now teaches her daughter to "internalize the revolution" as Sheryl Sandberg's feminism professes: sometimes you just have to push yourself forward. In the absence of a broader context and vocabulary of feminist collective action and solidarity, it would seem that Jenny has been left to adopt the language of individualized empowerment, grit, and resilience. She invests her feminist energy in her daughter's education and instilling in her daughter self-belief and self-confidence, as individualized gestures isolated from a broader feminist project. However, she seems incapable of challenging the traditional gender roles she has unwillingly assumed since quitting her job. Her sixteen-year-old feminist self haunts her, but she feels unable to reconnect with the girl that was, and to rock the boat.

Like Jenny, most of the women I interviewed were keen to instill confidence and individualized empowerment-type feminism in their daughters, and to ensure they received a good education (often in private schools) to put them in the best position to start their professional lives as independent and empowered women. At the same time, almost all the women I met admitted that they hoped their daughters would curb their ambitions and dreams so that their chosen profession was compatible with family life. For instance, former financial director Sara said she was keen for her daughter to have as many opportunities as possible, which was why she and her husband had decided to send her daughter to a private school. It was a financial sacrifice, she admitted, but one they deemed worthwhile, given the excellent education and possibilities it would provide. As far as professions are concerned, Sara reflected:

> It would be nice for my daughter to have a profession which fits with family life. She loves children and she's very good with children, so I think she will want to have a family of her own one day. I don't think she's going to be, you know, just a pure career girl with that aspect. So I would like for her to have something she could fall back on . . . Yes. But I mean I wouldn't expect her to choose a career based on that, but it would be quite nice if you were in a position where you could sort of . . . suggest, maybe you want to be a GP [general practitioner] rather than a cardiologist . . . Or maybe you want to be a teacher rather than a university professor.

I was struck by how many interviewees seemed unconsciously to embrace this contradiction: investing huge amounts of money and time in educating their daughters and equipping them with versatile skills, reiterating the message that they could be anything they wanted to be, while simultaneously guiding them to adjust to the cultural definition of femininity of being a mother and wife, and to heteronormative notions of family and relationships.

Katie recognized this call for adjustment was "a terrible thing to say," but nevertheless endorsed it as a pragmatic position to prepare her daughter for the future:

> It sounds like a terrible thing to say, but sometimes you think to yourself that if you want the best for your children, you want the best for your daughters, and you want them to grow up and be intelligent, independent women, but also to start a family. You almost want to say to them: you know, all that time you're going to spend studying, do think about what's going to happen when you have your family because it may be that if you want to be a stay-at-home mom you will have to give up something that you've studied years and years for so try to think about getting a job where you can carry on and maintain that afterwards . . . There are

certain careers where you can't just carry on, you know. And there are some careers that make it a little bit easier.

There was a similar sense among many of the women I interviewed that the reality out there was fixed: some jobs were inherently more family-friendly than others, and their children would have to navigate that reality and choose those jobs that were more compatible with family life. Also, most interviewees seemed unable to think outside a heteronormative framework; they mostly imagined their children in the future as parents in heterosexual nuclear families. There was little to no sense that this (perceived) reality could be changed, or that they or their children had the capacity to change it.

Strikingly, several of the women who were mothers to both boys and girls expressed different hopes for their daughters and sons. For instance, former journalist Maggie, who has three boys and a girl, said:

> I would like all of my children to find the job they want to do, but, maybe, as a daughter, and as a girl . . . that whole process of thinking about how children are going to fit in, and how you're going to manage that . . . find the sort of job where the childcare is . . . maybe things will have changed by then, you know, maybe there'll be . . . more, sort of, structured childcare, or . . .
>
> You know, it's still . . . the biggest assumption is that the woman will do the majority of the childcare, you know, so I've got to make her prepared for that. At the same time, it's not to say that I wouldn't like my sons to spend a lot of time with their children. But I would give different advice to her in terms of her career path.

The "biggest assumption" that a woman's primary role is to look after the children, which is perpetuated in numerous cultural representations, guides Maggie's thinking and action. She prepares her daughter to fit into an unequal system and adjust to what she identifies is the dominant definition of femininity. She hopes that "maybe things will have changed" by the time her daughter comes of age, but sees no role either for herself or for her daughter in changing it. Paula, whose mother in the 1950s was one of the first women directors in British television and who herself had been a successful lawyer, said she would not encourage her daughter "to do anything too high-flying" because she wants her to be ready to combine work and motherhood. "Would you say the same to your son?" I asked. She replied, clearly discomfited and embarrassed for giving the "wrong" answer, "Mmm . . . Good question . . . Hm, [silence] no, I wouldn't. I mean I . . . I . . . I'm not sure, I'm not sure I would . . . which is not good, is it, really? If you . . . if you're . . . well, I don't know [silence]. Yeah, it's just so much more . . . seems to fall on the mom. So much more, doesn't it?"

Echoing the hegemonic warning to parents in the 1950s and 1960s to avoid the risk of "awakening [girls'] interests and abilities" that "run counter to the present definition of femininity,"[44] Paula, Maggie, Katie, Jenny, Louise, and many of the other women I met are encouraging their daughters to curb their dreams, inhibit their desires, and consequently, like their mothers, to become "great ones for the status quo," to use Janet's words. The language of empowerment, confidence, choice, positivity, and resilience, and the idea that high-quality education will open the doors to girls to become anything they want, help to disguise a regressive message that the mothers deliver—however ambivalently—to their daughters: be a GP rather than a cardiologist. Adjust to, don't challenge, the status quo.

IMAGINING ALTERNATIVES: ANGER AND AGENCY

Many of the women I met were frustrated, sarcastic, and cynical about gender inequality in their lives and in society, yet were unable to critique, refuse, and challenge it. Rather, they adjusted, and encouraged their daughters' adjustment, to the narrow confines of gender attributes and definitions of femininity. Like the American mothers whom Julie Wilson and Emily Chivers Yochim interviewed in their study of mothering under advanced neoliberalism, so too many of the women I spoke to continuously modulated their anger and discontent, investing their emotional labor in "just not being angry."[45] The women I met felt that they were incapable of having the necessary conversations in which they could articulate their rage legibly. Maggie never had the conversation she declares she should have had with her husband seven years earlier when he was made redundant; Charlotte was unable to ask her husband to enable her to attend the interview for her dream job.

However, among the thirty-five women I interviewed, one stood out for what Angela McRobbie calls, after Judith Butler, "legible rage."[46] Beatriz, a forty-one-year-old mother of two, who had left paid employment three years earlier, grew up in Latin America where she worked for nine years as a journalist. From a young age, her mother, whom she describes as a "strong woman" who worked as a teacher, reiterated to Beatriz the significance of being financially independent: "Always earn your own money so your husband doesn't have to buy you knickers!" she used to tell her. In 2004, Beatriz was made redundant as a result of massive job cuts at her workplace. A few months earlier, she had met her future husband, an English man who had just graduated from university and was about to embark on a career as a lawyer. Beatriz moved with him to London, where initially, despite her work experience and master's degree from a prestigious university, she failed to find a job in journalism. For several months she worked as a barista before getting her first journalist job in the United Kingdom as a producer at the British Broadcasting Corporation (BBC). After three years on a fixed-term contract (which was renewed annually), she got pregnant. Well into her pregnancy, her department went through a major restructuring, and her employer informed her that her contract was to be terminated. She recalls:

> I was furious, because, you know, I had a plan! I want to go on maternity leave and I want to go back to work! And all of a sudden, everything changed. Um, and then, like, it was, like, a big fight. I got an employment lawyer involved . . . So I went on maternity leave, and my contract was ending soon after that. They said, "Yeah, that's it. No maternity pay. Absolutely nothing." And then I said, "No! If you won't give me my job back after maternity leave, at least you have to give me maternity pay. I've worked for you for three years, and that's the least that you can do for me." And then, in the end, they agreed to extend my contract to cover eighteen weeks maternity pay. So I got that in the end. Um, but it was quite . . . quite a difficult experience, because I felt like it's a second redundancy.

Beatriz found motherhood joyful: "a new world opening up." At the same time, it was difficult and lonely with no family around and a husband working in a full-time, highly demanding job. When her child was a few months old, Beatriz started applying for freelance journalist jobs and grasped whatever opportunities came up. For two years, she did freelance work from home. She then got pregnant with her second child and was unemployed for nine months. The juggling was too difficult, and the freelance work was unpredictable and poorly paid. Beatriz resolved to return to full-time paid work. "The only way this can work," she told herself, "is if I have a proper job." She started a new and stimulating job at her former workplace. However, the contract was temporary, and she was often asked to perform tasks at very short notice. The high level of uncertainty and unpredictability of the job made it extremely difficult to manage childcare. "Because I didn't have a permanent job," she explains, "I didn't see why I would pay for a full-time nursery, but then it meant that if I called the nursery on a short notice because I got a task to perform, they didn't always have a space."

When Beatriz's second child started preschool—a UK government provision at the time of two and a half hours a day[47]—she "started to get *really* frustrated." "What do I do? Two and a half hours a day is not enough! They want me to go to the office, and there's nothing really I can do from home." "I was so lost," she admits with anguish. Beatriz got help from a (male) career coach, whose advice resonated the popular notion that women's struggle with work and childcare is predominantly self-inflicted: "You put in a lot of self-imposed distress, so if your daughter is staying only another year at home, why don't you stop working and look after her . . . and try, you know, enjoy this moment! Then you can think about going back to work."

Echoing incitements to women to live in and savor the here and now, Beatriz's career coach's appeal that she should "enjoy this moment" diminishes a temporal horizon beyond the present moment—a horizon required for political mobilization and a vision for a better future.[48] "I didn't want to do it. It was very, very hard, but I took the decision to stop." Beatriz reluctantly obeyed the voice that tells women to "just wait a minute" and "enjoy the moment." She surrendered grudgingly to the unequal conditions and the voices that help justify and sustain them.

Ceding to her career coach's advice to enjoy the moment and leave paid employment unleashed frustration, bitterness, and rage in Beatriz. These pent-up feelings, which are largely ousted from the positive affect–driven appeals of neoliberal feminism, became deeper and more acute as Beatriz situated herself generationally. "I'm like my grandmother!" she mused.

"I'm basically like my grandmother who didn't have options and couldn't work because she had to look after the kids! But no, I have a choice!" From this moment on Beatriz's voice changed—in the interview, as in her life trajectory. "This is when all the differences between men and women really struck me," she announced. Beatriz became indignant:

> Why is it so difficult for women, so difficult for a woman to pursue her career dream *and* be a mother? Why for men it's never a problem? Why for them it's so straightforward? . . .
>
> Okay, so I am a mother. Yes! And I was . . . I worked full-time. Okay! So, you know . . . That's life. But no! It shouldn't be like that! It's a very easy situation for my husband because he doesn't need to do anything at all . . . he never needs to. He is happy with the situation at the moment, but he sees I'm very frustrated.

Here Beatriz enunciates her rage in a different way from any of the other women I spoke to: she connects the personal and the political, her own fate and women's fate as a collective, her own feelings and experience to gendered structures of power. It was only when for the first time in her life she made this connection and owned this fundamental indignation that Beatriz was able to name and critique her husband's attitude and behavior as sexist, and to dare to challenge it:

> When I was working, there were times where I needed my husband to be more present. There were difficult situations, because, um, you know . . . he's a high earner . . . And I, as a journalist, I didn't earn much. And there were situations where he could be quite nasty and say things like, "Why do you have to work hard if you anyway barely earn anything?!" . . . And [he would make] quite sexist comments as well . . . you know, "If I was fired, what would you do? . . . It was your choice [to quit the job]." Um . . . it's horrible.
>
> So we have really bad moments because I fight back. I fought back and said, "You know, you don't say that to me! My place is not in the kitchen! I'm happy to be in the kitchen, but I want to work! I'm overqualified. I love being a mother, but I'm not . . . it's not all that I am. I have a past!"

Beatriz's response became "legible rage": an animating force of feminist politics.[49] Naming her husband's attitude and behavior as sexist and nasty enabled Beatriz to critique and counter the narrative that the inequity she experienced at home was somehow inevitable, that her being at home to look after the children was the only possible order of things. It allowed her to locate her own injury in the broader societal context of gender inequality, identify its injustices, and demand that they be challenged—in her life and in society at large. Consequently, her agency was unleashed; Beatriz joined the UK Women's Equality Party, a recently established political party advocating equal gender representation in politics, business, industry, and throughout working life.[50] There she realized, "Oh, my God, I'm not alone!" The party offered her a social and a political space where she could refute the narrow confines of gender roles and definitions of femininity promoted by many contemporary narratives and echoed by her husband, and where she could move beyond living in the moment to imagining and designing alternative futures.

It is difficult to know for sure why, unlike the other women I interviewed, Beatriz reacted the way she did and became politicized, why she decided to rock the boat. Presumably, certain biographical factors played a role, for example, her mother's consistent and vocal insistence that she should be financially independent; Beatriz's participation as a teenager in antidictatorship protests in her country, which sensitized her to social injustice and the urgency of fighting it; and her painful experience of precarious employment in an increasingly neoliberalized workplace. However, what is particularly helpful in Beatriz's account is that it highlights the crucial role that language played in enabling her to come to terms with and make visible the injuries and injustices inflicted on her by the neoliberal, patriarchal system. In particular, the critiques of sexism, which in recent years have resurfaced in the mediated public sphere, furnished Beatriz with the vocabulary and alternative imaginary to articulate her rage and translate it into action. "It's only the beginning of the fight," she concluded our interview, with cautious optimism, "but . . . I hope that by the time my daughter is my age that she would feel more comfortable about being a woman in the workplace, and being a mother, and sharing things equally with her partner." Beatriz wished for her daughter the same things that most of the women I met wished for theirs, but unlike them, she refused to be patient.

Conclusion: Impatience

RETRO HOUSEWIVES?

One might wonder whether what we have seen in this book is no more than a return to an older version of femininity: relegation of women to the sphere of social reproduction within the private family. As suggested by terms such as "retro housewives" or "new traditionalists,"[1] one potentially could read the lives of the women whose accounts are presented in this book as a willful, nostalgic embrace of conservative gender roles. In particular, these women's deep investment in their roles as the CEOs of their families, and in mothering not just their children but the entire family, could be read as a retrogressive espousal of the traditional nineteenth-century sexual division of labor, where the woman is responsible not just for the material labor of housework and childrearing but also for cultivating and preserving the family's personal happiness and fulfillment.[2]

However, as I have argued, reading these women's accounts through such a lens would be misleading. None of the women whose stories appear in this book fits the description of the professional woman who unambivalently throws over her career for family and homemaking. In fact, they all rejected this description and sought actively to negotiate their lived realities after leaving paid employment, precisely in order to escape the trap of full-time motherhood, housewifery, and domesticity.

The accounts presented in this book show that these women's decisions to leave paid employment and their consequent life trajectories were shaped by a combination of factors, many of which were *not* of their own making. These factors include work structures and work cultures that are deeply discordant with family life, the denial of requests to work part-time, gender pay gaps, precarious work contracts, lack of suitable and sustained childcare support, and crucially, stubborn social perceptions and contradictory cultural representations against which women constantly are measured and judged by family, friends, employers, coworkers, media, government, and, most painfully, themselves. Thus, the women's choice to leave paid employment and their subsequent decisions were neither free nor private, nor entirely personal.

Like Betty Friedan's interviewees over half a century earlier, the women I interviewed had a deep yearning for "something more."[3] They longed to regain their own world and to realize themselves by connecting to—not divorcing from—the public world around them. However, what marks these contemporary women from their historical counterparts is that, paradoxically, the dominant cultural ideas of *their* time endorse, encourage, and validate their dreams and desires for something more. As feminist scholar Nancy Fraser notes, unlike in previous eras, today's liberal-individualist and gender-egalitarian imaginary insists that "women are the equals of men in every sphere, deserving of equal opportunities to realize their talents, including—perhaps especially—in the sphere of economic production."[4] Today, the idea that a woman should seek her feminine fulfillment as a wife and mother sounds absurd; a notion safely relegated to the past. The post-industrial capitalist economy is dependent on female labor, an economic necessity that helps fuel the proliferation of images and stories of confident, assertive, and self-reliant career women—images whose loss Friedan lamented in the 1960s. As we have seen, many contemporary images depict women as not only passionately involved in the world of economic production, "leaning in"[5] and cracking the "confidence code,"[6] but also as adeptly balancing their engagement in the world of paid work with their simultaneous responsibilities in the sphere of unpaid social reproduction, and crucially, as prospering in both spheres.

Today's ideal woman represents not just a very different version of femininity from that of the 1950s and 1960s but also a more mature, sober, and pragmatic variant of the 1980s image of "the woman with the flying hair"[7] and the 1990s and early 2000s heroines who sought to have it all. Specifically, the ideal woman in the second decade of the twenty-first century has emerged from the resounding failure of women who have tried to have it all; indeed, she might have read and identified with Anne-Marie Slaughter's much-cited formative account of the recognition of this failure—the 2012 *Atlantic* article "Why Women Still Can't Have It All." The contemporary ideal continues to strive for a felicitous work-life balance, and seeks to flourish in both the public sphere of economic production and the private sphere of social reproduction. However, unlike her earlier versions, she is encouraged to loosen her grip at home, and to "let it go" as Anne-Marie Slaughter urges, or to "drop the ball" as African American businesswoman and former director of the White House Project Tiffany Dufu advocates in a recent book with the same title.[8] While the "good mother" and the "happy housewife" continue to haunt the popular imagination,[9] many of the heroines of today's television shows, films, self-help guides, memoirs, chick-lit, and myriad websites, apps, and social media sites seem no longer to be required to be perfect happy mothers or housewives. Instead, they can be unabashedly non-normative and unruly, and more openly express their frustration, disappointment, and ingratitude. The "mompreneur" (discussed in chapter 5) is a typical iteration of this new woman-mother-worker, who reaps the rewards of the gig economy and seamlessly (if occasionally complainingly) combines running a successful home business with her caring responsibilities. Thus, the ideal woman of the second decade of the twenty-first century ostensibly has exorcised, or at the very least substantially eased, the longstanding contradictions of the gendered split between the public sphere of economic production (capital) and the sphere of social reproduction (care).[10]

THE CRUEL OPTIMISM OF THE NEOLIBERAL FEMINIST IMAGINARY

It is in the context of this liberal-individualist, progressive, and (supposedly) gender-egalitarian imaginary that the struggle of the women whose accounts are discussed in this book has to be understood as fundamentally distinct from previous eras. The earlier discourses of "girl power" that hailed them in the 1980s, and the later images and stories that represented and reinforced ideas of femininity, "choice feminism," confidence, empowerment, and balance, have profoundly shaped these women's self-understanding and nourished their dreams. Without exception, all the women I interviewed imagined realizing themselves as successful career women *and* fulfilled mothers. The images and cultural ideas that have surrounded them have provided a framework within and through which they could articulate their aspirations and make sense of their experiences—first as career women and later as mothers. It is also through these cultural ideals, which have consistently individualized and privatized female success, choice, empowerment, and balance, that the women I spoke with read their failure as personal pathology.

The women I interviewed were able to point to the social forces of inequality that had determined their life trajectories, and particularly their decision to leave paid employment. Yet they struggled to articulate this decision outside the narrow and individualized terms of the confidence culture,[11] which posits that the key to women's success in the workplace as well as in other domains of life is overcoming their internal confidence gap defect, by working on the transformation of their individual psyches and behaviors. They recounted career and personal trajectories marked by ambition, drive, determination, and commitment, yet they often interpreted their particular trajectories as failing to live up to the demands of "lean in" and the confidence culture: "There's something wrong with my personality," "I don't have the personality type of a professional mother," "I'm not a natural," "I was not cut out for this type of demanding job," "I didn't have the ambition it takes," "I lacked the confidence you need for this job," they told me. Having failed to "internalize the revolution" as Sheryl Sandberg calls on them to do, these women, instead, internalized the blame.

In the workplace, these women had repeatedly experienced structural inequalities and oppressive expectations that prevented them from becoming the balanced woman who felicitously balances work and family and public and private aspects of the self.[12] With husbands who were largely absent during the week, workplaces that could not or did not want to accommodate their needs, and competing demands made of them as workers on the one hand and mothers and wives on the other, they could not drop the ball or let it go in the home, and *also* flourish in the workplace. Yet, as we have seen, the seductive idea of the balanced woman helps to mute and cover up the structural conditions that prevented the women from balancing the two spheres. Rather than seeing their situation as an impossibility determined by the sheer incompatibility of family life and their and their husbands' work cultures, the women I spoke to experienced it as personal failure. Thus, the cultural ideal of the balanced woman flew in the face of these women's lived experience, yet they continued painfully to judge their experience and construct their desires through and in relation to it.

Perceiving themselves as having failed to approximate the balanced woman in their reinvented lives as stay-at-home mothers, my interviewees sought to make sense of their new role and experience. It is in this context that public stories and images of motherhood provided potent cultural models through which and against which they explained—to themselves and to others—their choices and negotiated their refashioned identities. Compounded by liberal discourses of egalitarianism and freedom of choice, these contemporary cultural narratives of motherhood and family furnished these women with the terms that helped them to rationalize their uneasy collusion with wifehood and to construct it as progressive. These discourses allow them to present their deeply unequal lives as an egalitarian partnership. And yet these women are faced with an overwhelming problem: the waning of their identity and the painful diminishing of their sense of self in this contradictory moment, in which a discourse of parenting has not displaced the prioritizing of motherhood and mothers as foundation parents, while value and social status still derive largely from professional and economic independence, and care and reproductive work continue to be severely devalued.

The cultural fantasy of the gig economy as a haven for thriving mompreneurs offered the women I interviewed a compelling solution that tailored the ideal of work-life balance to their new circumstances as stay-at-home mothers, and injected in them a sense of hope and optimism about their futures. However, this myth masks the very conditions that were preventing most of them from becoming that successful mompreneur. It obscures the fundamental insecurity of working in a market that has no institutional structure, the various risks of this precarious employment, and the fact that despite the flexibility, satisfaction, and freedom they would purportedly enjoy, as the foundation parents[13] and their families' CEOs, they are far from being either free or flexible. Nevertheless, this fantasy has retained a powerful hold on these women's imaginations and shaped their desires about the future in the most intimate and profound ways. Fundamentally, it directs them to seek individualized solutions to structural problems, and to deny the deep contradictions between their wish to get "out there" in the public world of work, and the obstacle in the way of its realization—the structural conditions that led them to leave their workplace and that keep them in the home to look after the children and manage their families.

The images and discourses of women, work, and family that circulate in and through current media and policy representations provide the women I interviewed with a meaningful discursive context for making sense of their past, their present, and their and their children's future lives. However, the imaginary that many of these very representations propel largely disavows the structural inequalities that these women experience, directing them, instead, to turn inward and to invest in overcoming their "internal barriers." It constructs a seemingly hopeful narrative of inevitable and natural progress toward greater societal gender equality, which requires patience, while simultaneously conveying a sense of fatalism, denying women's own ability to effect any larger, structural change. It offers these women a lens through which to read their own futures and those they desire for their children, in individualized terms of empowerment, self-confidence, and resilience, and without disturbing the status quo. This contemporary cultural imaginary encourages these women to deny the injurious structural forms of inequality that have affected their lives so deeply, and to bury their anger and indignation.

The feminine mystique of the 1950s and 1960s that Betty Friedan described was unambiguously oppressive. Its purveyors in magazines, newspapers, books, television panels, and "armies of marriage and child-guidance counselors, psychotherapists, and armchair psychologists"[14] were invested in establishing that women can find fulfillment only as mothers and wives. The contemporary cultural imaginary described in this book is as oppressive as that of Friedan's era. However, it is at once less monolithic and more insidious.[15]

It is less monolithic partly because of the sheer number and diversity of platforms, outlets, and media which make it difficult to refer to the promulgation of a singular mystique. The contemporary imaginary is also less monolithic because it is itself a response that seeks to defy past oppressive and narrow definitions of femininity. For example, the expansion of meanings of motherhood and the abundance of depictions of non-normative mothers have emerged, at least partly, in response to criticisms of the restricted and idealized models of motherhood in popular culture. In the contemporary mediated public sphere, conflicting messages circulate simultaneously: women are subjected to feminist discourses and economic necessity that construe them as independent workers in the public world, while they are called at the same time to take time out to have children and stay at home to rear them.[16]

This more contradictory and fragmented nature of today's representations of women, work, and family arguably makes the contemporary images and narratives harder to resist. My interviewees were buoyed by the vague and optimistic vision perpetuated in current public discourse of an inevitable change toward gender equality; the promise that "a new day is on the horizon," as proclaimed by Oprah Winfrey in her inspirational Golden Globes speech in January 2018, and amplified in numerous iterations related to the #MeToo movement.[17] At the same time, the women and men I interviewed concurrently endorsed the popular fatalist sentiment about the impossibility of challenging the larger structural conditions of inequality. They drew on popular liberal discourses of gender-egalitarian relationships while accepting dominant ideas about the role of women as primary caregivers.

The contradictory and less consistent nature of the current dominant imaginary of women, work, and family also makes it more insidious than imaginaries of previous eras. It promises to empower women and liberate them, while obfuscating the fundamental structural obstacles that lie in the way of realizing this promise. The series of disjunctions discussed in the book demonstrates how, despite the fact that their experience often flew in the face of media and policy representations of women, family, and work, these women would often interpret their lives and judge themselves through these very representations. Although definitions and ideals of femininity, motherhood, and success propagated by contemporary representations often failed to match their experience and feelings, they nevertheless became their "internal tyrants."[18]

Equipped with the consciousness and language of feminism that their mothers had lacked and which they had gained from the media and the wider culture, these women provided clear accounts of the profound social forces of inequality which had determined their and other women's life trajectories. However, most women, simultaneously, ascribed their decision to leave their career and the consequences of this decision to personal failure, whose sources and remedies can be found in the self. At the same time as painfully admitting to seamlessly "slipping into traditional gender roles," as one woman described it, they drew continuously on the liberal-individualist and gender-egalitarian imaginary to construct their family, and their marriage in particular, as a partnership of equals. In sum, the dominant cultural ideas about successful femininity, family, and work are largely incongruent with the experience of the women I interviewed. However, the women continued to draw on these ideas and used them as yardsticks against which they explained and lambasted their feelings, behaviors, achievements, and failures as personal and private affairs, disconnected from and unaffected by larger structural factors.

The contradiction faced by the women whose stories appear in this book is that they live in a society and a culture that are constantly telling them they have the individual capacity to live their lives as the equals of men in every sphere of life, and especially the sphere of economic production, but do not provide them with the necessary resources to realize this capacity. In what Lauren Berlant would regard as a "cruelly optimistic" fashion, the compelling narrative of the individual's capacity to achieve equality and success ignites a sense of possibility, drawing these women to desire equality and success while impeding their tackling the structural issues that obstruct the realization of this desire.[19]

GOING FOR A RUN, EXTINGUISHING DESIRE

In the interviews, the women talked about some of the meaningful pleasures and rewards they derive from having stepped off the work treadmill and invested time, skills, and emotional labor in their families. However, these accounts also exposed pent-up feelings of frustration, disappointment, and regret. Indeed, one clear pattern that emerged from all of the women's interviews was the continuous and concerted hushing of disappointment. There is a particularly telling incident in the interview with Helen, an accountant who had left her job nine years earlier after the birth of her first child. Determined to go back to paid work after the end of her maternity leave, Helen attended several job interviews, but for similar reasons to those cited by other women, she never achieved her aim of returning to paid employment. After quitting her job and embarking on her new role as a stay-at-home mother, Helen "was getting very anxious about having an empty life" and "always being at the bottom of the pile." In the first three years after she quit, she felt constantly that leaving the workplace had been a mistake, and frequently felt the urge to contact her old company; she experienced a repeated, "uncontrollable impulse" to pick up the phone and ask if they would take her back. However, when these thoughts and feelings arose, whenever she felt that urge, Helen would go for a run. "And then I'd calm down!" she exclaimed with laughter.

Indeed, going for a run or doing other forms of physical exercise is a strategy frequently recommended by contemporary self-help (including so-called feminist) experts, books, apps, and programs to deal with difficult feelings, conflict situations, and adversity.[20] It has a known short-term effect of triggering a positive feeling following the body's release of endorphins.[21] However, as a strategy on its own, it becomes a glib technique that encourages avoidance of painful and uncomfortable feelings. Like Helen, many of the women I met had chosen to go for metaphorical runs—to block out disappointments and anxieties that were too painful for them to face.

Repeated metaphorical (and actual) runs made these women feel better and crucially, as Helen put it, calm down. However, this self-silencing, this self-containment of their disappointment and soothing of their injury, are just what the individual spirit of the "happiness industry" and the confidence culture wants to encourage. It seeks to outlaw negative and difficult feelings—particularly anger and complaint—and to promote instead calm, happiness, and positive energy. These are the very "human values" that nineteenth century housewives were encouraged to and expected to nurture in themselves and their families.[22]

CREATING THE STRUCTURAL CONDITIONS FOR "THAT CONVERSATION"

Describing C. Wright Mills, whose *Sociological Imagination* inspired my study, the American sociologist Tod Gitlin wrote:

> [Mills] hammered home again and again the notion that people lived lives that were not only bounded by social circumstances but deeply shaped by social forces not of their own making, and that this irreducible fact had two consequences: it lent most human life a tragic aspect with a social

root, and also created the potential—if only people saw a way forward—of improving life in a big way by concerted action.[23]

I think that most of my interviewees would recognize their lives in the first part of Gitlin's observation: they described lives that had been shaped intensively by social, economic, cultural, and organizational forces. However, the majority could not see how to formulate a concrete way forward, "of improving life in a big way by concerted action."[24]

It is through the regrets these women expressed that a vision, however blurry, emerges of ways they could have improved their lives. "In hindsight," former teacher and mother of two Simone told me, "the one thing I would have done . . . I would have made a proper effort to define exactly what *I* would like to have." This might sound a trivial task, but decades of feminist writing and activism speak volumes about what a mountainous and daunting task defining, speaking out, and acting on one's desire has been and continues to be for a woman. It requires a "proper effort," as Simone accurately put it—that is, an intensive and sustained challenging of the systematic containment and suppression of female desire by the patriarchal order. "If I have any regret," many interviewees told me, "it is that I didn't have that conversation, about what I want, with myself, with my husband, and with my workplace."

This is not to suggest that had they had such discussions with their husbands and employers, their choice would necessarily have been different; some might still have decided to leave paid employment. Rather, what these women seemed to be saying is that by having "that conversation," they could have become more truly themselves and refused to act out others' fantasies.[25] Having "that conversation" would have allowed them to maintain or regain the recognition so many of them felt they had lost. As Betty Friedan observed, perhaps when a woman refuses to act out her husband's fantasy "he will suddenly wake up and see *her* again"[26]—he being her husband, but also the patriarchal order more broadly.

What my interviews with these women also show is that many of them lacked the resources and tools to have "that conversation" about their desires. In an era that encourages women's pursuit of their dreams and celebrates their individual fulfillment and self-realization, the stories of the women in this book reveal that they failed to talk about and to realize their desires. If such a group of educated and highly privileged women was unable to articulate and act on their desires, other women who lack their resources will arguably find it even more difficult.

The women I spoke to had failed to voice their desires not because of some internal flaw, but because the current political and cultural structures undercut the conditions required for the possibility to do so. In particular, the two central (patriarchal) institutions these women have experienced as adults—the workplace and the family—where "that conversation" could and arguably should have taken place, failed to furnish them a safe space conducive for articulating and acting on their desires. The dominant cultural, political, and policy representations and discourses of women, work, and family have largely supported this failure. Rather than facilitating and energizing a critical conversation about the structural conditions required for achieving equal gender relations, they generally discourage and help to diffuse that critical conversation. While the #MeToo campaign may have invigorated renewed discussions about structural inequalities—for example, in relation to sexual harassment in the workplace and the gender pay gap—it remains to be seen whether this lively debate will address in a bold and effective fashion the structural changes required to fight and overcome these entrenched inequalities.[27]

What do the accounts of the women in this book tell us about what specifically prevented this conversation from taking place, and what structural conditions might have enabled it?

The workplace

Louise, the former marketing director, noted that there is considerable "noise" about gender equality in the workplace. On any given day in the United States and the United Kingdom, there will be news stories related to gender diversity in the workplace, corporate reports on how to achieve it, or politicians' comments on the need to tackle it. However genuine this "noise" might be, it is fundamentally limited given its typical isolation from discussions about equality in the home. For Paula, it is of no consequence that her workplace offers flexible working arrangements if her husband, who occupies a very senior position in a media firm, generally does not arrive home until 10:30. Unless a serious conversation about equality takes place in both her *and* her husband's workplace and more widely in the public sphere (and crucially, as I discuss next, between Paula and her husband), and unless this conversation insists urgently on the need to look at the inextricable relationship between equality in the workplace and equality in the home, it is likely to remain mere noise.

In particular, what emerges most clearly from the interviews is that the long-hours work culture, which continues to characterize many workplaces, makes it extremely difficult, if not impossible, for women—and, importantly, their partners—to participate in family life in a meaningful way. Their husbands' workplaces may have been awarded numerous diversity badges and accreditations, but their demands on their employees to completely separate their public (workplace) selves from their private (home) selves—that is, to be maximal employees and minimal fathers and partners—undercut any attempt to create a more equal social order.

Indeed, the husbands of many of the women I interviewed often would not see their children awake during the week because of frequent business traveling and/or early starts and late homecomings. When they were at home, their involvement in fathering was often restricted and partial.[28] This arrangement, which operates at the expense of the children and the woman, treats fathering as though it were a peripheral, insignificant experience, as though it did not really matter. Both the husbands' workplaces and their families colluded in accepting the very limited involvement of fathers as a necessary compromise.

Arguably, this compromise is the exception. Recent research suggests that fathers, particularly those with higher education, are increasingly interested in active parenting, reflecting and in turn helping to shape the changing norms about gender roles and parenting, and policy efforts to encourage more equal gender roles.[29] However, as Charlotte Faircloth points out, there continues to be a considerable gap between policy, academic, and popular ideas of the "involved father," and men's experience and practice as fathers. [30] Despite commitment to "new fatherhood," the exhaustion and financial burden of parenting cause many fathers to revert to patriarchal habits.[31]

Indeed, there is abundant research showing that, consistently, women continue to shoulder more than half of the parenting and housework responsibilities, and that they experience the division of these responsibilities as unfair.[32] In the United Kingdom, on average men spend 16 hours a week doing unpaid care work, including childcare, laundry and cleaning, compared to women, who do 26 hours a week—making UK parents the worst in the developed world for sharing childcare responsibilities.[33] A 2018 survey by the charity Working Families of 2,761 working parents across the United Kingdom, found that parents consider and find that it is more acceptable for mothers rather than fathers to leave and/or take time out of work for childcare issues, and that parents believe that their employers expect the same gendered pattern.[34] In the United States, on average, the time mothers spend on childcare is twice as much as is expended by fathers: 15 hours a week compared to 7 hours.[35] In 2013, Jack O'Sullivan, cofounder of the Fatherhood Institute, declared men to be on the brink of an "extraordinary transformation." That has yet to occur.

Thus, whether exceptional or extreme, the model that the workplaces of the husbands of the women I interviewed foster, and which their families have adopted (if unwittingly), highlights a broader pattern of "father involvement deficit" in advanced capitalist societies.[36] Across developed countries, fathers' involvement in parenting is substantially more limited than mothers'. This is a result of multiple factors, including unequal entitlements to parenting leave during the first year when long-term parenting patterns and skills are established, low take-up of shared parental leave—in the United Kingdom between 1 percent and 3 percent according to recent estimates[37]—the persistent and in some cases widening gender pay gap between men and women, which worsens with parenthood, and stubborn cultural perceptions reinforced by stereotypical representations that mothers should be the primary parents. Hence, the husbands' minimal fathering is not the result of men being "feeble in sympathy,"[38] as the Victorians believed. Rather, it is a manifestation of "financialized capitalism's rapacious subjugation of reproduction to production."[39] It allows men's roles as caregivers to be trumped by their "more important" roles in the sphere of capitalist production, and as Fraser puts it, "free rides" on the women's and their—mostly female low-paid—helpers' reproductive labor while obscuring its value.

As the case studies in this book underscore, even when men work at home, which is a solution adopted by some workplaces and that is valorized as one of the gig economy's great promises, they still work long hours and contribute minimally to childcare and housework. Thus, challenging current work cultures is fundamental but needs to go hand in hand with a demand for equal investment in childrearing and a "desexing" of care work.

Working toward such fundamental change should include, among other things, a concerted effort to challenge cultural, political, and policy discourses which, as we have seen, largely reinforce and legitimize the devaluing of caregiving and the idea of women being the primary carers of the children. In particular, the model of minimal fathering is perpetuated by popular representations of men as uninvolved, useless, or hopeless fathers—what some have called the "Homer Simpson syndrome"—a view which, as we have seen, reverberates through women's accounts.[40] When men are depicted as involved fathers, these portrayals tend to focus on particular fun and educational activities, thus further devaluing the bulk of caregiving and domestic labor shouldered chiefly by women. Furthermore, popular culture and government encouragements to men to become more involved in family life, such as those described in chapter 2, seem to target almost exclusively working-class fathers. In so doing they legitimize the huge deficit of fathering in families like those explored in this book, implying that it is a justified sacrifice to allow *these* men to fully participate and succeed in the sphere of capitalist production. Men in high-powered jobs like those occupied by the husbands of many of the women I interviewed, typically are shown in popular films and dramas as dedicated almost exclusively to their exciting, action-packed, competitive, and long-hours waged work. One can readily recall images of the sleep-deprived senior detective or lawyer who stays in the office late at night to solve a case, but not images of his wife and female domestic helpers who look after the family and the home. The latter enable the work of the high-powered man (and by extension of the capitalist economy) but remain an invisible background condition.

Of course, there are changes taking place in representations of masculinity and of fatherhood in particular, but they are too small and too slow. While changes in the ways fathering and fathers are depicted are insufficient in themselves, they play an important role in conveying what is "normal," and in shaping what families, workers, and workplaces accept as normal and desirable. Representations of well-rounded rather than minimalist or ridiculous fathers, and depictions that puncture the valorization of productivity-driven lives and present alternative work, family, and relationship forms might help prompt "that conversation."

Another important aspect highlighted by the interviews concerns how both the women's and men's workplaces had frequently fallen silent at two critical moments when the conversation about women's equality could and should have taken place: when the woman was due to take up her maternity leave, and when she was due to return to work after her maternity leave. Many employers simply congratulated the expectant woman and her husband, but expressed no interest in the woman's returning after maternity leave and did not discuss in any detail possible avenues and arrangements for her return after the birth of the child, or explore possibilities to adjust her husband's work conditions. When these women informed their workplaces that they were not intending to return after the end of their maternity leave, most employers made no or only small efforts to talk through this decision, and some explicitly supported the woman's decision not to return. For instance, Christine, the former deputy head teacher, recalled:

> My boss said if I didn't want to come back, that would be okay, and they still wouldn't ask me to pay back maternity leave . . . I think she almost would have been surprised if I had said I was going to be going back, because she had a history of having very young, very driven deputy heads, who worked extremely long hours, and the teachers in the school who were parents really struggled. It wasn't an easy school in which to be a parent.

Christine's account reveals how the existing structures, conditions, and norms of work lead some employers to avoid discussing with the woman her decision to leave the workplace. They see how difficult it is for parents to combine parenting with paid work, but instead of initiating a conversation about how these conditions might be changed, they succumb to them as if they were a given. The result is a silence which reaffirms and reproduces the status quo at a key structural moment where it could be challenged.

This silence presumably is a result, at least partly, of the existing legal framework. While according to the statute in the United Kingdom, an employer can make informal inquiries about whether or not an employee intends to return from maternity leave, in practice this is a highly sensitive area. Employers are instructed that if they make such an inquiry, they must ensure that it cannot be construed as either harassment or breach of the implied mutual trust and confidence. Furthermore, such an inquiry should not be repetitive.[41] Of course, the law is there to protect women against discrimination; however, in this instance, the way in which it is followed in practice might be closing down a crucial opportunity for "that conversation" to happen. It might be closing down an important opportunity for women and men to explore, together with their employers, what both might want and need, and whether and how the workplace can make adjustments to accommodate these needs and the employees' desires to have meaningful work *and* family lives. Some of my interviewees' workplaces did initiate such conversations. However, that most of them did *not* suggests that for structural change to occur, the conversation perhaps needs to be more forcefully facilitated and encouraged by the law, to protect women but also to ensure institutional accommodation of care work.

Therefore, celebrating successful career women as role models whom other women are called on to emulate by "sitting at the table" (to use Sheryl Sandberg's popular exhortation), offers what Emma Goldman described over a century ago as "merely external emancipation,"[42] and for the very few, since it continues to ignore the dining tables that are served and wiped almost exclusively by women. In other words, it divorces discussion of and practices geared toward empowering women in the workplace from analysis of their continued subordination within the family, thus shrinking women's politics to the sphere of capitalist production. As Janet, the forty-three-year-old mother of two who had left her job as an actress eleven years earlier, put it so poignantly, "The family life is set up on me being here as a taxi service, as a collection point." To realize herself in the sphere of paid work, this family setup has to change radically, so Janet can "throw the table over and go: 'Mom wants a job! You know, you can't all just depend on me anymore. Mom wants a job!'" For women to be able to sit at the table in the workplace, the tables at work *and* in the home must be overturned.

The family

In parallel with what happens in their workplaces, there is also a lot of "noise" about equality in these women's families, and in particular, the idea of the couple as a partnership of equals geared toward the happiness and flourishing of their children. At the same time, there are continuous silences that mute the deeply unequal character of the couple's marriage.

Where the silencing and proscription of difficult feelings are perhaps most pronounced is in the women's avoidance of difficult conversations with their husbands. Part of Helen's project of going for a run in order to calm down is to avoid a serious discussion with her husband about her frustrations as a stay-at-home mother and wife. Consequently, the traditional gender split is reinstated quietly—"almost without talking about it with my husband," she confessed.

Strikingly, almost all the women I interviewed noted that they could not recall having had a proper conversation with their husbands or partners to discuss their decision to quit their jobs and what the consequences of this decision might be. Many imagined an arrangement that involved their eventual return to some form of paid employment, but they had never initiated a conversation to spell out their needs and discuss their wishes. The women's husbands seemed equally unable to instigate conversations about their own feelings, especially how they felt about the male breadwinner/female carer model they had adopted. Their repeated barbed comments, such as "How was your holiday today?" or "Who have you had coffee with today?"—as evidenced in the women's accounts related in earlier chapters—divulge the resentfulness many of these men felt toward what they depicted as their wives' easy lives. These feelings of anger and resentment derived, at least partly, from the men's extremely stressful and demanding jobs, and from the anxiety emanating from the huge burden of being the sole breadwinners, notwithstanding how much they benefited from their domestic arrangement, especially in career terms. However, the women's husbands rarely uttered or addressed these feelings directly to their wives. Like their wives, they avoided having "that conversation" to express their anxiety, dissatisfaction, and discontent, and to confront the enormous personal cost of assuming the role of sole breadwinner.[43]

The silences ensure that the family myths about an egalitarian partnership that the couple tells themselves and their children are not disrupted, and that marriage is never directly evoked as a site of injustice and domination. Tanya "gets the joke" when her husband teases her about her doing nothing all day; Tess feels upset but says nothing about serving herself food last, after her children and her husband; Liz suppresses her anger about the unequal distribution of labor in the house; Helen avoids responding to her husband's irritation at her underlining her coursework in bed; and Katie remains silent about her husband's active encouragement of her leaving the workplace and the consequent "emotional and psychological trauma" (her words) she suffered as a consequence of "leaving her life behind" (chapter 4). These silences underscore how, in addition to the various ways in which these women's lives are constrained by others—primarily their husbands and their husbands' careers—women constrain themselves.

There was a poignant moment in one of the interviews that represents a momentary refusal of silence. Maggie, the former journalist and stay-at-home mother for eleven years, whom we met in chapter 6, lamented not having "that conversation" about her desire to return to paid employment after her second child was born and then on two more occasions when her husband was made redundant. Recounting her regret at not exploiting the latter "window of opportunity," as she called it, Maggie tried to remember in what years her husband was made redundant. "Let me just shout up and ask him" she said, and called her husband to come down from upstairs.

"I'm on the toilet," he replied. "Oh, sorry!" she responded with a big laugh. I assured Maggie that the details of when exactly her husband was made redundant were not important and asked that she continue. Maggie continued telling me how excited she was at the possibility of returning to some form of paid employment and having her husband "at the helm of the family and the household!" His temporary (if enforced) withdrawal of male power enabled the unleashing of her deepest desire. But it was soon recontained: Maggie reflected with sadness on the window of opportunity that had closed—her husband found a new job, she never initiated the conversation, and her position as CEO of the family and wife was cemented.

Maggie then hears the sound of the flushing toilet upstairs. She calls her husband again, and the following exchange ensues:

Maggie: You know when you were made redundant the first time?
Husband (replies shouting from upstairs): Yes?
Maggie: How old were the children?
Husband: Well, ah . . . it's . . . it was end of 2007.
Maggie: Right. So Damian would have been about three?
Husband: Yes.
Maggie: And then, the second time you were made redundant, it was in 2009, wasn't it?
Husband: What?

Maggie: No . . . that can't be . . . just come down a second!
Husband: Where are you?
Maggie: I'm just . . . we're in the living room.

A few seconds later, Maggie's husband appears and leans against the doorway to the living room. "Right. Yes. Hello," he says, his body language and laconic replies exhibiting his utter reluctance to be there.

I nod to greet him and look down, feeling awkward to witness this exchange. Maggie asks him, "But that was the *second time* you were sacked, wasn't it?" "No!" he replies vehemently. "2007! Imogen was born in 2009. I was made redundant in 2011. Okay?!!" "Right. Okay. Thank you!" Maggie exclaimed.

Maggie's husband leaves the room, and Maggie turns to me. Smiling wryly, she says with a subtle sense of smugness, "Ha, I get the dates slightly wrong, well, but my idea was that he was at home, and then he was made redundant again more recently, and then I was thinking, actually, this could be my chance!"

Maggie's insistence that her husband come down to the living room where she and I were sitting was clearly about something other than getting the dates right. She demanded that he enter the space where she was recounting the painful containment of her desire, an injury that had enabled the smooth running of the family and had secured her husband's position exclusively in the public sphere of economic production. In this space—which, tellingly, he is disinclined to enter—she then humiliates him. She dwells on his injury—being "emasculated" twice—to claim her own enduring injury. Here in the presence of another woman (me), Maggie refuses to participate in the ongoing silencing in which she had been colluding. However indirect and fleeting, she finally utters her complaint, laden with anger and deep pain.

Maggie's articulation of her complaint exposes that there has been an absence of vital conversations between her and her husband at major moments of structural change, first when the children were born, and on two occasions later when he was fired from his jobs. Maggie's exit from the workforce following the birth of their second child led to a reshaping of the entire model on which the family was predicated and to a radical change in her and her husband's roles within it. Later, the two instances when her husband lost his job presented opportunities to rewrite these roles. Maggie's use of the metaphor "window of opportunity" highlights the potential of the family to be a flexible structure that accommodates changing circumstances and needs while allowing its members to take changing positions and roles within it.

However, having listened to Maggie and the accounts of the other women I interviewed, it appears that their family structures have mostly failed to offer that flexibility. Indeed, it seems that it is not just the work-places that have remained inflexible in the face of their employees' family demands. Crucially, the family also appears to be a stubbornly inflexible structure whose rigid roles both the women and their husbands have helped to reproduce and consolidate. The rigid gendered family struc-tures have largely failed the women I interviewed: they had curbed their desire and yielded to deep disappointment. Yet these very rigid struc-tures, and the heteronormative institution of marriage, continue to have an immensely powerful hold on the thinking, feelings, hopes, and actions of these women. Liz, the former academic whose story appeared earlier in the book, underlines the trade-off she was compelled to make between quitting her job and preserving her marriage (and the traditional heter-onormative family structure), and her ultimate decision at the age of 35 to choose the latter: "My husband's job was one of these City jobs of all hours . . . [Leaving my job] was a forced choice. I would say it was a forced choice; it wasn't my optimal life at all. But, it was like, I felt like if I wanted to stay married . . . I had to choose this path."[44]

Liz's somber admission illuminates the incredible affective grip of the institutions of marriage and the heteronormative family. Concerned with the survival of her marriage, she felt she was *forced*—a word she repeats twice in the short space of this quote—to give up not just years of educa-tion but fundamentally a huge part of her identity. Liz had chosen mar-riage and traditional family, and with it a life that serves the needs of her husband and the family, and which is light-years away from that "opti-mal" life she desired. Rather than changing the situation into which she was "forced," Liz, and the majority of the women I interviewed, chose to adapt to it.

Three decades since Hochschild's (with Machung) seminal study *The Second Shift*, the accounts of the women in this book suggest that hetero-normative marriage has remained "a magnet for the strains of the stalled revolution."[45] While discussions on flexibility seem to govern debates and policies related to workplace diversity and equality, and while some work-places have made considerable efforts to enable their workers flexibility, the idea of flexibility seems to have been largely ousted from discussions on family and marriage, and from the imaginations and lives of these women's families.

Shockingly, recent studies indicate that it is not just women and men of the generation I interviewed who struggle to imagine, let alone implement, flexible gender roles and family arrangements. A set of reports released in 2017 by the American nonprofit, nonpartisan Council on Contemporary Families found that young people aged 18 to 25—part of the millennials, heralded as the gender equality generation—are becoming increasingly convinced that it would be "much better for everyone involved if the man is the achiever outside the home and the woman takes care of the home and the family."[46] Fewer of these youngest millennials, the reports revealed, support egalitarian family arrangements than did the same age group twenty years earlier.[47]

One thing that is common to these young people and the women I inter-viewed is that the public discussion by which they are surrounded includes little talk about alternative, including nonheteronormative, family struc-tures and roles, or how to create more gender-flexible family arrange-ments. Notwithstanding changes in media and cultural representations and policy discourses about the family, public discourse remains largely dominated by a rigid and conservative view of family and the gender roles within it.[48]

UNMUTING DISAPPOINTMENT

Maggie's aggressive demand of her husband that he specify the exact dates he was made redundant is a potent if indirect evocation of their marital relations as a site of oppression and injustice. It helps to reveal gender biases that have been consistently naturalized, her collusion with them, and the injustice she suffered as a consequence. Importantly, this demand was uttered in front of an audience (me), thus rendering the injustice in a private relationship a matter of record and concern beyond the con-fines of the couple's intimate space. Maggie's utterance is an instance of what Lauren Berlant calls the female complaint, "a powerful record of patriarchal oppression"[49] that "observes struggles and registers the failure of the desired world, without wanting to break with"[50] or change the conditions of its author's struggle and suffering.

Berlant traces the female complaint as a genre in dominant modes of American female cultural discourse, and identifies some of its iterations in genres such as melodrama, television shows, situation comedies, and rap music. She argues that in the history of what she calls the "American female culture industry," complaints "have operated as 'safety valves' for surplus female rage and desire,"[51] that is, as modes dedicated to managing the resistance to masculine privilege and oppression. Complaints are thus simultaneously a genre of self-expression and self-circumscription: they constitute sites of resistance to the messages and practices of patriarchal dominance while implicitly foreclosing any action to change the fundamental condition of the complaint's production.

It seems to me that in the stories of the women that appear in this book we may have seen a further step in the containment of women's desire and rage in both the public and private spheres. These women not only put the lid on their rage and frustration, they frequently do not utter these feelings in the first place; they block them out of their imagination. Contemporary dominant representations and discourses of women, work, and family, many of which appeal particularly to these middle-class women, seem not just to contain but increasingly to outlaw rage and protest against male domination. If, as Berlant explains, in the female melodrama "the utmost importance is the staging of the complaint,"[52] then in many of the current "female" neoliberal feminist genres, many of which were discussed in this book, what is of paramount importance is the staging of confidence, balance, and happiness, *not* complaint. Unlike the melodrama, which allows for the clarification and recognition of female suffering (albeit, as Berlant critiques, as an end in itself), contemporary symbolic forms of the confidence culture and neoliberal feminism more broadly by and large repudiate female suffering, disappointment, and complaint.[53] They render such negative affects abhorrent, uninhabitable, and unimaginable.[54] Louise felt guilty because she judged herself against the oppressive cultural image of the balanced woman who manages the difficulties of combining career and motherhood "without making a big deal of it" (chapter 2). Christine deprecated herself for exhibiting stress to her children, mirroring and confirming the message and images that prohibit full-time mothers from experiencing stress or anxiety (chapter 3). Beatriz reluctantly followed her career coach's advice to deny her pain at being forced to abandon her career and to "enjoy the moment," and savor the "here and now," as various incitements to women cajole them to do (chapter 6).

Of course, this is not to say that female rage has disappeared from public discourse (and perhaps we are now witnessing its reinvigoration, in the wake of movements such as #MeToo and #TimesUp). Rather, the accounts of the women I interviewed suggest that that the conditions for the possibility of female rage are continuously under threat. The dominant messages the women I interviewed had received from their workplaces, husbands, the media, and government, and that they are passing on to their daughters, are "don't make a fuss, just get on with it," and "keep calm and carry on"—messages that in the past decade have become more broadly prevalent and popular responses to the uncertainties of economic collapse and austerity.[55] Therefore, it would seem that in the absence of sufficient structures and vocabularies that enable, let alone support or encourage the utterance of disappointment and anger, the women whose accounts appear in this book have almost completely abandoned complaint. They have abandoned critique of inequality in favor of compromise and adjustment to the requirement of masculine domination. In so doing, they have unwittingly muted their disappointment and colluded in muting capitalism's deep contradictions of capital and care, contradictions in which their lives are acutely caught up.

Beatriz's story, which was recounted in chapter 6, is particularly illuminating in this context, since it underscores the possibility opened up by the creation of safe spaces within the public sphere for sounding the female complaint and refusing that it remain a genre of self-circumscription. For Beatriz, this space was the Women's Equality Party; it furnished her with a structure and the tools for making the injustice she experienced in the private relationships with her husband and her employer a matter of both public record and public concern. It helped her to break away from the patriarchal conditions that kept her frustrated and disappointed, and gave her the vocabulary to critique them and the support she needed to change them in her life. For others this safe space may be a different forum, platform, community, or group. What Beatriz's story highlights so powerfully is the urgency of creating and protecting such collective spaces that refuse to privatize and individualize women's struggle, pain, and their solutions, and that advocate critique rather than adjustment, and of making such spaces visible and available within the contemporary public sphere.

The women whose accounts the book explored are clearly the exception, in their extraordinary financial privilege, the apparently retrogressive choice they made, and the non-normative position they adopted, leaving behind years of education, training, and achievement to become stay-at-home mothers. However, their experience sheds light on the normative position of our time, where in the guise of a progressive liberal narrative, women are required to deny their desires, maintain the deeply unequal gendered split, and bear its costly emotional and financial price. The disjunctions that run through the lives of the women in this book, between the promise of gender equality and the experience of continued gender injustice, run also, I believe, through the lives of many women in contemporary advanced capitalist societies. Juxtaposed against the cultural landscape within which they are produced, the accounts of these women—precisely because of the non-normative choice they represent and their authors' ambivalence about it—reveal some stark fault lines in the gendered public/private, capital/care division in advanced capitalism.

The middle-class women I interviewed are, as Angela McRobbie notes, the winners of the female population, who benefited from the feminism of the earlier period. They have been designated by culture, media, and policy as subjects of immense capacity, rendered by the neoliberal ethos of meritocracy, opportunity, and competition of the 1980s and 1990s, and of confidence, balance, and empowerment of the current decade. Yet their accounts expose how, as McRobbie observes, at the same time they are also the losers, who are subject to gender retrenchment, the containment of desire, and masculine domination.[56] Perceived as the fortunate beneficiaries of choice feminism who reaped the rewards of the abundant possibilities opened up to women of their generation, normatively, these women have no legitimate space to talk about their disappointment and to claim their needs and unrealized desires. They have internalized the voice that judgmentally questions how they can possibly be disappointed and want something more, when they had had all that infinite choice—a question strikingly redolent of patriarchal scathing voices of men like David Hubback in the 1950s, whom I cited at the beginning of the book.[57]

The current moment seems a particularly difficult one for these women to raise the issue of their own needs and desires. On the one hand, a discourse of parenting has not displaced the prioritizing and idealization of motherhood and the perception of mothers as foundation parents. On the other hand, value and social status still derive largely from paid work and from professional and economic independence. Thus, those outside the sphere of paid work supposedly have no right to express their dissatisfaction and disappointment, especially as they occupy a role that is still widely perceived as a woman's natural and most important job. In this contradictory moment in which only certain forms of work are being valued and valorized, and in which the heteronormative family and marriage continue to be central ideals with immense affective and disciplinary power, the women I spoke to are reticent about voicing their disappointment. To do so would require detaching from those dominant ideals and fantasies of gender, work, and family, and would unleash the force of critique, and with it some destabilizing and even devastating eruptions.

Yet the plea that I feel runs through the accounts of every one of the women in this book is to decontract from those powerful cultural fantasies and norms, and to reconnect to and excavate their buried desire, and make both the public *and* the private spheres safe for women to realize those desires.[58] It is a plea to unmute and deprivatize disappointment "until she bows down to it no longer,"[59] until she can safely enunciate her rage and demand the creation of social infrastructure that will bring about long overdue equality, both at work and at home.

APPENDIX 1

Interviewees' Key Characteristics

Women

	Name	Age	Nationality and ethnicity	Highest education	Former occupation	Husband's/partner's occupation	Number and age of children	Years since leaving paid employment
1	Alison	50	British, white	BA Fashion	Fashion designer	Marketing manager	2 (14, 11)	14
2	Anne	42	British, white	N/A	HR manager	IT consultant	3 (11, 9, 6)	11
3	Beatriz	41	Latin American, white	MBA	Journalist	Lawyer	2 (7, 4)	3
4	Carmen	40	European, white	BA English	Train driver	Financial director	1 (5)	5
5	Catherine	42	British, white	BA Fashion	Fashion designer	Engineer	3 (12, 9, 5)	5
6	Charlotte	46	British, white	MS Law	Lawyer	Lawyer	3 (13, 12, 10)	10
7	Christine	42	British, white	BA Education	Deputy head teacher	Lawyer	2 (11, 8)	10
8	Dana	49	British, white	BA Latin and Politics	Arts festival manager	Financial director	2 (10, 6)	10
9	Emily	47	European, white	MBA	Operation director	Divorced Former husband: Financial director	1 (15)	11
10	Fiona	38	British, mixed race	BA Business	Publishing manager	Senior health manager	2 (8, 5)	7
11	Geraldine	44	British, white	BA Law	Lawyer	Divorced Former husband: Lawyer	2 (13, 6)	13
12	Helen	45	British, white	BA Accounting	Accountant	Financial director	2 (10, 6)	9
13	Janet	43	British, white	BA Drama	Actress	Film producer	2 (9, 11)	11
14	Jenny	48	British, black	BE Engineering	Engineer	Lawyer	2 (13, 10)	3

No.	Name	Age	Ethnicity	Degree				
15	Joan	45	American, white	BA Liberal Arts	HR manager	Lawyer	2 (20, 9)	8
16	Julie	42	British, white	BA Education	Publisher	Senior manager in a publishing house	2 (10, 7)	9
17	Karen	43	British, white	BA English	Marketing director	Finance director	1 (11)	9
18	Katie	36	British, white	BA Accounting	Accountant	Insurance broker	2 (7, 4)	6
19	Laura	43	British, white	BA Classics and English	Software programmer	Floor trader	2 (7, 5)	7
20	Linda	51	American, mixed race	BS Economics	Banker	Financial director	3 (17, 15, 12)	17
21	Liz	43	British, white	PhD Criminology	Academic	Lawyer (partner in a firm)	2 (9, 7)	8
22	Louise	38	British, white	Russian Studies and politics	Marketing director	Engineer	1 (4)	3
23	Maggie	49	British, white	BA English, MA Journalism	Journalist	Communications director	4 (15, 11, 10, 6)	11
24	Marie	41	British, white	BA Law	Lawyer and then legal adviser	Lawyer	2 (5, 4)	3
25	Natalie	45	European, white	BA Law	Lawyer	Lawyer	3 (14, 11, 4)	10
26	Paula	43	British, white	BA Psychology and LLM	Lawyer	Media producer	2 (12, 10)	9
27	Rachel	46	British, white	BA Accounting	Accountant	Partner in an accountancy firm	3 (12, 10, 7)	10
28	Sara	42	British, white	BS Economics	Financial director	Banker	2 (6, 4)	3
29	Sharon	42	European, mixed race	MS Social Work	Director of social work department	Energy consultant	2 (5, 3)	3
30	Sheryl	36	American, white	BA Business	Fundraiser	CEO of technology firm	2 (5, 2)	3

(continued)

Women

	Name	Age	Nationality and ethnicity	Highest education	Former occupation	Husband's/partner's occupation	Number and age of children	Years since leaving paid employment
31	Simone	35	European, white	BA Education	Schoolteacher	Banker	2 (4, 6)	4
32	Susan	44	British, white	MBBS Medicine	Medical doctor	Financial consultant	3 (6, 9, 12)	11
33	Tanya	48	British, white	BA Law	Lawyer (partner in a firm)	Lawyer (partner in a firm)	2 (6, 9)	7
34	Tess	49	British, white	BA Journalism	News producer	Lawyer	2 (12, 10)	6
35	Wendy	43	European, white	BE Engineering	Software engineer	Manager at an IT firm	4 (12, 10, 4, 2)	9

Men

	Name	Age	Nationality and ethnicity	Education	Occupation	Wife's former occupation	Number and age of children	Years since wife left paid employment
1	Tim	46	British, white	MBA	CEO of technology firm	Art curator	2 (14, 10)	9
2	Roberto	39	Latin American, white	MS Economics	Financial adviser	Accountant	1 (5)	5
3	Richard	43	British, white	MBA	IT consultant	Engineer	4 (13, 10, 5, 2)	10
4	Peter	44	British, white	BE Engineering	Director of a technology firm	Teacher	2 (6, 9)	5
5	John	50	British, white	BE Engineering	Director at an energy firm	Engineer	2 (16, 12)	11

APPENDIX 2
List of Media and Policy Representations

Primary representations that were analyzed in detail are marked with an asterisk. Other representations listed are secondary: they inform the analysis but were not analyzed in detail in the book.

MEDIA REPRESENTATIONS

Advertisements: Outdoor ads

*Ad Council and National Responsible Fatherhood Clearinghouse, "Take Time to Be a Dad" campaign, 2015, https://www.fatherhood.gov/multimedia.

*BBH for Barclays, "Barclaycard: Today I will Stress Less," 2015, https://www.theguardian.com/lifeandstyle/2015/jul/18/do-it-all-dads-men-career-family-friends (third image from the top).

*British Airways, "What if Your Only Job Was Being a Mum?" 2017 (no hyperlink).

*Hometown, UK for Powwownow, "Powwownow: Here's to Flexible Working" (with mother), print advertisement, 2016, https://www.adsoftheworld.com/media/print/powwownow_heres_to_flexible_working_2.

*Hometown, UK for Powwownow, "Powwownow: Here's to Flexible Working" (with man), print advertisement, 2016, https://www.adsoftheworld.com/media/print/powwownow_heres_to _flexible_working_3.

*Nestlé, "Become a Superdad," 2015 (no hyperlink).

Paul O'Connor for Legal & General, superheroes print advertisement, 2015, https://the-dots.com/projects/paul-o-connor-for-legal -general-jwt-london-154001.

Commercials

BBDO India, "Ariel, #ShareTheLoad with English Subtitles," YouTube, February 24, 2016, https://www.youtube.com/watch?v =vwW0X9f0mME.

FiatUK," 'The Motherhood' feat. Fiat 500L," YouTube, December 13, 2012, https://www.youtube.com/watch?v=eNVde5HPhYo.

*United Airlines, "1988 United Airlines Commercial," YouTube, https://www.youtube.com/watch?v=Zgd6K2vi0wk.

Films

*Baby Boom, directed by Charles Shyer, released October 7, 1987, United Artists/Meyer/Shyer, theatrical.

Horrible Bosses, directed by Seth Gordon, released July 8, 2011, Warner Bros., theatrical and DVD.

Nine to Five, directed by Colin Higgins, released December 19, 1980, 20th Century Fox, theatrical.

The Wife, directed by Björn Runge, film festival release September 12, 2017, Tempo Productions Limited, Anonymous Content.

Working Girl, directed by Mike Nichols, released December 21, 1988, 20th Century Fox, theatrical.

Memes and images

Digital image, "I have so much housework . . . what movie should I watch?" https://uk.pinterest.com/pin/14566398778723544.

Digital image, "Taking naps sounds so childish. I prefer to call them horizontal life poses," https://uk.pinterest.com/ pin/512636370061977284/.

*Digital image in Jon Card, "What Entrepreneurs Want from the 'Self-Employment Revolution,'" *Guardian*, October 6, 2016, http://www.theguardian.com/small-business-network/2016/oct/06/what-entrepreneurs-want-from-self-employment-revolution.
*Digital image in Lucy Tobin, "How the Google Campus Creche Is Revolutionising Workplace Childcare," *Evening Standard*, October 20, 2016, https://www.standard.co.uk/lifestyle/london-life/how-the-google-campus-creche-is-revolutionising-workplace-childcare-a3374221.html.

Mobile applications

Cozi Inc., Cozi Family Organizer, available on Google Play.
*Ministère des Droits des Femmes, Leadership Pour Elles, available on Google Play.
TimeTune Studio, TimeTune, available on Google Play.
Tsurutan, Inc., Daily Check: Routine Work, available on Google Play.
WonderApps AB, ATracker Pro, available on ITunes.

News stories

*Al Jazeera, "WEF: Gender Wage Gap Will Not Close for 170 Years," October 26, 2016, http://www.aljazeera.com/news/2016/10/index-gender-wage-gap-close-170-years-161026071909666.html.
*Rachel Aroesti, "Take That, Patriarchy! The Horrific, Cack-Handed 'Feminism' of Netflix's Girlboss," *Guardian*, May 10, 2017, https://www.theguardian.com/tv-and-radio/2017/may/10/girlboss-netflix-horrific-cack-handed-feminism-sophia-amoruso.
*Associated Press, "Report: Women Won't Earn as Much as Men for 170 Years," October 26, 2016, https://apnews.com/114bfd7fb7f94d3085d353b94db689ab.
*BBC, "BBC Interview with Robert Kelly Interrupted by Children Live on Air," March 10, 2107, https://www.bbc.com/news/av/world-39232538/bbc-interview-with-robert-kelly-interrupted-by-children-live-on-air.
BBC, "Facebook's Sheryl Sandberg in Call to Help Working Mothers," BBC Business, May 14, 2017, https://www.bbc.com/news/business-39917277.

Lisa Belkin, "The Opt-Out Revolution," *New York Times Magazine*, October 26, 2003, 42–47, http://www.nytimes.com/2003/10/26/magazine/the-opt-out-revolution.html.

*Elizabeth S. Bernstein, "Why Is Obama Sticking It to Stay-at-Home Moms?" *Washington Post*, April 3, 2015, https://www.washingtonpost.com/opinions/why-is-obama-sticking-it-to-stay-at-home-moms/2015/04/03/c0aeaaf0-c756-11e4-aa1a-86135599fb0f_story.html.

*Jon Card, "What Entrepreneurs Want from the 'Self-employment Revolution,'" *Guardian*, October 6, 2016, http://www.theguardian.com/small-business-network/2016/oct/06/what-entrepreneurs-want-from-self-employment-revolution.

*Kerry Close, "Moms in the Midwest Are More Likely to Work Outside the Home than Anywhere Else in the US," *Time*, May 6, 2016, http://time.com/money/4320772/midwest-highest-rate-working-moms/.

*Lauren Davidson, "Gender Equality Will Happen—but Not Until 2095," *Telegraph*, October 24, 2014, http://www.telegraph.co.uk/finance/economics/11191348/Gender-equality-will-happen-but-not-until-2095.html.

* MacLellan Lila, "The Canada-US task force of women CEOs in a photo opp with Trump and Trudeau seems to have 'vaporized,'" Quartz, April 26, 2017, https://qz.com/966970/trump-and-trudeaus-canada-us-task-force-of-women-ceos-seems-to-have-disappeared-two-months-after-its-photo-opp/.

*Peter Dominiczak, "We Have Done Enough for 'Admirable' Stay-at-Home Parents, Insists Clegg," *Daily Telegraph*, March 29, 2013.

*Peter Dominiczak and Rowena Mason, "David Cameron's 'Slur' on Stay-at-Home Mothers," *Telegraph*, March 19, 2013, http://www.telegraph.co.uk/news/politics/9941492/David-Camerons-slur-on-stay-at-home-mothers.html.

*Steve Doughty, "Working Mothers Risk Damaging Their Child's Prospects," *Daily Mail*, N.D., http://www.dailymail.co.uk/news/article-30342/Working-mothers-risk-damaging-childs-prospects.html.

Maggie Haberman, "Ivanka Trump Swayed the President on Family Leave. Congress is a Tougher Sell," *New York Times*, May 21, 2017, https://www.nytimes.com/2017/05/21/us/politics/ivanka-trump-parental-leave-plan.html.

Felicity Hannah, "80 percent of Self-Employed People in Britain Live in Poverty: Freelance Perks Mask Growing Fears of Financial Ruin for Millions," *Independent*, June 8, 2016, http://www.independent.co.uk /money/spend-save/80-of-self-employed-people-in-britain-live-in -poverty-a7070561.html.

Mina Haq, "The Face of 'Gig' Work Is Increasingly Female—and Empow- ered, Survey Finds," *USA Today*, April 4, 2017, https://www.usatoday .com/story/money/2017/04/04/women-gig-work-equal-pay-day -side-gigs-uber/99878986/.

Nathan Heller, "Many Liberals Have Embraced the Sharing Economy. But Can They Survive It?" *New Yorker*, May 15, 2017, http://www .newyorker.com/magazine/2017/05/15/is-the-gig-economy -working.

*Issie Lapowseky, "Want More Women Working in Tech? Let Them Stay Home," *Wired*, June 4, 2015, http://www.wired.com/2015/04 /powertofly/.

*Wednesday Martin, "Poor Little Rich Women," *New York Times*, May 16, 2015, http://www.nytimes.com/2015/05/17/opinion/sunday /poor-little-rich-women.html.

*Claire Miller, "A Darker Theme in Obama's Farewell: Automation Can Divide Us," *New York Times*, January 12, 2017, https://www.nytimes .com/2017/01/12/upshot/in-obamas-farewell-a-warning-on -automations-perils.html.

*Erika Rackley, "So, Lord Sumption Says to Be Patient—We'll Have a Diverse Bench . . . in 2062," *Guardian*, November 20, 2012, https:// www.theguardian.com/law/2012/nov/20/judiciary-uk-supreme -court.

*Samantha Simmons, "The Election—Is Imposter Syndrome to Blame?" *Huffington Post*, June 12, 2017, http://www.huffingtonpost.co.uk /samantha-simmonds/the-election-is-imposter-_b_17017264.html.

*Anne-Marie Slaughter, "Why Women Still Can't Have It All," *Atlantic*, July/August, 2012, https://www.theatlantic.com/magazine /archive/2012/07/why-women-still-cant-have-it-all/309020/.

Jennifer Steinhauer, "Even Child Care Divides Parties. Ivanka Trump Tries Building a Bridge," *New York Times*, March 11, 2017, https:// www.nytimes.com/2017/03/11/us/politics/ivanka-trump-women -policy.html.

*Lucy Tobin, "How the Google Campus Creche Is Revolutionising Workplace Childcare," *Evening Standard*, October 20, 2016, https://www.standard.co.uk/lifestyle/london-life/how-the-google-campus-creche-is-revolutionising-workplace-childcare-a3374221.html. In hard copy this article appeared as: Lucy Tobin, "Bringing Up Baby (While Launching an Online Empire)," *Evening Standard*, October 20, 2016.

*Jill Treanor, "Gender Pay Gap Could Take 170 Years to Close, Says World Economic Forum," *Guardian*, October 25, 2016, https://www.theguardian.com/business/2016/oct/25/gender-pay-gap-170-years-to-close-world-economic-forum-equality.

Popular fiction

Amy Chua, *Battle Hymn of the Tiger Mother* (London: Penguin, 2011).
*Helen Fielding, *Bridget Jones: Mad About the Boy* (New York: Knopf, 2013).
Allison Pearson, *I Don't Know How She Does It* (New York: Anchor: 2003).
Allison Pearson, *How Hard Can It Be?* (London: Borough, 2017).

Popular scholarly studies

*Ernest Dichter, *The Strategy of Desire* (London and New York: T. V. Boardman, 1960).
*Catherine Hakim, *Work-Lifestyle Choices in the 21st Century: Preference Theory* (Oxford: Oxford University Press, 2000).
*Carmen Nobel, "Men Want Powerful Jobs More than Women Do," *Harvard Business School Working Knowledge*, September 23, 2015, http://hbswk.hbs.edu/item/men-want-powerful-jobs-more-than-women-do.
*Heather Sarsons and Guo Xu, "Confidence Gap? Women Economists Tend to Be Less Confident than Men When Speaking Outside Their Area of Expertise," *LSE Impact Blog*, July 2, 2015, http://blogs.lse.ac.uk/impactofsocialsciences/2015/07/02/confidence-gap-women-economists-less-confident-than-men/.
Felice Schwartz, "Management Women and the New Facts of Life," *Harvard Business Review* (January-February 1989), https://hbr.org/1989/01/management-women-and-the-new-facts-of-life.

Self-help and guide books

Tiffany Duffy, *Drop the Ball* (New York: Flatiron, 2017).

* Helena Morrissey, *A Good Time to Be a Girl: Don't Lean In, Change the System* (London: William Collins, 2018).

*Katty Kay and Claire Shipman, *The Confidence Code: The Science and Art of Self-Assurance—What Women Should Know* (New York: Harper Collins, 2014).

*Sharon Meers and Joanna Strobber, *Getting to 50/50: How Working Couples Can Have It All by Sharing It All* (Berkeley: Viva Editions, 2009).

*Sheryl Sandberg, *Lean In: Women, Work, and the Will to Lead* (London: WH Allen, 2013).

* Anne-Marie Slaughter, *Unfinished Business: Women, Men, Work, Family* (London: Oneworld, 2015).

* Ivanka Trump, *Women Who Work: Rewriting the Rules for Success* (New York: Portfolio, 2017).

Social media campaigns

Dove US, "Baby Dove | #RealMoms," YouTube, April 5, 2017, https://www.youtube.com/watch?v=9dE9AnU3MaI.

Everyday Sexism Project, http://everydaysexism.com (accessed June 13, 2018).

Hollaback Project, http://www.ihollaback.org (accessed June 13, 2018).

*#MeToo, Twitter, https://twitter.com/hashtag/metoo (accessed June 13, 2018).

*Motherhood Challenge, Facebook, 2016.

Television shows

Ally McBeal, created by David E. Kelly, 1997–2002, Fox.

*Big Little Lies, created by David E. Kelley, 2017, HBO.

Borgen, created by Adam Price, 2010–2013, DR Fiktion.

Commander-in-Chief, created by Rod Lurie, 2005–2006, ABC.

Desperate Housewives, created by Marc Cherry, 2004–2012, ABC.

Doctor Foster, created by Mike Bartlett, 2015–2017, BBC.

*The Good Wife, created by Robert King and Michelle King, 2009–2016, CBS.

Grace and Frankie, created by Marta Kauffman and Howard Morris, 2015–present, Netflix.

Homeland, developed by Howard Gordon and Alex Gansa, 2011–present, 20th Century Fox.

The Killing (US), developed by Veena Sud, 2011–2014, AMC/Netflix.

Mad Men, created by Matthew Weiner, 2007–2015, AMC.

Married with Children, created by Michael Moye and Ron Leavitt, 1987–1997, Fox.

Mom, created by Chuck Lorre, Eddie Gorodetsky, and Gemma Baker, 2013–present, CBS.

Motherland, created by Graham Linehan and Sharon Horgan, 2017–present, BBC.

Nurse Jackie, created by Liz Brixius, Evan Duncky, and Linda Wallem, 2005–2015, Showtime.

Orange Is the New Black, created by Jenji Kohan, 2013–present, Netflix.

The Real Housewives franchise, 2006–present, Bravo.

The Replacement (UK), written and directed by Joe Ahearne, 2017, BBC.

Rita (Denmark), created by Christian Torpe, 2012–present, SF Film Production.

Roseanne, created by Matt Williams, 1988–1997, ABC.

Sex and the City, created by Darren Star, 1998–2004, HBO.

The Simpsons, created by Matt Groening, 1989–present, Fox.

Weeds, created by Jenji Kohan, 2005–2012, Showtime.

Websites, blogs, and social media posts

Angela Ahrendts, "Apple's Angela Ahrendts: Always Be Present," *Leaders and Daughters*, March 6, 2017, http://leadersanddaughters.com/2017/03/06/always-be-present-read-the-signs-stay-in-your-lane-and-never-back-up-more-than-you-have-too/.

*Amy Cuddy, "Your Body Language May Shape Who You Are," TEDGlobal, June 2012, https://www.ted.com/talks/amy_cuddy_your_body_language_shapes_who_you_are.

*Black Career Women's Network (BCWN), https://bcwnetwork.com (accessed June 13, 2018).

Brittany Frey, *Handcrafted Brunette* blog, February 17, 2017, https://www.truthinkapparel.com/single-post/2017/02/17/Handcrafted-Brunette, last accessed October 24, 2017.

*Jessica Mairs, " 'Women Are the Salt of Our Lives. They Give it Flavour,' says Santiago Calatrava," *De Zeen*, February 17, 2017, https://www .dezeen.com/2017/02/17/women-salt-lives-architecture-gender -discrimination-santiago-calatrava/.

Mothers at Home Matter (MAHM), http://mothersathomematter.co.uk / (accessed June 13, 2018).

Mumsnet: By Parents for Parents, https://www.mumsnet.com/ (accessed June 13, 2018).

*Sheryl Nance-Nash, "How I (Successfully!) Started an Etsy Store," *Muse*, N.D., https://www.themuse.com/advice/how-i-successfully-started -an-etsy-store.

Dana Smithers, "Enjoy the Present Moment," *Law of Attraction Blog*, March 12, 2014, http://www.empoweredwomeninbusiness.com /enjoy-the-present-moment/.

*Ivanka Trump, Twitter post, September 23, 2016, https://twitter.com /ivankatrump/status/779304354817773569.

POLICY REPRESENTATIONS

Corporate and non-governmental organizations' policy reports

*Joanna Barsh and Lareina Yee, "Unlocking the Full Potential of Women at Work," McKinsey & Company, 2012, https://www.mckinsey.com /business-functions/organization/our-insights/unlocking-the-full -potential-of-women-at-work.

*Charted Management Institute, "Women in Management: The Power of Role Models," 2014, https://www.managers.org.uk/~/media /Research%20Report%20Downloads/The%20Power%20of%20Role %20Models%20-%20May%202014.pdf.

*Katie McCracken, Sergio Marquez, Caleb Kwong, Ute Stephan, Adriana Castagnoli, and Marie Dlouhá, "Women's Entrepreneurship: Closing the Gender Gap in Access to Financial and Other Services and in Social Entrepreneurship," European Parliament, Policy Department C: Citizen's Rights and Constitutional Affairs, 2015, http://www .europarl.europa.eu/RegData/etudes/STUD/2015/519230/IPOL _STU(2015)519230_EN.pdf.

*McKinsey & Company, "Women Matter 2: Female Leadership, a Competitive Edge for the Future," 2008.

*Klynveld Peat Marwick Goerdeler (KPMG), "KPMG Women's Leadership Study: Moving Women Forward into Leadership Roles," 2015, http://womensleadership.kpmg.us/content/dam/kpmg-womens -leadership-golf/womensleadershippressrelease/FINAL%20Womens %20Leadership%20v19.pdf, p. 12.

Government reports, speeches, and announcements

Lorely Burt, "The Burt Report: Inclusive Support for Women in Enterprise," February 2015, http://www.weconnecteurope.org /sites/default/files/documents/Burt_Report.pdf.

*David Cameron, "PM Transcript: Start-up Britain Speech in Leeds," January 23, 2012, https://www.gov.uk/government/speeches /pm-transcript-start-up-britain-speech-in-leeds.

*David Cameron, "David Cameron on Families," August 18, 2014, https:// www.gov.uk/government/speeches/david-cameron-on-families.

*David Cameron, "Prime Minister's Speech on Life Chances," January 11, 2016, https://www.gov.uk/government/speeches/prime-ministers -speech-on-life-chances.

Department for Digital, Culture, Media & Sport, "Women and the Economy Action Plan," 2013, https://www.gov.uk/government /publications/women-and-the-economy-government-action-plan.

Emily Gosden and Steven Swinford, "David Cameron's 30-Hour Free Childcare Plan 'Underfunded,'" *Telegraph*, June 1, 2015, http://www .telegraph.co.uk/news/politics/conservative/11642734/David -Camerons-30-hour-free-childcare-plan-underfunded.html.

*Philip Hammond and Theresa May, "Spring Budget 2017: Support for Women Unveiled by Chancellor," March 8, 2017, https://www.gov .uk/government/news/spring-budget-2017-support-for-women -unveiled-by-chancellor.

*Barack Obama, "Remarks by the President on Women and the Economy," October 31, 2014, https://obamawhitehouse.archives .gov/the-press-office/2014/10/31/remarks-president-women-and -economy-providence-ri.

*Donald J. Trump, "Remarks at Aston Community Center in Aston, Pennsylvania," September 13, 2016, http://www.presidency.ucsb .edu/ws/index.php?pid=119193.

APPENDIX 3
Study Methodology

RECRUITING PARTICIPANTS

To search for educated women who left paid employment after having children who would (hopefully!) be willing to share their experiences with me, I posted notes on parents' mailing lists in schools in middle-class and upper-middle-class neighborhoods in London, on various London social media mothers' groups where there was likely to be a high concentration of highly educated mothers, and on notice boards in local libraries, community centers, and leisure/sport clubs in these neighborhoods. I also posted a message calling for research participants in the alumni newsletter of the London School of Economics and Political Science, the university where I work. Some of the women I interviewed referred me to other women they knew, and some friends and colleagues referred me to women they knew who met the criteria, as well as to some of the men I interviewed.

INTERVIEWEE SAMPLE

Relying on these networks, snowball sampling, and referrals, my aim was to include a variety of experiences, professional backgrounds, and perspectives, including years outside the workforce, number and age of children, and areas of London. The various and diverse sources (listed above) from which I recruited participants helped to ensure wide variability of perspectives and experiences. While I aimed for as much diversity as possible within this group of women, my qualitative findings are not representative of all educated stay-at-home mothers. I adopted a purposive rather than a representative sampling strategy.[1] Thus, for example, the sample consisted mostly of white women, and included only one black woman and three mixed-race women. That said, the distribution of stay-at-home mothers in the United Kingdom (see appendix 4) shows that the vast majority are white (72 percent).

The sample includes thirty-five women who live in London and who had left paid employment between three and seventeen years earlier. The size of the sample was determined by the "saturation point"—the point when the researcher starts to hear very similar themes to those already collected. Pamela Stone, who used a similar sampling strategy, notes that the "prevailing guidelines for a study of this sort recommend sample sizes that range anywhere from twenty to fifty."[2] Appendix 1 presents the interviewees' key characteristics.

While the women in the sample are married to men whose wages allow the family to live on a single income, none belong to what the Great British Class Survey terms "elite."[3] Some are in the second wealthiest class group of the "established middle class": a comfortably off, secure section of the British population, and the largest of the seven classes identified by the survey. Some belong to the "new affluent workers"—a class group with middle levels of economic capital that includes the offspring of the "traditional working class," which has been fragmented by de-industrialization, mass unemployment, immigration, and a shift from manufacturing to services-based employment. All interviewees were home owners, but not all of them could afford to live in a house. Some lived in flats in middle-class neighborhoods; others had lodgers whose rents augmented the household's single income and allowed the family to live in a private house.

London, the city in which the people I interviewed live, has the highest percentage of stay-at-home mothers across UK regions (see appendix 4). It is a global financial center and is home to leading global firms where many of the women I interviewed used to work and which currently employ their partners or husbands. As the accounts of the women in the book demonstrate, some of the factors that influenced their decision to leave their job are intimately related to life in London. They include the work culture, especially of financial and legal firms in

London's financial center—"the City," where many of the women and their husbands worked—the long commutes to and from work demanded by many London jobs, the high costs of living in the capital, and the large number of high-skilled migrants (some of my interviewees included) and low-paid migrants (often my interviewees' childcarers and domestic helpers) living in London. Most of the interviewees lived far from their extended families, had elderly parents and parents-in-law who could not supply regular help, or had no living parents or parents-in-law. Some of the characteristics of London are particular, but many of these aspects on which the women and men reflected in the interviews are typical of the experience of families living in big cities and are likely to resonate with readers with similar socioeconomic backgrounds in other cities around the world.

The presence and influence of American culture in London is also worth noting. While all the interviewees live in London, and their experiences and cultural points of reference are often particular to the United Kingdom and sometimes to London, at the same time many of the issues, debates, images, and examples to which they referred and through which they interpreted their experience are American. There seems to be what researchers Yvonne Tasker and Diane Negra call a high degree of "discursive harmony"[1] between my interviewees' accounts of their experiences as educated women living in London, predominantly in middle-class neighborhoods, and American representations, cultural reference points, and ideas. It seems important also to note that nearly half of my interviewees referred to the United States in the context of their own former and/or their husbands' workplaces, either because they had been taken over or were strongly influenced by American companies. For this reason, I juxtapose the interview accounts with representations from both British and American media and policy.

HOW THE INTERVIEWS WERE CONDUCTED

The calls I posted for participants, especially on parent mailing lists, yielded initially seventeen responses within a few days of posting. This relatively high response rate was perhaps due to my "gatekeepers"— parents known to these women who had forwarded my message to the various groups. Some of the women who replied and expressed interest in being interviewed "warned" me that it was a very sensitive issue and that they were likely to cry during the interview.

All interviews except one were face-to-face; in one case, the woman could not meet me in person so the interview was conducted on the phone. As mentioned in the introduction, about half of the interviews were conducted in the interviewees' homes, and the rest in coffee shops or other public places in the vicinity of their homes. All the interviewees gave informed consent for the interviews to be audiotaped and transcribed verbatim, and for the interview material to be used for the purposes of this research but without identifying them.

Interviewees were first given a brief and broad description of the study's purpose. Then I opened the interview with the broad question, "Can you take me from the last couple of years of being in paid employment to where you are now?" The purpose was to invite interviewees to recount their life stories, giving them the freedom to express what was important to them and to construct their account in a way that made sense to them.[5] From this moment on, I kept my interventions to a minimum. I focused on listening, following up with questions or requests for clarifications when I identified potential contradictions or if details did not stack up.

My interview guide included questions related to three central themes: women's experience in paid employment, the decision to leave paid employment, and their lives since leaving paid employment. I rarely asked all of the questions in my guide since most interviewees addressed them organically in their responses to the opening question. I deliberately avoided asking direct questions about media or policy stories and images *per se*, since I was interested in whether and when direct or indirect references to media and policy representations and discourses occurred, and if they did, what this might say about the way they shaped and structured the women's accounts of their lives.

However, in addition to the broad opening question, I did pose two specific questions if (and often because) they had not been addressed organically: "What do you find satisfying in your current life?" and "How do you imagine your life when the children are grown?" Both these questions were directly inspired by the questions Betty Friedan asked her respondents,[6] and aimed to situate the women's account *vis-à-vis* their 1950s counterparts. Historical comparison between the women I interviewed in

London and the women of their mothers' generation whom Friedan interviewed in America runs throughout the book.

The interviews with men were conducted, upon their request, in their offices or a workplace-related space (e.g., one interview was conducted at a corporate conference venue). They followed a similar approach and principle although they raised some different issues and challenges. The opening question was adapted to "Can you take me from the last couple of years before you had children?" following which I asked several questions in an effort to understand how the wife's decision to quit her job came about, their involvement in and view of her decision and its aftermath, their life today, including a particular question about the distribution of labor between them and their wives (tellingly, something most of the women talked about unprompted), what they found satisfying in their current lives, and how they imagined the future when the children were grown. The five men who responded to my call for participants were very confident, assertive, and talkative. While they candidly shared some of their regrets and conflicted feelings about their wives' decisions to quit their jobs, they expressed very limited recognition of the influence they may have had on this decision and its consequences for their wives' lives. As I mentioned earlier, the book focuses primarily on women's accounts. Examples are drawn from interviews with men when they illuminate something important or provide another perspective from those of the women interviewed.

HOW THE INTERVIEWS WERE ANALYZED

The interview analysis was strongly influenced by the work of Valerie Walkerdine and her colleagues[7] and was conducted in three stages, representing three levels. First, like much qualitative research, I examined individual narratives to ascertain the overall plot, its key events, characters, themes, and scenes. On this basis, each interview was mapped onto its interviewee's life trajectory. Drawing on the themes that were identified in each interview, during the second stage, a thematic analysis was conducted across the interviews. It consisted of looking for similarities and differences across the themes in all of the interviews and then clustering them. For instance, the theme of work-life balance recurred in almost all interviews, as did the theme of distribution of labor in the home. Inter-viewees' mothers' disapproval of their daughters' decision to quit their job figured in just over two-thirds of the interviews, while children's health as one of the factors that influenced women's decision to quit their jobs emerged in five interviews. The most prevalent themes were used to frame the discussion and correspond largely to the topics of the chapters in this book. Some of the less frequently mentioned themes were also included in the discussion, depending on the context.

Given my interest in the constructed nature of experience, and how women's subjectivities, visions, fantasies, and deepest desires are consti-tuted by and in relation to media and policy representations and discourses, the third stage focused on a deeper interpretative level of analysis. At this level, I examined closely *how* interviewees accounted for their lives and experiences: the particular words, images, metaphors, discourses, tone, and register they used; their occurrence and recurrence; the inconsistencies, tensions, ambiguities, subtleties, and contradictions within their accounts; and crucially, the omissions, avoidances, and silences—what often was not said, what women struggled to say, the words they could not find. This level of discourse analysis provides valuable insights into the relationships between women's thinking and feeling and cultural discourses, and, in par-ticular, into moments in which these discourses failed them but simultane-ously shaped their thinking, feelings, behavior and sense of self.

MEDIA AND POLICY REPRESENTATIONS SAMPLE

Charting the cultural landscape within which the experiences of the educated stay-at-home mothers are constituted, and upon which these women draw and which they negotiate in their everyday lives, is a daunt-ing task. It is impossible to capture all of the social and cultural images, narratives, and discourses related to gender, work, and family that circu-late in contemporary culture: they are numerous and circulate in multiple media, sites, and across many years. As explained in the introduction, my aim was rather to devise a sample of *illustrative* as opposed to represen-tative examples of media and policy representations and discourses (see appendix 2), which resonate with and/or are in tension with the accounts of the interviewees' lived experience.

The material drawn on includes advertising, films, newspaper articles and other news stories, self-help and guide books, popular fiction, television shows, websites, social media (e.g., blogs, Instagram memes), and popular scholarly texts. These last refer to academic publications that are treated as part of the data since they give access to ways of talking and thinking about women, work, and family.

Public discourse about women, work, and family is shaped significantly by policy debates, and interviewees frequently made reference to these debates. Therefore, I also included policy representations in the sample. However, since it is such a vast field I restricted the data collected to two types of accounts: government policy reports, speeches, and announcements, and corporate and non-governmental organizations' policy reports and papers, such as reports on gender equality policies in the workplace. Unlike empiricist approaches to public policy, in this book I treat policy as discourse; the focus is on the social construction of policy problems and issues, rather than the details of policy and its implementation.[8] In some instances I refer to political discourse, such as political leaders' speeches or announcements, however, these always relate to policy discussions.

The sample of media and policy representations is presented in appendix 2 and focuses almost exclusively on the United Kingdom and the United States because of the close discursive relationships between the two cultures (discussed above), and the particular confluence of reference points from British and American cultures in women's accounts.

The thematic and discursive analyses of the interviews provided the basis for identifying media and policy representations.[9] When interviewees mentioned particular examples of cultural, media, and policy representations, I included them in the sample for analysis. Other representations were retrieved drawing on the anthropologist George Marcus's essay on multi-sited ethnography as a research strategy for "tracing a cultural formation across and within multiple sites of activity."[10] It involved establishing interconnections between topics, genres, and forms in three main sites: women's self-narratives, media representations, and policy representations. Marcus lists various techniques to trace the objects of study within different settings of a complex cultural phenomenon. Although I did not conduct a multi-sited ethnography, two of these techniques or "practices of construction,"[11] as Marcus describes them, proved particularly productive for my exploration. The first, "follow the metaphor,"[12] which resembles a Foucauldian genealogical approach,[13] focuses on tracing ways of thinking and talking about certain issues at various discursive locations, and making connections between tropes in what seemingly are separate and disconnected locations of cultural production. For instance, one of the metaphors interviewees used repeatedly to account for their experiences of work and family, and especially for what they perceived as their personal failure, was balance and lack of balance. Following this prominent metaphor led me to search for its presence and use in contemporary and some older (e.g., Ernest Dichter's 1940s writings, which I discuss in chapter 2) media and policy representations related to women, family, and work.

The second technique, "follow the plot, story, or allegory,"[14] looks for connections, associations, and relationships between narratives and plots across different sites of cultural production. This served as an especially useful methodological practice for identifying the relationships between the fantasies women articulated in the interviews and cultural fantasies and myths that media and policy representations mobilize and (re) produce. For example, the discussion in chapter 5 of the "mompreneur" includes various examples of representations in media and policy that perpetuate the myth of the mother working from home while simultaneously looking after her young children. These representations were identified and included in the sample by following the prominence of this fantasy in women's accounts.

Additionally, as Marcus notes, following stories and myths invites one to look for narratives, plots, and allegories that threaten and disturb dominant visions. For example, I collected examples of media representations and discourses that challenge and puncture the fetishization and idealization of motherhood, and discuss how they shape women's thinking and feeling, and what they simultaneously obscure. Thus, Marcus's techniques informed the selection of media representations that resonate with, confirm, reinforce, as well as challenge and offer alternative visions to those offered by other representations and to those interviewees articulated in their accounts. Moreover, some media and policy representations were selected by drawing on existing scholarship on media and policy representations of women, family, and work.

Finally, given the book's focus on stay-at-home mothers and women's own preoccupation with this identity term, it was important to gain a robust understanding of how stay-at-home mothers are represented in UK and US media and policy. Therefore, to complement the above methods, I conducted a focused search to identify key patterns in depictions of stay-at-home mothers in media and policy. This yielded an extensive sample of representations, including 299 newspaper articles, and another 118 representations from magazines, film, popular fiction, self-help/guide books, celebrity, advertising, social media, popular academic accounts, and policy reports, speeches, and texts.

HOW MEDIA AND POLICY REPRESENTATIONS WERE ANALYZED

I conducted content analysis on the 299 newspaper articles (with Sara De Benedictis). The analysis examined UK newspaper coverage of the figure of the stay-at-home mother during the global recession and its aftermath (2008–2013). The analysis, which is reported in full elsewhere,[15] provided the basis for the discussion in chapter 3 of the depiction of stay-at-home mothers in media and policy discourse, and informed the discussion throughout the book.

Of the remaining 118 representations in the sample, 62 were analyzed using qualitative interpretive methods, particularly discourse and visual analyses. They are marked with an asterisk in appendix 2. My interpretation of media texts and images draws on the rich feminist scholarship that uses semiotics to analyze the construction of gender in media representations, and particularly Roland Barthes's work on myth in the analysis of popular culture.[16] It is profoundly influenced and informed also by Foucault's work and its influence in cultural and media analysis. Specifically, the present analysis focuses on the ways in which media and policy representations construct meanings that discipline and regulate women's thinking, most intimate feelings, judgments, and deepest desires.

APPENDIX 4

Characteristics of UK Stay-at-Home Mothers

Percentage of stay-at-home mothers with:

Age of youngest child:

- under 2	25
- 2 to 4	29
- 5 to 9	23
- 10 to 15	16
- 16 to 18	5

Number of children:

- one	38
- two	35
- three	18
- four plus	9

Partnership:

- married	53
- cohabiting	15
- single, previously married	11
- single, never married	21

Percentage of stay-at-home mothers with:

Age:

- less than 25	10
- 25 to 29	18
- 30 to 34	20
- 35 to 39	18
- 40 to 44	15
- 45 and over	20

Highest qualification:

- degree	19
- higher education	7
- A Level	16
- GCSE	26
- other	15
- none	17

Ethnicity:

- white	72
- Asian	16
- black	6
- other/mixed	6

Percentage of stay-at-home mothers across UK regions:

North East	4
North West	11
Yorkshire/Humberside	9
East Midlands	7
West Midlands	10
Eastern	9
London	18
South East	11
South West	6
Wales	4
Scotland	8
Northern Ireland	3

Note: Sample is 5,791 mothers outside the labor force from Labour Force Survey 2015 Q2 to 2017 Q1. Analysis conducted by Gillian Paull, Frontier Economics.

Notes

INTRODUCTION

1. A form of public or social housing built by local municipalities in the United Kingdom and Northern Ireland.
2. For an excellent discussion of the changing economic, social, and cultural scenario during the 1980s and 1990s and how it shaped working-class girls' lives, see Valerie Walkerdine, Helen Lucey, and June Melody, *Growing Up Girl: Psychosocial Explorations of Gender and Class* (Basingstoke, UK: Palgrave, 2001).
3. Isabella Bakker, "Women's Employment in Comparative Perspective" in *Feminization of the Labour Force: Paradoxes and Promises*, ed. J. Jenson, E. Hagen, and C. Reddy (Cambridge: Polity Press, 1988), 17.
4. Walkerdine, Lucey, and Melody, *Growing Up Girl*, 158.
5. This theme is developed in chapter 2, drawing on Catherine Rottenberg's concept of the "balanced woman." See Catherine Rottenberg, "Happiness and the Liberal Imagination: How Superwoman Became Balanced," *Feminist Studies* 40, no. 1 (2014): 144–168.
6. Allison Pearson, *I Don't Know How She Does It* (New York: Knopf, 2002).
7. See Walkerdine, Lucey, and Melody, *Growing Up Girl*.
8. Rosalind Gill, "Sexism Reloaded, or, It's Time to Get Angry Again!" *Feminist Media Studies* 11, no. 1 (2011): 66.
9. US figures are based on "Women, Work and Children: The Return of the Stay-at-Home Mother," *Economist*, April 19, 2014. UK figures are based on analysis of the UK Labour Force Survey 1997–2017. Presentation by Shani Orgad and Gillian Paull (Frontier Economics) to the Policy Lab and Government Equalities Office, July 17, 2017.
10. Betty Friedan, *The Feminine Mystique* (1963; reprint, London: Penguin, 2000), 49. Judith Hubback raised a similar question in relation to UK women in her 1957 book *Wives Who Went to College* (London: Heinemann, 1957).
11. Friedan, *Feminine Mystique*, 34.
12. Friedan, 198.
13. Sheryl Sandberg, *Lean In: Women, Work, and the Will to Lead* (London: WH Allen, 2013).

14. Sarah Banet-Weiser, *Empowered: Popular Feminism and Popular Misogyny* (Durham, NC: Duke University Press, 2018); Catherine Rottenberg, *The Rise of Neoliberal Feminism* (Oxford: Oxford University Press, 2018); Anne-Marie Slaughter, "Why Women Still Can't Have It All," *Atlantic*, July/August, 2012, https://www.theatlantic.com/magazine /archive/2012/07/why-women-still-cant-have-it-all/309020.

15. See Anne-Marie Slaughter, *Unfinished Business: Women, Men, Work, Family* (London: One-world, 2015).

16. See, for instance, Business in the Community, "Business in the Community Toolkit," 2017, https://gender.bitc.org.uk/all-resources/toolkits/business-case-gender-diversity; Berkeley Executive Education, "Berkeley Insight," 2017, http://executive.berkeley.edu/thought -leadership/blog/business-case-gender-diversity; Vivian Hunt, Dennis Layton, and Sara Prince, "Why Diversity Matters," January 2015, http://www.mckinsey.com/business -functions/organization/our-insights/why-diversity-matters; Carline Turner, "The Business Case for Gender Diversity: Update 2017," *Huffington Post*, April 30, 2017, http://www .huffingtonpost.com/entry/the-business-case-for-gender-diversity-update-2017 _us_590658cbe4b05279d4edbd4b.

17. Angela McRobbie, *The Aftermath of Feminism: Gender, Culture and Social Change* (London: Sage, 2009); see discussion in chapter 1.

18. The UK figures are based on Figure 2 in Office for National Statistics, Labour Force Survey (2018), https://www.ons.gov.uk/employmentandlabourmarket/peopleinwork /employmentandemployeetypes/bulletins/uklabourmarket/latest (accessed July 9, 2018). Employment includes those undertaking any paid work, including employees and the self-employed. The employment proportions are seasonally adjusted and are for women aged 16 to 64. The US figures are based on US Department of Labor, "Women in the Labor Force," Women's Bureau, 2016, https://www.dol.gov/wb/stats/NEWSTATS/facts /women_lf.htm (accessed July 9, 2018).

19. See, for instance, Alison Wolf, *The XX Factor: How Working Women Are Creating a New Society* (London: Profile, 2013).

20. Spencer Thompson and Dalia Ben-Galim, *Childmind the Gap: Reforming Childcare to Support Mothers into Work* (London: Institute for Public Policy Research, 2014), 2.

21. "Professional" women are defined here as those working in or who have worked in the top three occupational categories in the UK Labour Force Survey: 1. Managers, directors, senior officials; 2. Professionals; 3. Associate professionals, technical. The analysis in table 1 was prepared by Gillian Paull for presentation by Shani Orgad and Gillian Paull (Frontier Economics) to the Policy Lab and UK Government Equalities Office, July 17, 2017.

22. Landivar's analysis of US employment trends found that "women with preschool-age children were 1.9 times more likely to be out of the labor force than women without children" and that women who gave birth in the past were twice as likely to be out of the labor force than women without children. Liana Cristin Landivar, *Women at Work: Who Opts Out?* (Boulder, Colo.: Lynne Rienner, 2017), 84.

23. Claudia Goldin and Joshua Mitchell, "The New Life Cycle of Women's Employment: Disappearing Humps, Sagging Middles, Expanding Tops," *Journal of Economic Perspectives, American Economic Association* 31, no. 1 (2017): 161–182. Data from the UK Office for National Statistics indicate that the average age of women having children in

England and Wales is 30.3 years, with rates in older women rising since the mid-1970s; UK Office for National Statistics, "Statistical Bulletin: Births by Parents' Characteristics in England and Wales: 2015," November 29, 2016, https://www.ons.gov.uk /peoplepopulationandcommunity/birthsdeathsandmarriages/livebirths/bulletins /birthsbyparentscharacteristicsinenglandandwales/2015.

24. Pew Research Center, "Parenting in America," *Pew Research Center*, December 17, 2015, http://www.pewsocialtrends.org/2015/12/17/1-the-american-family-today/.

25. Gillian Paull, "The Impact of Children on Women's Paid Work," *Fiscal Studies* 27, no. 4 (2006): 506, 508. The conventional wisdom is that children's school entry is a key time for mothers to *return* to paid employment. In fact, it is a time when a substantial proportion of mothers leave employment.

26. Slaughter, *Unfinished Business*, 54.

27. UK Labour Force Survey (2015). Analysis prepared by Gillian Paull (Frontier Economics) for presentation by Shani Orgad and Gillian Paull to the Policy Lab and Government Equalities Office, July 17, 2017. See Shani Orgad, "Heading Home: Public Discourse and Women's Experience of Family and Work" (London: London School of Economics and Political Science, 2017), http://eprints.lse.ac.uk/81486/.

28. John Bingham, "Middle Class Mothers Deserting Workplace to Care for Children, Government Study Shows," *Telegraph*, January 30, 2014, http://www.telegraph.co.uk /women/10608528/Middle-class-mothers-deserting-workplace-to-care-for-children -Government-study-shows.html.

29. Based on analysis of the UK Labour Force Survey 1997–2017. Presentation by Shani Orgad and Gillian Paull (Frontier Economics) to the Policy Lab and UK Government Equalities Office, July 17, 2017. See note 21.

30. Landivar, *Women at Work*, 92.

31. See, for example, Catherine Hakim, *Work-Lifestyle Choices in the 21st Century: Preference Theory* (Oxford: Oxford University Press, 2000).

32. Hakim, *Work-Lifestyle Choices*. Hakim's theory is discussed in greater detail in chapter 1.

33. Lydia Saad, "Children a Key Factor in Women's Desire to Work Outside the Home," *Gallup*, October 7, 2015, http://www.gallup.com/poll/186050/children-key-factor-women -desire-work-outside-home.aspx.

34. For example, Anne Mari Ronquillo, "Why I Chose to Be a Stay-at-Home Mom," *I Am Claire* blog, August 25, 2017, https://www.iamclaire.com/story/2017-08-25/why-i -chose-to-be-a-stay-at-home-mom; Nicole Caruso, "Why I Chose to Be a Stay-at-Home Mom," December 2, 2016, https://nicolemcaruso.com/motherhood/why-i-chose-to-be -a-stay-at-home-mom; Jamie Smith, "Why I Don't Regret Being a Stay-at-Home Mom," *Huffington Post*, November 3, 2017, http://www.huffingtonpost.com/jamie-davis-smith /why-i-dont-regret-being-a-stay-at-home-mom_b_3849263.html.

35. See, for example, discussion of the representation of Jools Oliver as a stay-at-home mother, in Sara De Benedictis and Shani Orgad, "The Escalating Price of Motherhood: Aesthetic Labour in Popular Representations of 'Stay-at-Home' Mothers," in *Aesthetic Labour: Rethinking Beauty Politics in Neoliberalism*, ed. Anna Sofia Elias, Rosalind Gill, and Christina Scharff (London: Palgrave Macmillan, 2017), 101–116. See also Candace Bure, *Balancing It All: My Story of Juggling Priorities and Purpose* (Nashville, Tenn.: B&H Publishing, 2014).

36. Kate Conger, "Exclusive: Here's the Full 10-Page Anti-Diversity Screed Circulating Internally at Google [Updated]," *Gizmodo*, May 8, 2017, https://gizmodo.com/exclusive-heres-the-full-10-page-anti-diversity-screed-1797564320.

37. Angela Saini," Silicon Valley's Weapon of Choice against Women: Shoddy Science," *Guardian*, August 7, 2017, https://www.theguardian.com/commentisfree/2017/aug/07/silicon-valley-weapon-choice-women-google-manifesto-gender-difference-eugenics.

38. Katerina Gould, "Is Lack of Confidence Getting in the Way of Your Return to Work?" *Working Mums*, June 1, 2017, https://www.workingmums.co.uk/is-lack-of-confidence-getting-in-the-way-of-your-return-to-work-2/.

39. Keith Kendrick, "Maternity Leave Mums Suffer Confidence Crisis After 11 Months," *Huffington Post*, May 22, 2015, http://www.huffingtonpost.co.uk/2014/08/14/maternity-leave-mums-suffer-confidence-crisis-after-11-months_n_7367786.html.

40. These concepts are discussed in detail in chapter 1 of this book.

41. Francesca Gino, Caroline Ashley Wilmuth, and Alison Wood Brooks, "Compared to Men, Women View Professional Advancement as Equally Attainable, but Less Desirable," *Proceedings of the National Academy of Sciences of the United States of America* 112, no. 40 (2015): 12354–12359, http://www.pnas.org/content/112/40/12354.

42. Lisa Miller, "The Retro Wife," *New York* magazine, March 17, 2013, http://nymag.com/news/features/retro-wife-2013-3/.

43. Victoria Coren Mitchell, "Women Can Still Have It All. Can't They?" *Guardian*, June 11, 2017, https://www.theguardian.com/commentisfree/2017/jun/11/girls-depression-can-women-still-have-it-all.

44. Pamela Stone, *Opting Out? Why Women Really Quit Careers and Head Home* (Berkeley: University of California Press, 2007).

45. A related work is Bernie Jones's *Women Who Opt Out*, which corroborates Stone's thesis that women are being pushed out by a work environment that is hostile to women, children, and demands of family caregiving. As an edited collection, it inevitably provides a broad overview of debates and questions rather than a systematic, in-depth account of women's experience. However, it pays very limited attention to the influence of other social (e.g., husbands' work conditions, unequal household work) and cultural factors, and specifically media and policy representations. See Bernie Jones, ed. *Women Who Opt Out: The Debate over Working Mothers and Work-Family Balance* (New York: New York University Press, 2012).

46. See Banet-Weiser, *Empowered*; Rosalind Gill, "Post-postfeminism? New Feminist Visibilities in Postfeminist Times," *Feminist Media Studies* 16, no. 4 (2016): 610–630; Rottenberg, *Rise of Neoliberal Feminism* (Oxford: Oxford University Press, 2018).

47. For example, Heather Addison, Mary Kate Goodwin-Kelly, and Elaine Roth, *Motherhood Misconceived: Representing the Maternal in US Films* (Albany: State University of New York Press, 2009); Heather L. Hundley and Sara Hayden, *Mediated Moms: Contemporary Challenges to the Motherhood Myth* (New York: Peter Lang, 2016); Rebecca Feasey, *From Happy Homemaker to Desperate Housewives* (New York: Anthem Press, 2012); May Friedman, *Mommyblogs and the Changing Face of Motherhood* (Toronto: University of Toronto Press, 2013); Jones, *Women Who Opt Out*.

48. Hochschild with Machung, *Second Shift*; Rosalind Coward, *Our Treacherous Hearts: Why Women Let Men Get Their Own Way* (London: Faber & Faber, 1993).

49. Hochschild with Machung, *Second Shift*, 59–60.

50. This critique is discussed in: Cynthia Carter and McLaughlin, "The Tenth Anniversary Issue of *Feminist Media Studies*: Editors' Introduction," *Feminist Media Studies* 11, no. 1 (2011): 1–5; Margaret Gallagher, "Media and the Representation of Gender," in *The Routledge Companion to Media and Gender*, ed. C. Carter, L. Steiner, and L. McLaughlin (Abingdon, UK: Routledge, 2014.); Laura Grindstaff and Andrea Press, "Too Little but Not Too Late: Sociological Contributions to Feminist Studies," in *Media Sociology*, ed. S. Waisbord (Cambridge: Polity, 2014), 151–167; McRobbie, *Aftermath of Feminism*.

51. For two exceptions, see Lara Descartes and Conrad P. Kottak, *Media and Middle Class Moms: Images and Realities of Work and Family* (New York: Routledge, 2009), and Rachel Thomson, Mary Jane Kehily, Lucy Hadfield, and Sue Sharpe, *Making Modern Mothers* (Bristol, UK: Policy, 2011).

52. Charles Wright Mills, *The Sociological Imagination* (Oxford: Oxford University Press, 1959).

53. Mills, *Sociological Imagination*, 8.

54. Mills, 8.

55. Nicholas Gane and Les Back, "C. Wright Mills 50 Years On: The Promise and Craft of Sociology Revisited," *Theory, Culture & Society* 29, no. 7–8 (2012): 6–7.

56. Richard Sennett and Jonathan Cobb, *The Hidden Injuries of Class* (Cambridge: Cambridge University Press, 1972), 152.

57. See Shani Orgad, *Media Representation and the Global Imagination.* (Cambridge: Polity, 2012).

58. Mills, 8.

59. Joan Wallach Scott, "The Evidence of Experience," *Critical Inquiry* 17, no. 4 (1991): 773–797.

60. Friedan, 296.

61. Janice Radway, *Reading the Romance: Women, Patriarchy, and Popular Literature* (Chapel Hill: University of North Carolina Press, 1984).

62. Valerie Walkerdine, "Some Day My Prince Will Come: Young Girls and the Preparation for Adolescent Sexuality," in *Gender and Generation*, ed. A. McRobbie and M. Nava (Bath, UK: MacMillan, 1984), 162–184; Walkerdine, Lucey, and Melody, *Growing Up Girl*.

63. Kim Akass, "Motherhood and Myth-Making: Despatches from the Frontline of the US Mommy Wars," *Feminist Media Studies* 12, no. 1 (2012): 137–141; Melissa A. Milkie, Joanna R. Pepin, Kathleen E. Denny, and Trinity University, "What Kind of War? 'Mommy Wars' Discourse in U.S. and Canadian News, 1989–2013," *Sociological Inquiry* 86, no. 1 (2016): 51–78.

64. Michèle Lamont, *Money, Morals, and Manners: The Culture of the French and the American Upper-Middle Class* (Chicago: University of Chicago Press, 1992). For feminist accounts of "studying up," see, for example, Joey Sprague, *Feminist Methodologies for Critical Researchers: Bridging Differences* (Oxford: AltaMira, 2005); Michelle Fine, "Working the Hyphens: Reinventing Self and Other in Qualitative Research" in *The Landscape of Qualitative Research: Theories and Issues*, ed. N. Denzin and Y. Lincoln (Thousand Oaks, Calif.: Sage, 1998), 130–155.

65. Mike Savage, Fiona Devine, Niall Cunningham, Mark Taylor, Yaojun Li, Johs Hjellbrekke, Brigitte Le Roux, Sam Friedman, and Andrew Miles, "A New Model of Social Class? Findings from the BBC's Great British Class Survey Experiment," *Sociology* 47, no. 2 (2013): 219–250.

66. Laura Nader, "Up the Anthropologist: Perspectives Gained from Studying Up," in *Reinventing Anthropology*, ed. D. Hymes (New York: Pantheon, 1972): 284–311.

67. See Hochschild with Machung, 19.

68. Friedan, 15.

69. The feminist scholar Rosalind Gill calls (albeit in another context) for the urgency of holding together privilege and exploitation in our analysis. See Rosalind Gill, "Academics, Cultural Workers and Critical Labour Studies," *Journal of Cultural Economy* 7, no. 1 (2014): 12–30.

70. Virginia Nicholson, *Perfect Wives in Ideal Homes: The Story of Women in the 1950s* (Stirlingshire, UK: Penguin, 2015), 193.

71. Nicholson, *Perfect Wives*, 195–196.

72. The feminist scholar Joan Williams points out that "choice concerns the everyday process of making decisions within constraints." Joan Williams, *Unbending Gender: Why Family and Work Conflict and What to Do about It* (New York: Oxford University Press, 2000), 37.

73. Sennett and Cobb, *Hidden Injuries of Class*, 23.

74. Sennett and Cobb, 45.

75. I thank Dafna Lemish for this point.

76. Les Back, "Broken Devices and New Opportunities: Re-imagining the Tools of Qualitative Research," *NCRM Working Paper Series*, 2010, http://eprints.ncrm.ac.uk/1579/1/0810 _broken_devices_Back.pdf. Back draws on several critical discussions of the interview, including Roland Barthes's commentary on the interview situation, Paul Atkinson and David Silverman's well-known critique of the "interview society," and Howard Becker's exploration of how knowledge about society is communicated through different forms of telling. See: Roland Barthes, *The Grain of the Voice: Interviews 1962-1980* (London: Cape, 1985); Paul Atkinson and David Silverman, "Kundera's Immorality: The Interview Society and the Invention of the Self," *Qualitative Inquiry* 3, no. 3 (1997): 304–325; Howard Becker, *Telling about Society* (Chicago: University of Chicago Press, 2007); David Silverman, *A Very Short, Fairly Interesting and Reasonably Cheap Book About Qualitative Research* (Los Angeles: Sage, 2007), 56.

77. See Ann Crittenden, *The Price of Motherhood: Why the Most Important Job in the World Is Still the Least Valued* (New York: Picador, 2001); Silvia Federici, *Revolution at Point Zero: Housework, Reproduction, and Feminist Struggle* (New York: Common Notions, 2012); Nancy Fraser, "Contradictions of Capital and Care," *New Left Review* 100 (July-August 2016).

78. Lauren Berlant, *Cruel Optimism* (Durham, N.C.: Duke University Press, 2011).

79. Berlant, *Cruel Optimism*.

1. CHOICE AND CONFIDENCE CULTURE/TOXIC WORK CULTURE

1. See Angela McRobbie, *The Aftermath of Feminism: Gender, Culture and Social Change* (London: Sage, 2009), for review of the new sexual contract in the UK during the 1980s and 1990s.

2. Heather L. Hundley and Sara Hayden, *Mediated Moms: Contemporary Challenges to the Motherhood Myth* (New York: Peter Lang, 2016); Emily Nussbaum, "Shedding Her Skin: 'The Good Wife's Thrilling Transformation," *New Yorker*, October 13, 2014, https://www .newyorker.com/magazine/2014/10/13/shedding-skin; Kathleen Rowe Karlyn, "Feminist Dialectics and Unrepentant Mothers: What I Didn't Say, and Why," keynote lecture

at the University of Warwick, UK: Television for Women Conference, 2013; Suzanna D. Walters and Laura Harrison, "Not Ready to Make Nice: Aberrant Mothers in Contemporary Culture," *Feminist Media Studies* 14, no. 1 (2014): 38–55.

3. Arlie Hochschild with Anne Machung, *The Second Shift: Working Families and the Revolution at Home* (New York: Penguin, 1989), 1.

4. Hochschild with Machung, *Second Shift*, 22.

5. For an interesting review of the cultural ideal of the supermom in the American press from the 1970s to the 2010s, see Amanda Westbrook Brennan, "The Fantasy of the Supermom," *Gnovis* (April 26, 2013), http://www.gnovisjournal.org/2013/04/26/the -fantasy-of-the-supermom/.

6. United Airlines, "1988 United Airlines Commercial," YouTube, https://www.youtube.com /watch?v=Zgd6K2vi0wk.

7. While the majority of working-class women always undertook some kind of paid work outside the home, the growing number of middle-class families during the 1920s resulted in consignment of the majority of middle-class women to the role of housewives. Many middle-class women returned to full-time occupations during the Second World War, but were forced to return to the home after the war, and it was not until the late 1960s and 1970s that they re-entered the labor force in substantial numbers. For the UK figures of female employment, see Figure 2 in Office for National Statistics, Labour Force Survey, 2017, http://www.ons.gov.uk/employmentandlabour market/peopleinwork/employmentandemployeetypes/bulletins/uklabourmarket /latest (accessed July 9, 2018).; for the US figures, see United States Department of Labor, "Women in the Labor Force," 2016, http://www.dol.gov/wb/stats/facts_over _time.htm (accessed July 9, 2018).

8. Miriam Peskowitz, *The Truth Behind the Mommy Wars: Who Decides What Makes a Good Mother?* (Berkeley, CA: Seal Press, 2005), quoted in Janet McCabe and Kim Akass, eds., *Reading 'Desperate Housewives': Beyond the White Picket Fence* (London: I. B. Tauris, 2006), 99. See also, Imelda Whelehan, *Modern Feminist Thought: From the Second Wave to Post-Feminism* (New York: NYU Press, 1995).

9. Shelley Budgeon, "Individualized Femininity and Feminist Politics of Choice," *European Journal of Women's Studies* 22, no. 3 (2015): 303–318.

10. Budgeon, "Individualized Femininity," 304.

11. Rosalind Gill, "Postfeminist Media Culture: Elements of a Sensibility," *European Journal of Cultural Studies* 10, no. 2 (2007): 147–166.

12. Gill, "Postfeminist Media Culture."

13. Hannah Gavron, *The Captive Wife: Conflicts of Housebound Mothers* (London: Routledge & Kegan Paul, 1966).

14. Catherine Hakim, *Work-Lifestyle Choices in the 21st Century: Preference Theory* (Oxford: Oxford University Press, 2000).

15. Susan Faludi, *Backlash: The Undeclared War against Women* (London: Chatto & Windus, 1992); Arielle Kuperberg and Pamela Stone, "The Media Depiction of Women Who Opt Out," *Gender & Society* 22, no. 4 (2008): 497–517; Joan Williams, *Unbending Gender: Why Family and Work Conflict and What to Do About It* (Oxford: Oxford University Press, 2000).

16. Kuperberg and Stone, "Media Depiction of Women," 512.

17. Hochschild with Machung, *Second Shift*, 59–60.

18. Betty Friedan, *The Feminine Mystique* (London: Penguin, 2000 [1963]), 29.
19. Sheryl Sandberg, *Lean In: Women, Work, and the Will to Lead* (London: WH Allen, 2013), 8
20. Sandberg, *Lean In*, 100.
21. Sandberg, *Lean In*, 49.
22. For critiques of Sandberg, see Rosalind Gill and Shani Orgad, "The Confidence Cult(ure)," *Australian Feminist Studies* 30, no. 86 (2015): 324–344; Angela McRobbie, "Feminism, the Family and the New 'Mediated' Materialism," *New Formations* 80 (2013): 119–137; Catherine Rottenberg, "The Rise of Neoliberal Feminism," *Cultural Studies* 28, no. 3 (2014).
23. Sandberg, *Lean In*, 33.
24. Sandberg, *Lean In*, 8.
25. Katty Kay and Claire Shipman, *The Confidence Code: The Science and Art of Self-Assurance— What Women Should Know* (New York: Harper Collins, 2014), xv.
26. Anne-Marie Slaughter, *Unfinished Business: Women, Men, Work, Family* (London: Oneworld, 2015), 148.
27. Gill and Orgad, "The Confidence Cult(ure)"; Rosalind Gill and Shani Orgad, "Confidence Culture and the Remaking of Feminism," *New Formations* 91 (2017): 16–34; Shani Orgad and Rosalind Gill, *Confidence Culture* (Durham, NC: Duke University Press, forthcoming).
28. Gill and Orgad, "Confidence Culture and the Remaking of Feminism."
29. Gill and Orgad, "The Confidence Cult(ure)."
30. Quoted in David Hochman, "Amy Cuddy Takes a Stand," *New York Times*, September 21, 2014, http://www.nytimes.com/2014/09/21/fashion/amy-cuddy-takes-a-stand-TED -talk.html.
31. Ervin Goffman, *Gender Advertisements* (New York: Harper & Row, 1979).
32. Hochman, "Amy Cuddy Takes a Stand."
33. For a detailed analysis of the show *The Good Wife*, see Shani Orgad, "The Cruel Optimism of *The Good Wife*: The Fantastic Working Mother on the Fantastical Treadmill," *Television and New Media* 18, no. 2 (2017): 165–183.
34. I thank Rosalind Gill for this insightful point.
35. Orgad, "Cruel Optimism of *The Good Wife*."
36. For references to KPMG's leadership on gender diversity, see, for example, Slaughter, *Unfinished Business*; Sandberg, *Lean In*; Pamela Stone, *Opting Out? Why Women Really Quit Careers and Head Home* (Berkeley: University of California Press, 2007).
37. Klynveld Peat Marwick Goerdeler (KPMG), "KPMG Women's Leadership Study: Moving Women Forward into Leadership Roles," http://womensleadership.kpmg.us/content /dam/kpmg-womens-leadership-golf/womensleadershippressrelease/FINAL%20Womens %20Leadership%20v19.pdf, p. 12.
38. "KPMG Women's Leadership Study," 12.
39. Joanna Barsh and Lareina Yee, "Unlocking the Full Potential of Women at Work," McKinsey & Company, 2012, 17; emphases added.
40. Katie McCracken, Sergio Marquez, Caleb Kwong, Ute Stephan, Adriana Castagnoli, and Marie Dlouhá, "Women's Entrepreneurship: Closing the Gender Gap in Access to Financial and Other Services and in Social Entrepreneurship," European Parliament: Policy Department C: Citizen's Rights and Constitutional Affairs, 2015, http://www .europarl.europa.eu/RegData/etudes/STUD/2015/519230/IPOL_STU(2015)519230_EN .pdf, p. 3.

41. Charted Management Institute, "Women in Management: The Power of Role Models," 2014, https://www.managers.org.uk/~/media/Research%20Report%20Downloads/The%20Power%20of%20Role%20Models%20-%20May%202014.pdf.

42. Heather Sarsons and Guo Xu, "Confidence Gap? Women Economists Tend to Be Less Confident than Men When Speaking Outside Their Area of Expertise," *LSE Impact Blog*, July 2, 2015, http://blogs.lse.ac.uk/impactofsocialsciences/2015/07/02/confidence-gap-women-economists-less-confident-than-men/; emphasis added.

43. Carmen Nobel, "Men Want Powerful Jobs More than Women Do," *Harvard Business School Working Knowledge*, September 23, 2015, http://hbswk.hbs.edu/item/men-want-powerful-jobs-more-than-women-do; Ines Wichert, "What Does Success Look Like for Women Today?" *Guardian*, October 28, 2015, http://www.theguardian.com/women-in-leadership/2015/oct/28/what-does-success-look-like-for-you.

44. Wichert, "What Does Success Look Like," bullet point 5.

45. Alison Wood Brooks, one of the study's authors, added in an interview. "The findings in the paper could be construed as anti-feminist, but one could also argue that they represent true feminist ideals . . . It's fascinating that women have more goals than men. At this point in Western culture, women are pursuing more things. It's empowering to have a long list of goals, and to try to pursue them all. We hope our findings encourage men and women to be more aware of their own goals and preferences, and respectful of others." See Nobel, "Men Want Powerful Jobs More Than Women Do."

46. Susan Douglas and Meredith W. Michaels, *The Mommy Myth: The Idealization of Motherhood and How It Has Undermined All Women* (New York: Free Press, 2004), 205.

47. Betty Friedan's observation is as true today as it was in 1963: "For this is not just the private problem of each individual woman. There are implications of the feminine mystique that must be faced on a national [or societal] level." Friedan, *Feminine Mystique*, 296.

48. Emma Cahusac and Shireen Kanji's study shows similar patterns and norms in the working lives of the professional and managerial mothers in London they interviewed. See Cahusac and Kanji, "Giving Up: How Gendered Organizational Cultures Push Mothers Out," *Gender, Work & Organization* 21, no. 1 (2013): 57–70.

49. Slaughter, *Unfinished Business*, 218, 58.

50. Several women confessed they too had suffered from depression when they were in paid employment and/or after they left.

51. Slaughter, *Unfinished Business*, 218, 58, paraphrasing Joan Williams, *Unbending Gender*.

52. Shelley J. Correll, Stephen Benard, and In Paik, "Getting a Job: Is There a Motherhood Penalty?" *American Journal of Sociology* 112, no. 5 (2007): 1297–1339; Clair Cain Miller, "The Gender Pay Gap Is Largely Because of Motherhood," *New York Times*, May 13, 2017, https://www.nytimes.com/2017/05/13/upshot/the-gender-pay-gap-is-largely-because-of-motherhood.html; Slaughter, *Unfinished Business*, 54; Sean Coughlan, "'Motherhood Penalty' in Worse Pay at Work," BBC, April 11, 2017, http://www.bbc.com/news/education-39566746.

53. Joeli Brearley, "Pregnant but Screwed: The Truth about Workplace Discrimination," *Guardian*, May 12, 2015, http://www.theguardian.com/women-in-leadership/2015/may/12/pregnant-but-screwed-the-truth-about-workplace-discrimination.

54. Stone, *Opting Out?*

55. Slaughter, *Unfinished Business*, 15.

2. THE BALANCED WOMAN/UNEQUAL HOMES

1. Betty Friedan, *The Feminine Mystique* (London: Penguin, 2000 [1963]), 185.
2. Sean Nixon, "Cultural Intermediaries or Market Device? The Case of Advertising" in *The Cultural Intermediaries Reader*, ed. J. Smith Maguire and J. Matthews (London: Sage, 2013), 24.
3. Friedan, *Feminine Mystique*, 167.
4. Friedan, *Feminine Mystique*, 168.
5. Ernest Dichter, *The Strategy of Desire* (London/New York: Boardman, 1960), 185.
6. Friedan, *Feminine Mystique*, 169, 168; see also Ernest Dichter Papers, Accession 2407 (Wilmington, DE: Hagley Museum and Library), http://findingaids.hagley.org/xtf/view?docId=ead/2407.xml.
7. Dichter, *Strategy of Desire*, 185.
8. Friedan, *Feminine Mystique*, 169.
9. Dichter, *Strategy of Desire*, 187.
10. Dichter, *Strategy of Desire*, italics in original.
11. Dichter, *Strategy of Desire*, 188.
12. Dichter, *Strategy of Desire*.
13. Cited in Friedan, *Feminine Mystique*, 169. The bibliographic details of the original citation are not provided. Friedan mentions only that she was given access to Dichter's studies by the Institute for Motivational Research in Croton-on-Hudson, New York.
14. Friedan, *Feminine Mystique*, 185.
15. For a discussion of the enduring power of the happy housewife, see Sara Ahmed, *The Promise of Happiness* (Durham, NC: Duke University Press, 2010).
16. Arlie Hochschild with Anne Machung, *The Second Shift: Working Families and the Revolution at Home* (New York: Penguin, 1989), 1.
17. Note that the UK Office for National Statistics figures refer to women aged 16 to 64 in 2017, whereas the US Department of Labor data refer to women aged 16+ in 2015. Office for National Statistics, Statistical Bulletin: UK Labour Market: August 2017, http://www.ons.gov.uk/employmentandlabourmarket/peopleinwork/employmentand employeetypes/bulletins/uklabourmarket/latest (accessed 9 July, 2018); US Department of Labor, "Women in the Labor Force," 2017, http://www.dol.gov/wb/stats/stats_data.htm (accessed 9 July, 2018); US Bureau of Labor Statistics, *Women in the Labor Force: A Databook* (Washington, DC: United States Department of Labor, 2017), https://www.bls.gov/opub/reports/womens-databook/2016/pdf/home.pdf (accessed 9 July, 2018).
18. Based on analysis of the UK Labour Force Survey 1996–2017, conducted by Gillian Paull for this study. Employment includes those undertaking any paid work, including employees and the self-employed. The employment proportions are for mothers and fathers aged 16 to 64.
19. US Bureau of Labor Statistics, "Employment Characteristics of Families Summary," 2017, https://www.bls.gov/news.release/famee.nr0.htm.
20. Hochschild with Machung, *The Second Shift*, 4.
21. Catherine Rottenberg, "The Rise of Neoliberal Feminism," *Cultural Studies* 28, no. 3 (2014): 151.

22. Sheryl Sandberg, *Lean In: Women, Work, and the Will to Lead* (London: WH Allen, 2013), 49.

23. Working-class and single mothers were depicted in American popular culture in the 1980s and 1990s in a significantly different manner, and often as rebellious. For instance, the popular sitcom *Roseanne*, which centered on a working mother who had no choice but to stay in the workforce while raising her children, "mooned romantic notions of motherhood week-in and week-out" (Susan Douglas and Meredith W. Michaels, *The Mommy Myth: The Idealization of Motherhood and How It Has Undermined All Women* (New York: Free Press, 2004, 206). Similarly, the sitcom *Murphy Brown* revolved around a revolutionary working woman who decides to have and raise a child out of wedlock, and to return to her job as an investigative journalist and news anchor. The show was famously criticized in 1992 by Vice President Dan Quayle, who said the character of Murphy Brown was "mocking the importance of fathers, by bearing a child alone, and calling it just another 'lifestyle choice.'" See Jacey Fortin, "That Time 'Murphy Brown' and Dan Quayle Topped the Front Page," *New York Times*, January 26, 2018, https://www.nytimes.com/2018/01/26/arts/television/murphy-brown-dan-quayle.html.

24. See Helena Morrissey, *A Good Time to Be a Girl: Don't Lean In, Change the System* (London: William Collins, 2018).

25. Rottenberg, "Rise of Neoliberal Feminism," 156. See also Catherine Rottenberg, "Happiness and the Liberal Imagination: How Superwoman Became Balanced," *Feminist Studies* 40, no. 1 (2014): 144–168.

26. Rottenberg, "Happiness and the Liberal Imagination," 156.

27. Abigail Gregory and Susan Milner, "Editorial: Work-Life Balance: A Matter of Choice?" *Gender, Work & Organization* 16, no. 1 (2009): 1–13.

28. Gregory and Milner, "Work-Life Balance," 4.

29. Gregory and Milner, "Work-Life Balance," 2.

30. Kathryn A. Cady, "Flexible Labor: A Feminist Response to Late Twentieth-century Capitalism?" *Feminist Media Studies* 13, no. 3 (2013): 395–414; Melissa Gregg, "The Normalisation of Flexible Female Labour in the Information Economy," *Feminist Media Studies* 8, no. 3 (2008): 285–299.

31. Gregg, "The Normalisation," 287.

32. "Interview: Rebecca Asher, Producer and Writer," *The Scotsman*, April 3, 2011, http://www.scotsman.com/lifestyle/culture/books/interview-rebecca-asher-producer-and-writer-1-1572297; see also Rebecca Asher, *Shattered: Modern Motherhood and the Illusion of Equality* (New York: Vintage, 2011), 6.

33. Gregg, "The Normalisation," 287.

34. Gregory and Milner, "Work-Life Balance."

35. Office for National Statistics, "Annual Survey of Hours and Earnings: 2016 Provisional Results, Labour Force Survey, Quarter 2 (April to June) 2016, Table EMP04, https://www.ons.gov.uk/employmentandlabourmarket/peopleinwork/earningsandworkinghours/bulletins/annualsurveyofhoursandearnings/2016provisionalresults.

36. Amna Silim and Alfie Stirling, *Women and Flexible Working: Improving Female Employment Outcomes in Europe*, Institute for Public Policy Research, 2014, http://www.ippr.org/files/publications/pdf/women-and-flexible-working_Dec2014.pdf.

37. US Bureau of Labor Statistics, "Labor Force Statistics from the Current Population Survey," https://www.bls.gov/web/empsit/cpseea06.htm; figures are for July 2017.

38. Hochschild with Machung, *The Second Shift*, 1.

39. See, for example, one blogger's recommended list of apps for working mothers' better work-life balance: Cindy Goodman, "Working Mothers Share Best Apps for Work Life Balance," *Miami Herald*, July 5, 2014, http://miamiherald.typepad.com/worklife balancingact/2014/05/working-mothers-share-best-apps-for-work-life-balance.html; see also Elena Prokopets, "14 Smart Apps to Improve Your Work/Life Balance," Lifehack, http://www.lifehack.org/275194/14-smart-apps-improve-your-worklife-balance (accessed June 13, 2018).

40. Kelli Orrella, "6 Top Apps to Help Make Work Life Balance a Reality (Not Just a Fantasy)," *Working Mother*, January 27, 2016, http://www.workingmother.com/6-top -apps-to-help-make-work-life-balance-reality-not-just-fantasy.

41. Shani Orgad, "The Cruel Optimism of *The Good Wife*: The Fantastic Working Mother on the Fantastical Treadmill," *Television and New Media* 18, no. 2 (2017): 165–183.

42. Orgad, "Cruel Optimism."

43. Sandberg, *Lean In*, 113.

44. This discourse is overwhelmingly heteronormative, hence my reference to the woman's partner as male.

45. Jonathan Scourfield and Mark Drakeford, "New Labour and the 'Problem of Men,'" *Critical Social Policy* 22, no. 4 (2002): 619–640.

46. Ad Council, US Department of Health and Human Services, and National Responsible Fatherhood Clearinghouse, "A Message to Fathers across America: Take Time to Be a Dad Today," *PR Newswire*, June 18, 2015, http://www.multivu.com/players/English/7552651 -ad-council-fatherhood-psa/; Gaby Hinsliff, "I Don't Know How He Does It! Meet the New Superdads," *Guardian*, July 18, 2015, http://www.theguardian.com/lifeandstyle/2015 /jul/18/do-it-all-dads-men-career-family-friends; Jane Levere, "Ads Urge Fathers to 'Take Time' to Be a Dad," *New York Times*, October 18, 2010, http://www.nytimes.com /2010/10/19/business/media/19adnewsletter1.html.

47. In a 2016 Indian ad for Ariel detergent, which was praised and shared virally by Sheryl Sandberg, a father apologizes to his daughter for setting a bad example as a father who did not share the load of domestic housework. He watches his daughter, a young professional woman, in a married relationship that reproduces similar domestic inequalities, her husband totally failing to share the work. However, even in this more progressive ad, which tackles the issue of unequal domestic labor, the man apologizes to his daughter, not his wife. Furthermore, tackling this issue seems "safe" when depicting an "old-fashioned" "eastern" family. A similar ad set in a white, middle-class American or English family has yet to appear. See Sophie Haslett, "Share the Load, Men!" *Daily Mail*, March 2, 2016, http://www.dailymail.co.uk/femail/article-3472171/Ariel-India-advert -encourgaing-men-Share-Load-goes-viral.html.

48. Office for National Statistics, "Women Shoulder the Responsibility of 'Unpaid Work,'" November 10, 2016, https://www.ons.gov.uk/employmentandlabourmarket/peopleinwork /earningsandworkinghours/articles/womenshouldertheresponsibilityofunpaid work/2016-11-10.

49. US Bureau of Labor Statistics, "American Time Use Survey: Household Activities," 2016, https://www.bls.gov/tus/charts/household.htm.

50. Notably, the dominant framework of these discourses is heteronormative.

51. Anne-Marie Slaughter, *Unfinished Business: Women, Men, Work, Family* (London: Oneworld, 2015), 161, 169.

52. Slaughter, *Unfinished Business*, 155.

53. Catherine Hakim, *Work-Lifestyle Choices in the 21st Century: Preference Theory* (Oxford: Oxford University Press, 2000).

54. Rottenberg, "The Rise of Neoliberal Feminism," 152–153; italics in original.

55. *The Modern Families Index 2018*, Working Families, 5, https://www.workingfamilies.org.uk/publications/mfindex2018/.

56. For example, Slaughter shows how even when firms support flex policies, employees often do not ask because of deep culture and norms where "asking for flexibility to fit your work and your life together is tantamount to declaring that you do not care as much about your job as your co-workers do"—an observation corroborated by several of my interviewees, especially those who worked in the corporate legal and financial sectors. Slaughter, *Unfinished Business*, 62.

57. According to a 2018 survey of UK working parents, parents believe and find that it is more acceptable for mothers than for fathers to leave and/or take time out of work for childcare issues, and parents believe that their employers have similar expectations. See *Modern Families Index 2018*, 19.

58. Angela McRobbie, *The Aftermath of Feminism: Gender, Culture and Social Change* (London: Sage, 2009), 80–81.

59. Public policy in the United Kingdom, as in the United States, reinforces the belief that women should be the primary caregivers for children; see Sandberg, *Lean In*, 107.

60. See, for example, Heather L. Hundley and Sara Hayden, *Mediated Moms: Contemporary Challenges to the Motherhood Myth* (New York: Peter Lang, 2016). Michel Foucault's concept of normalization has been particularly useful in explaining the power to regulate through a description of what is deemed normal and what is not. As Rosalind Gill notes in *Gender and the Media*, "These procedures of normalization operate upon every aspect of our intimate lives." Gill, *Gender and the Media*, 64.

61. Sarah Macharia, *Who Makes the News? Global Media Monitoring Project 2015*, World Association for Christian Communication, http://cdn.agilitycms.com/who-makes-the-news/Imported/reports_2015/global/gmmp_global_report_en.pdf, p. 8.

62. Macharia, *Who Makes the News?* 9.

63. Cristal Williams Chancellor, Diahann Hill, Katti Gray, Cindy Royal, and Barbara Findlen, *The Status of Women in the US Media 2017*, Women's Media Center, http://wmc.3cdn.net/10c550d19ef9f3688f_mlbres2jd.pdf.

64. Cécile Guillaume and Sophie Pochic, "What Would You Sacrifice? Access to Top Management and the Work-Life Balance," *Gender, Work & Organization* 16, no. 1 (2009): 14–36.

65. Lauren G. Berlant, *Cruel Optimism* (Durham, NC/London: Duke University Press, 2011).

66. Berlant, *Cruel Optimism*, 166.

3. CUPCAKE MOM/FAMILY CEO

1. Roberto's talk of "my wife," and his not mentioning her name, recalls Goffman's observation that "to speak of a woman as one's wife is to place this person in a category of which there can only be one current member, yet a category is nonetheless involved and she is merely a member of it . . . at the centre is a full array of socially standardized anticipations that we have regarding her conduct and nature as an instance of the category 'wife.'" Ervin Goffman, *Stigma: Notes on the Management of Spoiled Identity* (London: Penguin, 1990 [1963]), 70.

2. Wednesday Martin, "Poor Little Rich Women," *New York Times*, May 16, 2015, http://www.nytimes.com/2015/05/17/opinion/sunday/poor-little-rich-women.html.

3. Susan Faludi, *Backlash: The Undeclared War against Women* (London: Chatto & Windus, 1992), 70–71. On the idealization of women as housewives and mothers in the Victorian era, see Eli Zaretsky, *Capitalism, the Family and Personal Life* (London: Pluto, 1976).

4. Faludi, *Backlash*, 106; see also Susan Douglas and Meredith W. Michaels, *The Mommy Myth: The Idealization of Motherhood and How It Has Undermined All Women* (New York: Free Press, 2004) for a discussion of the media frenzy following the publication of Schwartz's article, and the depiction of stay-at-home mothers in popular television shows such as *thirtysomething*.

5. Felice Schwartz, "Management Women and the New Facts of Life," *Harvard Business Review* (January-February 1989), https://hbr.org/1989/01/management-women-and-the-new-facts-of-life.

6. Douglas and Michaels, *Mommy Myth*, 207; Kathryn A. Cady, "Flexible Labor: A Feminist Response to Late Twentieth-century Capitalism?" *Feminist Media* 13, no. 3 (2013): 395–414.

7. Catherine Hakim, *Work-Lifestyle Choices in the 21st Century: Preference Theory*, (Oxford: Oxford University Press, 2000).

8. Hakim, *Work-Lifestyle Choice*, 161. For detailed critique of Hakim's theory, see Mary Leahy and James Doughney, "Women, Work and Preference Formation: A Critique of Catherine Hakim's Preference Theory," *Journal of Business Systems, Governance and Ethics* 1, no. 1 (2014): 37–48; Patricia Lewis and Ruth Simpson, "Hakim Revisited: Preference, Choice and the Postfeminist Gender Regime," *Gender, Work & Organization* 24, no. 2 (2017): 115–133; Susan McRae, "Constraints and Choices in Mothers' Employment Careers: A Consideration of Hakim's Preference Theory." *British Journal of Sociology* 54, no. 3 (2003): 317–338.

9. Lisa Belkin, "The Opt-Out Revolution," *New York Times Magazine*, October 26, 2003, 42–47, http://www.nytimes.com/2003/10/26/magazine/the-opt-out-revolution.html.

10. Pamela Stone, *Opting Out? Why Women Really Quit Careers and Head Home* (Berkeley: University of California Press, 2007), 4.

11. Arielle Kuperberg and Pamela Stone, "The Media Depiction of Women Who Opt Out," *Gender & Society* 22, no. 4 (2008): 503.

12. Kuperberg and Stone, "Media Depiction," 506.

13. Kuperberg and Stone, "Media Depiction," 512.

14. Daisy Sands, "The Impact of Austerity on Women," (London: Fawcett Society, 2012). Research conducted by the UK House of Commons Library in 2017 revealed that women

have borne 86 percent of the burden of austerity since 2010. See Heather Stewart, "Women Bearing 86 percent of Austerity Burden, Commons Figures Reveal," *Guardian*, March 9, 2017.

15. Shani Orgad and Sara De Benedictis, "The 'Stay At Home' Mother, Postfeminism and Neoliberalism: Content Analysis of UK News Coverage," *European Journal of Communication* 30, no. 4 (2015): 418–436.

16. Orgad and De Benedictis, "The 'Stay-At-Home' Mother."

17. See Peter Dominiczak, "We Have Done Enough for 'Admirable' Stay-at-Home Parents, Insists Clegg," *Daily Telegraph*, March 29, 2013.

18. See, for example, Kim Akass, "Motherhood and Myth-Making: Dispatches from the Frontline of the US Mommy Wars," *Feminist Media Studies* 12, no. 1 (2012): 137–141. Akass argues that UK and US news reporting and popular media representations during the recession promoted a backlash, restoring an old-fashioned familial model of male bread winner/dependent female carer emphasizing women as "willingly returning to their 'traditional' roles in the home." See also Kim Akass, "Gendered Politics of a Global Recession: A News Media Analysis," *Studies in the Maternal* 4, no. 2 (2012): 2.

19. Diane Negra and Yvonne Tasker, *Gendering the Recession: Media and Culture in an Age of Austerity* (Durham, NC: Duke University Press, 2014). See also Rebecca Bramall, *The Cultural Politics of Austerity: Past and Present in Austere Times* (Hampshire, UK: Palgrave Macmillan Memory Studies, 2013) for a discussion of "austerity nostalgia."

20. On the construction of working-class mothers as abject figures, see Angela McRobbie, "Feminism, the Family and the New 'Mediated' Maternalism," *New Formations* 80 (2013): 119–137; Jessica Ringrose and Valerie Walkerdine, "Regulating the Abject," *Feminist Media Studies* 8, no. 3 (2008): 227–246.

21. Orgad and De Benedictis, "The 'Stay-at-Home Mother.'"

22. Kim Allen and Yvette Taylor, "Placing Parenting, Locating Unrest: Failed Femininities, Troubled Mothers and Rioting Subjects," *Studies in the Maternal* 4, no. 2 (2012): 1–25; Carolyn Bronstein and Linda Steiner, "Weighing Mothers Down: Diets, Daughters, and Maternal Obligation," *Feminist Media Studies* 15, no. 4 (2015): 608–625; Douglas and Michaels, *Mommy Myth*; McRobbie, "Feminism, the Family," 135.

23. Jo Littler, "The Rise of the 'Yummy Mummy': Popular Conservatism and the Neoliberal Maternal in Contemporary British Culture," *Communication, Culture & Critique* 6, no. 2 (2013): 233.

24. Steve Doughty, "Working Mothers Risk Damaging Their Child's Prospects," *Daily Mail*, http://www.dailymail.co.uk/news/article-30342/Working-mothers-risk-damaging -childs-prospects.html (accessed June 13, 2018).

25. Anne-Marie Slaughter, *Unfinished Business: Women, Men, Work, Family* (London: Oneworld, 2015), xii.

26. McRobbie, "Feminism, the Family," 121.

27. Donald J. Trump, "Remarks at Aston Community Center in Aston, Pennsylvania," September 13, 2016.

28. Ivanka Trump, Twitter, September 23, 2016, https://twitter.com/ivankatrump/status /779304354817773569.

29. David Cameron, "Prime Minister's Speech on Life Chances," January 11, 2016, https:// www.gov.uk/government/speeches/prime-ministers-speech-on-life-chances.

30. Paula Cocozza, "Is David Cameron Right to Praise the 'Tiger Mother'?" *Guardian*, January 12, 2016, http://www.theguardian.com/lifeandstyle/2016/jan/12/david-cameron-amy-chua-battle-hymn-of-the-tiger-mother-parenting-abuse.

31. Douglas and Michaels, *The Mommy Myth*; Michael J. Lee and Leigh Moscowitz, "The 'Rich Bitch': Class and Gender on the *Real Housewives of New York City*," *Feminist Media Studies* 13, no. 1 (2013): 64–82; Littler, "Rise of the 'Yummy Mummy'"; Shani Orgad, "Incongruous Encounters: Media Representations and Lived Experiences of Stay-at-Home Mothers," *Feminist Media Studies* 16, no. 3 (2016): 478–494; Mary Vavrus, "Opting Out Moms in the News," *Feminist Media Studies* 7, no. 1 (2007): 47–63.

32. See, for example, studies cited in Spencer Thompson and Dalia Ben-Galim, *Childmind the Gap: Reforming Childcare to Support Mothers into Work* (London: Institute for Public Policy Research, 2014); see also Lisa Belkin, "(Yet Another) Study Finds Working Moms Are Happier and Healthier," *Huffington Post*, October 22, 2012, http://www.huffingtonpost.com/lisa-belkin/working-mothers-happier_b_1823347.html; Stephanie Coontz, "The Triumph of the Working Mother," *New York Times*, June 1, 2013, http://www.nytimes.com/2013/06/02/opinion/sunday/coontz-the-triumph-of-the-working-mother.html; compare with Friedan's discussion of the frightening figures published in the 1950s of children abandoned and rejected because their mothers worked; Friedan, *Feminine Mystique*, 156.

33. Memes are humorous media artifacts produced by users.

34. "I Have So Much Housework . . ." digital image, https://uk.pinterest.com/pin/14566398778723544; "Taking Naps . . ." digital image, https://uk.pinterest.com/pin/512636370061977284/.

35. Lee and Moscowitz, "The 'Rich Bitch.'"

36. Helen Fielding, *Bridget Jones: Mad About the Boy* (New York: Knopf, 2013), 4–5.

37. Fielding, *Mad About the Boy*, 354.

38. For a detailed analysis of Bridget Jones's depiction of stay-at-home motherhood, see Sara De Benedictis and Shani Orgad, "The Escalating Price of Motherhood: Aesthetic Labour in Popular Representations of 'Stay-at-Home' Mothers," in *Aesthetic Labour: Rethinking Beauty Politics in Neoliberalism*, ed. A. Elias, R. Gill, and C. Scharff (London: Palgrave Macmillan, 2017), 101–116.

39. The Obama administration was consistent in promoting specific policies that provided targeted support to women in the workforce, especially mothers.

40. Barack Obama, "Remarks by the President on Women and the Economy," October 31, 2014, https://obamawhitehouse.archives.gov/the-press-office/2014/10/31/remarks-president-women-and-economy-providence-ri.

41. Department of Education and Employment 1998, cited in Gillian Paull, "Can Government Intervention in Childcare Be Justified?" *Economic Affairs* 34, no. 1 (2014): 18.

42. Jonathan Scourfield and Mark Drakeford, "New Labour and the 'Problem of Men,'" *Critical Social Policy* 22, no. 4 (2002): 619–640.

43. Jill Rubery and Anthony Rafferty, "Gender, Recession and Austerity in the UK," in *Women and Austerity: The Economic Crisis and the Future for Gender Equality*, ed. M. Karamessini and J. Rubery (London: Routledge, Taylor & Francis, 2014), 123–143.

44. Emily Gosden and Steven Swinford, "David Cameron's 30-Hour Free Childcare Plan 'Underfunded,'" *Telegraph*, June 1, 2015, http://www.telegraph.co.uk/news/politics/conservative/11642734/David-Camerons-30-hour-free-childcare-plan-underfunded.html.

45. Philip Hammond and Theresa May, "Spring Budget 2017: Support for Women Unveiled by Chancellor," March 8, 2017, https://www.gov.uk/government/news /spring-budget-2017-support-for-women-unveiled-by-chancellor.

46. Katherine Rake, "Gender and New Labour's Social Policies," *Journal of Social Policy* 30, no. 2 (2001): 209–231.

47. Steven Swinford, "George Osborn Accused of 'Patronising' Stay-at-Home Mothers," *Telegraph*, August 5, 2013, http://www.telegraph.co.uk/news/politics/10223383/Fury -over-George-Osbornes-snub-to-stay-at-home-mums.html, emphasis added.

48. Peter Dominiczak and Rowena Mason, "David Cameron's 'Slur' on Stay-at-Home Mothers," *Telegraph*, March 19, 2013, http://www.telegraph.co.uk/news/politics /9941492/David-Camerons-slur-on-stay-at-home-mothers.html.

49. Dominiczak and Mason, "David Cameron's 'Slur.'"

50. See, for example, Dominiczak and Mason, "David Cameron's 'Slur'"; James Mildred, "PM Has Devalued Stay at Home Mothers," *Christian Action Research & Education*, December 9, 2015, http://www.care.org.uk/news/latest-news/pm-has-devalued-stay-home-mothers; Laura Perrins, "The Government Is 'Discriminating' Against Stay-at-Home Mothers," *Telegraph*, April 17, 2013, http://www.telegraph.co.uk/women/mother-tongue/10001069 /Laura-Perrins-The-Government-is-discriminating-against-stay-at-home-mothers .html.

51. Nancy Fraser, "Contradictions of Capital and Care," *New Left Review* (July-August 2016): 99–117.

52. McRobbie, "Feminism, the Family," 121.

53. London's Bond Street is famous for its expensive stores selling exclusive brands, designer fashion, luxury goods, fine jewels, art, and antiques.

54. This rejection of the idea that women who leave the workplace are "home-centered" is echoed by Pamela Stone's study in the United States, which shows that women's decisions to leave the workplace do *not* represent a nostalgic return to the 1950s. Stone, *Opting Out?*

55. In 2015, the Conservative government introduced a shared parental leave system to enable mothers and fathers to share childcare during a child's first year.

56. Judy Wajcman, *Pressed for Time: The Acceleration of Life in Digital Capitalism* (Chicago: University of Chicago Press, 2016).

57. Friedan, *Feminine Mystique*, 201.

58. Friedan, *Feminine Mystique*, 196.

59. Judith Warner, *Perfect Madness: Motherhood in the Age of Anxiety* (London: Vermilion, 2006).

60. This is, of course, a deliberate play on Friedan's formulation 'Occupation: Housewife,' 27.

61. "Interview: Rebecca Asher, Producer and Writer," *The Scotsman*, April 3, 2011, http:// www.scotsman.com/lifestyle/culture/books/interview-rebecca-asher-producer-and -writer-1-1572297; see also Rebecca Asher, *Shattered: Modern Motherhood and the Illusion of Equality* (New York: Vintage, 2011), 6; Pamela Stone makes a similar observation about the women she studied: "Women frequently overlooked the influence of prevailing gendered norms in understanding how these are being enacted in their own families," Stone, *Opting Out?* 71.

62. Ann Crittenden, *The Price of Motherhood: Why the Most Important Job in the World Is Still the Least Valued* (New York: Picador, 2010); Douglas and Michaels, *Mommy Myth*; Heather L. Hundley and Sara Hayden, *Mediated Moms: Contemporary Challenges to the Motherhood Myth* (New York: Peter Lang, 2016).

63. Friedan, *Feminine Mystique*.

64. Friedan, *Feminine Mystique*.

65. Crouch End is a middle-class neighborhood in north London.

66. Annette Lareau, *Unequal Childhoods: Class, Race, and Family Life*, 2nd ed., (Berkeley: University of California Press, 2011).

67. Melissa Milkie and Catharine Warner, "Status Safeguarding: Mothers' Work to Secure Children's Place in the Status Hierarchy," in *Intensive Mothering: The Cultural Contradictions of Modern Motherhood*, ed. L. Ennis (Bradford, ON: Demeter Press), 66–85. See also Frank Furedi, *Paranoid Parenting: Why Ignoring the Experts May Be Best for Your Child*. 3rd ed. (London: Continuum, 2008); Sharon Hays, *The Cultural Contradictions of Motherhood* (New Haven, CT: Yale University Press, 1996); Lareau, *Unequal Childhoods*; Warner, *Perfect Madness*.

68. George Monbiot, "Aspirational Parents Condemn Their Children to a Desperate, Joyless Life," *Guardian*, June 9, 2015. http://www.theguardian.com/commentisfree/2015/jun/09/aspirational-parents-children-elite.

69. Larry Elliott, "Each Generation Should Be Better Off than Their Parents? Think Again," *Guardian*, February 14, 2016, http://www.theguardian.com/business/2016/feb/14/economics-viewpoint-baby-boomers-generation-x-generation-rent-gig-economy; John H. Goldthorpe, "Social Class Mobility In Modern Britain: Changing Structure, Constant Process," *Journal of the British Academy* 4, (2016): 89–111.

70. In this regard this is a continuation of the feminine mystique of the 1950s, which encouraged women to give up their own dreams and education and live through their children: the "absorption" of the child's personality by the middle-class mother. See Friedan, *Feminine Mystique*, 232.

71. Arlie Hochschild with Anne Machung, *The Second Shift: Working Families and the Revolution at Home* (New York: Penguin, 1989), 93.

72. Hays, *Cultural Contradictions of Motherhood*.

73. I thank Catherine Rottenberg for this observation. See also Catherine Rottenberg, *The Rise of Neoliberal Feminism* (Oxford: Oxford University Press, 2018).

4. ABERRANT MOTHERS/CAPTIVE WIVES

1. Tiziana Barghini, "Educated Women Quit Work as Spouses Earn More," *Reuters*, March 8, 2012, http://www.reuters.com/article/us-economy-women-idUSBRE8270AC20120308.

2. Arlie Hochschild with Anne Machung, *The Second Shift: Working Families and the Revolution at Home* (New York: Penguin, 1989), 32.

3. Hochschild with Machung, *Second Shift*, 32–33.

4. Heather Addison, Mary Kate Goodwin-Kelly, and Elaine Roth, *Motherhood Misconceived: Representing the Maternal in US Films* (Albany: State University of New York Press, 2009), 5.

5. Imogen Tyler, "Pregnant Beauty: Maternal Femininities under Neoliberalism" in *New Femininities: Postfeminism, Neoliberalism and Subjectivity*, ed. R. Gill and C. Scharff (Hampshire, UK/New York: Palgrave MacMillan, 2011), 22.

6. Addison, Goodwin-Kelly, and Roth, *Motherhood Misconceived*; Melissa Gregg, "The Normalisation of Flexible Female Labour in the Information Economy," *Feminist Media*

Studies 8, no. 3 (2008): 285–299; Heather L. Hundley and Sara Hayden, eds., *Mediated Moms: Contemporary Challenges to the Motherhood Myth* (New York: Peter Lang, 2016); Jo Littler, "The Rise of the 'Yummy Mummy': Popular Conservatism and the Neoliberal Maternal in Contemporary British Culture," *Communication, Culture & Critique* 6, no. 2 (2013): 227–243; Robyn Longhurst, "YouTube: A New Space for Birth?" *Feminist Review* 93, no. 1 (2009): 46–63; Angela McRobbie, "Feminism, the Family and the New 'Mediated' Maternalism," *New Formations* 80 (2013): 119–137; Shani Orgad and Sara De Benedictis, "The 'Stay-at-Home' Mother, Postfeminism and Neoliberalism: Content Analysis of UK News Coverage," *European Journal of Communication* 30, no. 4 (2015): 418–436; Valerie Palmer-Mehta and Sherianne Shuler, "'Devil Mammas' of Social Media: Resistant Maternal Discourses in Sanctimommy" in *Mediated Moms*, ed. Hundley and Hayden, 221–245; Pamela Thoma, "What Julia Knew: Domestic Labor in the Recession-Era Chick Flick," in *Gendering the Recession: Media and Culture in an Age of Austerity*, ed. D. Negra and Y. Tasker (Durham, NC/London: Duke University Press, 2014), 107–135; Suzanna D. Walters and Laura Harrison, "Not Ready to Make Nice: Aberrant Mothers in Contemporary Culture," *Feminist Media Studies* 14, no. 1 (2014): 38–55.

7. Rebecca Collins, "Content Analysis of Gender Roles in Media: Where Are We Now and Where Should We Go?" *Sex Roles* 64, no. 3 (2011): 290–298; Iñaki Garcia-Blanco and Karin Wahl-Jorgensen, "The Discursive Construction of Women Politicians in the European Press," *Feminist Media Studies* 12, no. 3 (2012): 422–442; Erving Goffman, *Gender Advertisements* (New York: Harper & Row, 1979); Gaye Tuchman, "The Symbolic Annihilation of Women in the Media," in *Hearth and Home: Images of Women in the Mass Media*, ed. G. Tuchman, A. Daniels, and J. Benet (Oxford: Oxford University Press, 1978), 3–38 .

8. Arielle Kuperberg and Pamela Stone, "The Media Depiction of Women Who Opt Out," *Gender & Society* 22, no. 4 (2008): 497–517; Joan Williams, *Unbending Gender: Why Family and Work Conflict and What to Do About It* (Oxford/ New York: Oxford University Press, 2000).

9. Orgad and De Benedictis, "The 'Stay-at-Home' Mother."

10. Susan Douglas and Meredith W. Michaels, *The Mommy Myth: The Idealization of Motherhood and How It Has Undermined All Women* (New York: Free Press, 2004).

11. In her analysis of political rhetoric on "austerity parenting" in Britain, Sara De Benedictis observes how, drawing on Thatcherism's pathologization of lone parents, and following New Labour's stress on the individual responsibility of lone parents to gain employment, the 2010–2015 Coalition government constructed lone mothers as "feral mothers": uncontrollable, irresponsible, destructive, "leeching" on society, and unable to discipline their children. See Sara De Benedictis, "'Feral' Parents: Austerity Parenting under Neoliberalism," *Studies in the Maternal* 4, no. 2 (2012): 1–21.

12. See, for example, Emily Harmer's analysis of politicians' wives in British election campaign coverage. Emily Harmer, "Public to Private and Back Again: The Role of Politicians' Wives in British Election Campaign Coverage," *Feminist Media Studies* 16, no. 5 (2015): 1–17.

13. Rachel Thomson, Mary Jane Kehily, Lucy Hadfield, and Sue Sharpe, *Making Modern Mothers* (Bristol, UK: Policy, 2011), 6.

14. See, for example, Palmer-Mehta and Shuler, "'Devil Mammas.'"

15. Alicia Blum-Ross and Sonia Livingstone, "Sharenting: Parent Blogging and the Boundaries of the Digital Self," *Popular Communication* 15, no. 2 (2017): 110–125.

16. Adopting the format of the viral challenge popularized by examples such as the ALS Ice Bucket Challenge, No Make-Up Selfie for Cancer Research, and the Duct Tape Challenge, the Motherhood Challenge implores women to contribute by posting a series of photos that make them "happy to be a mother," and tag other women they consider to be "great mothers." Unlike some other viral challenges with discernibly worthier goals, such as fundraising for a charity or enhancing awareness of disease, the Motherhood Challenge is aimed at self-demonstration of one's "natural" success as a mother, and namechecking of other mothers considered to be doing a similarly sterling job. As might be expected, the Facebook challenge was criticized by many as a boastful and hubristic parade of happiness that damagingly legitimizes and reinforces a long history of fetishizing and idealizing motherhood. See, for example, Alice Judge-Talbot, "Why Are Women Falling for the Facebook Motherhood Challenge?" *Telegraph*, February 4, 2016, http://www.telegraph.co.uk/women/family/why-are-women-falling-for-the-facebook-motherhood-challenge/; Flic Everett, "Facebook's Motherhood Challenge Makes Me Want to Punch My Computer Screen," *Guardian*, February 2, 2016, https://www.theguardian.com/commentisfree/2016/feb/02/facebook-motherhood-challenge. The Motherhood Challenge not only exacerbated cultural pressure to airbrush, glorify, and idealize motherhood, it also contributed to expanding surveillance and tagging of mothers as "good" or "bad," and to the heightened self-regulation mothers are demanded to perform by constantly assessing themselves against some elevated benchmarks. See Angela McRobbie, "Notes on the Perfect," *Australian Feminist Studies* 30, no. 83 (2015): 3–20.

Similarly, a survey by the London-based mothers' meet-up app Mush found that more than 80 percent of mother respondents said "mommy bloggers" who post photographs of their "perfect" lives on platforms such as Instagram and Facebook "added pressure to be the perfect mum," and made them deeply anxious. See Mark Blunden, "'Perfect' Lives of Instamums Are Making London Mothers Feel Inadequate," *Evening Standard*, February 16, 2017, http://www.standard.co.uk/lifestyle/london-life/perfect-lives-of-instamums-are-making-london-mothers-feel-inadaquate-a3468426.html.

17. Richard Hayton, "Conservative Party Modernisation and David Cameron's Politics of the Family," *Political Quarterly* 81, no. 4 (2010): 497.

18. David Cameron, "David Cameron on Families," August 18, 2014, https://www.gov.uk/government/speeches/david-cameron-on-families.

19. In his 2016 "Life Chances" speech, David Cameron described *all* parents as needing help with parenting, and introduced his government's plan to significantly expand the parenting provision, and make it aspirational to attend parenting classes. David Cameron, "Prime Minister's Speech on Life Chances," January 11, 2016, https://www.gov.uk/government/speeches/prime-ministers-speech-on-life-chances.

20. Hayton, "Conservative Party Modernisation," 492.

21. At the time of writing, the UK government had not released official statistics on take-up of shared parental leave. The estimates according to small-size surveys are 1 to 3 percent take-up levels. Source: https://www.ft.com/content/2c4e539c-9a0d-11e7-a652-cde3f882dd7b.

22. Amy Chua, *Battle Hymn of the Tiger Mother* (London: Penguin, 2011).

23. As Richard Hayton notes, Cameron "has put the [traditional] family at the heart of his policy agenda and his public image" and continuously reiterated the family as the

fundamental institution for mending "Britain's broken society" and renewing the societal fabric. In some key respects, Cameron's (and May's) policy and rhetoric represent a clear continuation of his predecessors Duncan Smith and Howard. Hayton, "Conservative Party Modernisation," 497.

24. Gillian Pascall, "Women and the Family in the British Welfare State: The Thatcher /Major Legacy," *Social Policy & Administration* 31, no. 3 (1997): 294.

25. Pascall, "Women and the Family," 295.

26. Thomson et al., *Making Modern Mothers.*

27. Thomson et al., *Making Modern Mothers*, 4. See also De Benedictis, "'Feral' Parents."

28. "Interview: Rebecca Asher, producer and writer," April 3, 2011, http://www.scotsman .com/lifestyle/culture/books/interview-rebecca-asher-producer-and-writer-1-1572297; see also Rebecca Asher, *Shattered: Modern Motherhood and the Illusion of Equality* (New York: Vintage, 2011), 90.

29. A 2013 survey of British social attitudes, by Jacqueline Scott and Elizabeth Clery for NatCen, revealed that there has been very little change (from 41 percent in 1989 to 45 percent in 2012) in the proportion of people believing that the role of the housewife is just as fulfilling as the role of worker. The answers indicate more limited change in the public's perceptions of how women regard and experience a caring role in practice. Scott and Clery, "Gender Roles: An Incomplete Revolution?" NatCen Social Research, 2013, http://www.bsa.natcen.ac.uk/media/38457/bsa30_gender_roles_final.pdf.

    In a 2014 International Omnibus Survey conducted to mark International Women's Day, YouGov found that women around the world overwhelmingly prioritize being a mother over having a career, although most—particularly younger women—prefer to have both. Around four in five British women said being a mother is more important than having a career, and the belief that being a mother comes first is shared by 71 percent of women in the United States. William Jordan, "Most Women Put Motherhood Ahead of Career," YouGov.UK, March 7, 2014, https://yougov.co.uk/news/2014/03/07 /mult-country-survey-most-women-put-motherhood-ahea/.

30. See Thomson et al., *Making Modern Mothers*, 4, 5.

31. Douglas and Michaels, *The Mommy Myth*, 4; for a discussion of new representations of motherhood in contemporary media, see Rebecca Feasey, *From Happy Homemaker to Desperate Housewives: Motherhood and Popular Television* (London: Anthem, 2012); Hundley and Hayden, *Mediated Moms*; Emily Nussbaum, "Shedding Her Skin: *The Good Wife*'s Thrilling Transformation," *New Yorker*, October 13, 2014, http://www.newyorker.com /magazine/2014/10/13/shedding-skin; Kathleen Rowe Karlyn, "Feminist Dialectics and Unrepentant Mothers: What I Didn't Say, and Why," keynote lecture at the University of Warwick, UK, Television for Women Conference, 2013; Shani Orgad, "The Cruel Optimism of *The Good Wife*: The Fantastic Working Mother on the Fantastical Treadmill," *Television and New Media* 18, no. 2 (2017): 165–183; Walters and Harrison, "Not Ready to Make Nice."

32. These shows are discussed in Douglas and Michaels, *The Mommy Myth*, 215.

33. Walters and Harrison, "Not Ready to Make Nice," 38.

34. Alicia Florrick is a mature, confident, and "unabashedly sexual and refreshingly professional" (Walters and Harrison, "Not Ready to Make Nice," 47). As I show elsewhere (Orgad, "The Cruel Optimism"), she is often shown working in her apartment or the office while her children eat dinner, or engaged in work-related phone calls that prevent

her from responding even when her children seek her attention directly. Her demanding job and preoccupation with her sexual affair with her boss cause her to miss out on
her children's experiences, including serious matters like her son's girlfriend's abortion,
which she discovers only months later. At the same time, Alicia is depicted as a caring
mother who enjoys a strong bond and shares many intimate moments with her children.

35. Betty Draper is wholly disinterested in her children; her parenting "is cursory at best
and often downright dismissive of any demands on her attention" (Walters and Harrison,
"Not Ready to Make Nice," 41). Yet it is not unequivocally intended to be read as bad
mothering. Rather, it could be understood partly as a response to the oppressive feminine
mystique of the 1950s to which she has to conform (based on Walters and Harrison,
"Not Ready to Make Nice," 42).

36. *Rita* centers on a schoolteacher and single mother who radically deviates from and is
resolutely indifferent to norms of "intensive mothering". She is outspoken, messy, sexually driven, and often inconsiderate to the point of being neglectful of her children; yet
she is constructed as unruly and ambivalent, rather than a "bad mother." For a similar
observation about other representations, see Sharon R. Mazzarella, "It Is What It Is: *Here
Comes Honey Boo Boo*'s 'Mama' June Shannon as Unruly Mother," in *Mediated Moms*, ed.
Hundley and Hayden, 123–142.

37. Walters and Harrison, "Not Ready to Make Nice," 39; see also Hundley and Hayden, *Mediated Moms*; Karlyn, "Feminist Dialectics."

38. FiatUK, "'The Motherhood' Feat. Fiat 500L," YouTube, December 13, 2012, https://www
.youtube.com/watch?v=eNVde5HPhYo; Dove US, "Baby Dove | #RealMoms," YouTube,
April 5, 2017, https://www.youtube.com/watch?v=9dE9AnU3MaI.

39. Palmer-Mehta and Shuler, "'Devil Mammas.'" In another study of mommy blogs and
mommy bloggers' books related to alcohol use, Tasha Dubriwny found that an important
feature of these blogs is the venting of frustrations regarding caregiving. "By singling
in on the frustrations associated with caregiving," Dubriwny writes, "mothers debunk
at least one essential leg on which the institution of motherhood operates: namely,
that women are innately suited to and enjoy the mundane tasks associated with childrearing." Tasha Dubriwny, "Mommy Blogs and a Disruptive Possibilities of Transgressive
Drinking," in *Mediated Moms*, ed. Hundley and Hayden, 214. See also Leslie Husbands,
"Blogging the Maternal: Self-Representations of the Pregnant and Postpartum Body,"
Atlantis, 32, no. 2 (2008): 68–79; Julie A. Wilson and Emily Chivers Yochim, *Mothering
through Precarity: Women's Work and Digital Media* (Durham, NC/London: Duke University
Press, 2017); Sarah Pedersen, "The Good, the Bad and the 'Good Enough' Mother on the
UK Parenting Forum Mumsnet," *Women's Studies International Forum*, 59 (2016): 32–38.

40. See also Lisa Baraitser, *Maternal Encounters: The Ethics of Interruption*, Women and Psychology series (New York: Routledge, 2008).

41. Kuperberg and Stone, *Media Depiction*, 512.

42. Eli Zaretsky, *Capitalism, the Family and Personal Life* (London: Pluto, 1976).

43. Rosemary Crompton, "Employment, Flexible Working, and the Family," *British Journal of
Sociology* 53, no. 4 (2002): 537–558. See also Angela McRobbie's discussion of Crompton's
work in *The Aftermath of Feminism*, 79.

44. Nancy Fraser, "Contradictions of Capital and Care," *New Left Review* 100 (2016): 102.

45. Helier Cheung, "Why Did People Assume an Asian Woman in BBC Viral Video Was the Nanny?" BBC, March 11, 2017, http://www.bbc.co.uk/news/world-asia-39244325.

46. "BBC Interview with Robert Kelly Interrupted by Children Live on Air," BBC, March 10, 2107, https://www.bbc.com/news/av/world-39232538/bbc-interview-with-robert-kelly-interrupted-by-children-live-on-air. A spoof of the original video imagined how the scene would have unfolded had the wife been the expert interviewee, and suggested that rather than ignoring and trying to shoo away her children, she would have continued the interview while feeding her child, cleaning a toilet, cooking dinner, and defusing a bomb! For her, the spaces of work and home are fully integrated.

47. John Gray, *Men Are from Mars, Women Are from Venus* (London: Harper Collins, 1992).

48. Rachel O'Neill, "Feminist Encounters with Evolutionary Psychology," *Australian Feminist Studies* 30, no. 86 (2015): 345–350; Anne Perkins, "It's Official—Women Are Nicer than Men. Is This Really Science?" *Guardian*, October 10, 2017, https://www.theguardian.com/commentisfree/2017/oct/10/official-women-nicer-men-really-science.

49. In their study of American work-at-home mothers, Julie A. Wilson and Emily Chivers Yochim observe a similar dynamic: "Men 'veg out' while women feel compelled to keep working and working for the family," Wilson and Yochim, *Mothering through Precarity*, 23–24.

50. See Gill on the function of notions of sexual differences in postfeminist discourses: Rosalind Gill, "Postfeminist Media Culture: Elements of a Sensibility," *European Journal of Cultural Studies* 10, no. 2 (2007): 147–166.

51. McRobbie, "Feminism, the Family," 130.

52. Margaret Wetherell, Hilda Stiven, and Jonathan Potter, "Unequal Egalitarianism: A Preliminary Study of Discourses Concerning Gender and Employment Opportunities," *British Journal of Social Psychology* 26, no. 1 (1987): 59–71.

53. Wetherell, Stiven, and Potter, "Unequal Egalitarianism," 64.

54. Hochschild, *The Second Shift*, 44.

55. Betty Friedan, *The Feminine Mystique* (London: Penguin, 2000 [1963]).

56. For example, "I Have So Much Housework . . ." https://uk.pinterest.com/pin/14566398778723544/; "Taking Naps . . ." https://uk.pinterest.com/pin/512636370061977284/.

57. Pamela Stone, *Opting Out? Why Women Really Quit Careers and Head Home* (Berkeley: University of California Press, 2007).

58. Katie's account is also discussed in Shani Orgad, "Incongruous Encounters: Media Representations and Lived Experiences of Stay-at-Home mothers," *Feminist Media Studies* 16, no. 3 (2016): 478–494.

59. Hochschild and Machung, *Second Shift*, 53.

60. For a discussion of iterations of postfeminist fatherhood, see Hannah Hamad, *Postfeminism and Paternity in Contemporary US Film: Framing Fatherhood* (New York/London: Routledge, 2014).

61. Hochschild and Machung describe a similar move by one of their respondents, Jessica, who "colluded in the idea that [her husband] was the helpless captive of his profession and neurotic personality," Hochschild and Machung, *Second Shift*, 120.

62. Stone, *Opting Out?* 156–157.

63. See Judy Wajcman's critique of the productivity-driven culture, where being busy and having action-packed lives have become valorized. Judy Wajcman, *Pressed for Time: The Acceleration of Life in Digital Capitalism* (Chicago: University of Chicago Press, 2016).

64. Walters and Harrison, "Not Ready to Make Nice," 47.

65. Friedan, *Feminine Mystique*, 10.

5. THE MOMPRENEUR/INARTICULATE DESIRE

1. Betty Friedan, *The Feminine Mystique* (London: Penguin, 2000 [1963]), 44.

2. Friedan, *Feminine* Mystique, 44.

3. Sophie Boutillier, "The Theory of the Entrepreneur: From Heroic to Socialised Entrepreneurship," *Journal of Innovation Economics & Management* 2, no. 14 (2014): 9–40.

4. Joanne Duberley and Marylyn Carrigan, "The Career Identities of 'Mumpreneurs': Women's Experiences of Combining Enterprise and Motherhood," *International Small Business Journal* 31, no. 6 (2013): 633.

5. Duberley and Carrigan, "Career Identities," 644. Duberley and Carrigan draw on Alistair Anderson and Lorriane Warren, "The Entrepreneur as Hero and Jester: Enacting the Entrepreneurial Discourse," *International Small Business Journal* 29, no. 1 (2011): 1–21.

6. Margaret Tally, "She Doesn't Let Age Define Her: Sexuality and Motherhood in Recent 'Middle-aged Chick Flicks,'" *Sexuality & Culture* 2, no. 10 (2006): 33–55.

7. Jo Littler, *Against Meritocracy: Culture, Power and Myths of Mobility* (London: Routledge, 2018), 179.

8. Janet Newman, "Enterprising Women: Images of Success," in *Off-Centre: Feminism and Cultural Studies*, ed. S. Franklin, C. Lury, and J. Stacey (London: Routledge, 1991), 241, cited in Littler, *Against Meritocracy*, 195.

9. Littler, *Against Meritocracy*.

10. Littler, *Against Meritocracy*, 187.

11. Duberley and Carrigan, "Career Identifiers"; Carol Ekinsmyth, "Challenging the Boundaries of Entrepreneurship: The Spatialities and Practices of UK 'Mumpreneurs,'" *Geoforum* 42, no. 1 (2011): 105; Littler, *Against Meritocracy*.

12. Candice Harris, Rachel Morrison, Marcus Ho, and Kate Lewis, "Mumpreneurs: Mothers in the Business of Babies," in *Proceedings of the 22nd Annual Australian and New Zealand Academy of Management Conference (ANZAM)* (2008): 1–17.

13. This is discussed in Ekinsmyth, "Challenging the Boundaries," 105.

14. Ekinsmyth, "Challenging the Boundaries," 111.

15. David Cameron, "PM Transcript: Start-up Britain Speech in Leeds," January 23, 2012, https://www.gov.uk/government/speeches/pm-transcript-start-up-britain-speech-in-leeds.

16. Department for Digital, Culture, Media & Sport, "Female Entrepreneurs Set to Benefit from Superfast Broadband," May 13, 2014, https://www.gov.uk/government/news/female-entrepreneurs-set-to-benefit-from-superfast-broadband; see also Department for Business, Innovation & Skills, "The Burt Report: Inclusive Support for Women in Enterprise," February 2015, https://assets.publishing.service.gov.uk/government/uploads/system/uploads/attachment_data/file/403004/BIS-15-90_Inclusive_support_for_women_in_enterprise_The_Burt_report_final.pdf.

17. Cited in MacLellan Lila, "The Canada-US task force of women CEOs in a photo op with Trump and Trudeau seems to have 'vaporized,'" *Quartz*, April 26, 2017, https://qz.com/966970/trump-and-trudeaus-canada-us-task-force-of-women-ceos-seems-to-have-disappeared-two-months-after-its-photo-opp/.

18. Jo Littler gives the example of the popular 2008 book *Kitchen Table Tycoon*, whose back cover blurb reads: "Many mothers are quitting their day jobs and starting up on their own, eager to cut out the nursery fees and see more of their kids." Littler, *Against Meritocracy*, 180.

19. Kate V. Lewis, "Public Narratives of Female Entrepreneurship: Fairy Tale or Fact?" *Labour & Industry: A Journal of the Social and Economic Relations of Work* 24, no. 4 (2014): 336.

20. Littler, *Against Meritocracy*; Stephanie Taylor, "A New Mystique? Working for Yourself in the Neoliberal Economy," *Sociological Review* 63 (2015): 175. In the United Kingdom, self-employed workers now make up 1 in 7 of the population, while in 2015, 10.1 percent of total US employment was self-employment. US Bureau of Labor Statistics, "Self-employment in the United States," March 2016, https://www.bls.gov/spotlight/2016/self-employment-in-the-united-states/pdf/self-employment-in-the-united-states.pdf.

21. Taylor, "A New Mystique?" 181.

22. Cited in Felicity Hannah, "80% of Self-employed People in Britain Live in Poverty: Freelance Perks Mask Growing Fears of Financial Ruin for Millions," *Independent*, June 8, 2016, http://www.independent.co.uk/money/spend-save/80-of-self-employed-people-in-britain-live-in-poverty-a7070561.html.

23. Nathan Heller, "Is the Gig Economy Working? Many Liberals Have Embraced the Sharing Economy. But Can They Survive It?" *New Yorker*, May 15, 2017, http://www.newyorker.com/magazine/2017/05/15/is-the-gig-economy-working.

24. Claire Miller, "A Darker Theme in Obama's Farewell: Automation Can Divide Us," *New York Times*, January 12, 2017, https://www.nytimes.com/2017/01/12/upshot/in-obamas-farewell-a-warning-on-automations-perils.html.

25. Jon Card, "What Entrepreneurs Want from the 'Self-employment Revolution,'" *Guardian*, October 6, 2016, http://www.theguardian.com/small-business-network/2016/oct/06/what-entrepreneurs-want-from-self-employment-revolution.

26. Duberley and Carrigan, "Career Identities," 631.

27. Ekinsmyth, "Challenging the Boundaries"; Taylor, "A New Mystique?"

28. Lisa Adkins and Maryanne Dever, "Gender and Labour in New Times: An Introduction," *Australian Feminist Studies* 29, no. 79 (2014): 5.

29. Issie Lapowseky, "Want More Women Working in Tech? Let Them Stay Home," *Wired*, June 4, 2015, http://www.wired.com/2015/04/powertofly/.

30. Melissa Gregg, "The Normalisation of Flexible Female Labour in the Information Economy," *Feminist Media Studies* 8, no. 3 (2008): 291–292.

31. Kerry Close, "Moms in the Midwest Are More Likely to Work Outside the Home than Anywhere Else in the US," *Time*, May 6, 2016, http://time.com/money/4320772/midwest-highest-rate-working-moms/.

32. Heller, "Is the Gig Economy Working?"

33. Aaron Smith, "Gig Work, Online Sharing and Home Sharing," Pew Research Center, November 17, 2016, http://www.pewinternet.org/2016/11/17/gig-work-online-selling-and-home-sharing/.

34. Brhmie Balaram, Josie Warden, and Fabian Wallace-Stephens, "Good Gigs: a Fairer Future for the UK's Gig Economy,""Royal Society for the Encouragement of Arts, Manufactures and Commerce, April 2017, https://www.thersa.org/globalassets/pdfs/reports/rsa _good-gigs-fairer-gig-economy-report.pdf; Sarah O'Connor, "Gig Economy Is a Man's World, Data Show; Labour market," *Financial Times*, April 27, 2017, https://www.ft.com /content/5b74dd26-2a96-11e7-bc4b-5528796fe35c.

35. Douglas Holtz-Eakin, Ben Gitis, and Will Rinehart, "The Gig Economy Research and Policy Implications of Regional, Economic, and Demographic Trends," Aspen Institute, January 2017, https://assets.aspeninstitute.org/content/uploads/2017/02/Regional-and -Industry-Gig-Trends-2017.pdf.

36. Hyperwallet, "The Future of Gig Work Is Female: A Study on the Behaviors and Career Aspirations of Women in the Gig Economy," April 10, 2017, https:// www.hyperwallet.com/app/uploads/HW_The_Future_of_Gig_Work_is_Female .pdf; Trebor Scholz, *Uberworked and Underpaid: How Workers Are Disrupting the Digital Economy* (Cambridge/Malden: Polity, 2017); Anna Sussman and Josh Zumbrun, "Contract Workforce Outpaces Growth in Silicon-Valley Style 'Gig' Jobs," *Wall Street Journal*, March 25, 2016, https://www.wsj.com/articles/contract-workforce-outpaces -growth-in-silicon-valley-style-gig-jobs-1458948608.

37. Brooke Duffy, "Gendering the Labor of Social Media Production," *Feminist Media Studies* 15, no. 4 (2015): 710; Erin Duffy and Emily Hund, " 'Having It All' on Social Media: Entrepreneurial Femininity and Self-Branding Among Fashion Bloggers," *Social Media + Society* 1, no. 2 (2015): 2.

38. Smith, "Gig Work, Online."

39. Mina Haq, "The Face of 'Gig' Work is Increasingly Female—and Empowered, Survey Finds," *USA Today*, April 4, 2017, https://www.usatoday.com/story/money/2017/04/04 /women-gig-work-equal-pay-day-side-gigs-uber/99878986/.

40. See, for example, Manon DeFelice, "Why Women Can—and Should—Cash In on the Gig Economy," *Forbes*, March 15, 2017, https://www.forbes.com/sites/manondefelice /2017/03/15/why-women-can-and-should-cash-in-on-the-gig-economy /#2b9a6f341fb3; Jenny Galluzzo, "How the Gig Economy Is Changing Work for Women," *Entrepreneur*, October 12, 2016, https://www.entrepreneur.com/article/282693; Amanda Schneider "GigaMom: How the 'Gig Economy' Is Opening Up Opportunities for Women Who Love Work and Life," *Huffington Post*, April 15, 2017, http://www.huffingtonpost .com/amanda-schneider/gigamom-how-the-gig-econo_b_9691588.html; Michelle Wright, "The Gig Economy—A Helpful Spur for Female Entrepreneurs?" *Huffington Post*, February 15, 2016, http://www.huffingtonpost.co.uk/michellewright/the-gig-economy-_b _9235512.html.

41. Kate Lewis, Candice Harris, Rachel Morrison, and Marcus Ho, "The Entrepreneur-ship-Motherhood Nexus: A Longitudinal Investigation from a Boundaryless Career Perspective," *Career Development International* 20, no. 1 (2015): 23.

42. CNN Money, cited in Ursula Huws, "Logged Labour: A New Paradigm of Work Organisa-tion?" *Work Organisation, Labour and Globalisation* 10 (2016): 12–13.

43. Jason Malinak, *Etsy-preneurship: Everything You Need to Know to Turn Your Handmade Hobby into a Thriving Business* (Hoboken, NJ: Jon Wiley, 2013).

44. Sheryl Nance-Nash, "How I (Successfully!) Started an Etsy Store," *Muse*, https://www.themuse.com/advice/how-i-successfully-started-an-etsy-store (accessed June 13, 2018). In a similarly celebratory fashion, an American Express Open Forum piece cajoles women to "take inspiration, and advice, from . . . successful 'mompreneurs.'" Samantha Cortez, "How 3 Stay-at-Home Moms Balance Business and Family," American Express, August 12, 2012, http://www.americanexpress.com/us/small-business/openforum/articles/how-3-stay-at-home-moms-balance-business-and-family/.

45. Brittany Frey, *Handcrafted Brunette* blog, February 17, 2017, https://www.truthinkapparel.com/single-post/2017/02/17/Handcrafted-Brunette. Last accessed October 24, 2017.

46. Duffy and Hund, "'Having It All' on Social Media," 8.

47. Susan Luckman, "Women's Micro-entrepreneurial Homeworking: A 'Magical Solution to the Work–Life Relationship?" *Australian Feminist Studies* 30, no. 84 (2015): 154, 148. See also Michele White, "Working eBay and Etsy: Selling Stay-at-Home Mothers," *Producing Women: The Internet, Traditional Femininity, Queerness, and Creativity* (Abingdon/New York: Taylor & Francis, 2015), 33–64; Julie A. Wilson and Emily Chivers Yochim, *Mothering through Precarity: Women's Work and Digital Media* (Durham, NC/London: Duke University Press, 2017).

48. White, "Working eBay and Etsy."

49. Duffy and Hund, "'Having It All.'"

50. Angela McRobbie, *Be Creative: Making a Living in the New Culture Industries*, (Cambridge: Polity, 2016), 89.

51. Duffy and Hund, "'Having It All,'" 4.

52. "'Having It All,'" 5.

53. Brooke Duffy, "The Romance of Work: Gender and Aspirational Labour in the Digital Culture Industries," *International Journal of Cultural Studies* 19, no. 4 (2016): 454.

54. Elizabeth Nathanson, "Dressed for Economic Distress: Blogging and the 'New' Pleasures of Fashion," in *Gendering the Recession: Media and Culture in an Age of Austerity*, ed. D. Negra and Y. Tasker (Durham, NC/London: Duke University Press, 2014), 39. See also Doris Ruth Eikhof, Juliette Summers, and Sara Carter, "Women Doing Their Own Thing: Media Representations of Female Entrepreneurship," *International Journal of Entrepreneurial Behaviour & Research* 19 (2013): 547–564. This review of profiles of women entrepreneurs in UK women's magazines argues that these representations both mirror and reproduce existing gender inequalities in entrepreneurial activity.

55. Anne-Marie Slaughter, *Unfinished Business: Women, Men, Work, Family* (London: Oneworld, 2015), 210.

56. Slaughter, *Unfinished Business*, 211.

57. Of the 160 parents enrolled in the London campus, 85 percent are mothers. Lucy Tobin, "How the Google Campus Creche Is Revolutionising Workplace Childcare," *Evening Standard*, October 20, 2016, https://www.standard.co.uk/lifestyle/london-life/how-the-google-campus-creche-is-revolutionising-workplace-childcare-a3374221.html.

58. Tobin, "Google Campus Creche."

59. Lucy Tobin, "Bringing Up Baby (While Launching an Online Empire)," *Evening Standard*, October 20, 2016, 38.

60. Friedan, *Feminine Mystique*, 345.

61. Taylor, "A New Mystique?" 175.

62. Taylor, "A New Mystique?" 174.

63. Anthony Giddens, *Modernity and Self Identity: Self and Society in the Late Modern Age* (Cambridge: Polity Press in association with Basil Blackwell, 1991), 32; see also Eva Illouz, *Saving the Modern Soul: Therapy, Emotions, and the Culture of Self-help* (Berkeley: University of California Press, 2008).

64. Illouz, *Saving the Modern Soul*, 184.

65. Friedan, *Feminine Mystique*, 284.

66. "Interview: Rebecca Asher, Producer and Writer," *The Scotsman*, April 3, 2011, http://www.scotsman.com/lifestyle/culture/books/interview-rebecca-asher-producer-and-writer-1-1572297; see also Rebecca Asher, *Shattered: Modern Motherhood and the Illusion of Equality* (New York: Vintage, 2011), 6.

67. Littler, *Against Meritocracy*.

68. Friedan, *Feminine Mystique*, 192.

69. Littler, *Against Meritocracy*, 187.

70. Stephanie Taylor and Susan Luckman, *The New Normal of Working Lives: Critical Studies in Contemporary Work and Employment* (London: Palgrave Macmillan, 2018).

71. Rosalind Gill, "'Life Is a Pitch': Managing the Self in New Media Work," in *Managing Media Work*, ed. M. Deuze (Thousand Oaks, California: Sage, 2010), 249–262; Wilson and Yochim, *Mothering through Precarity*, 176.

72. Friedan, *Feminine Mystique*, 280.

73. Friedan, *Feminine Mystique*, 281.

74. Littler, *Against Meritocracy*, 187.

6. INEVITABLE CHANGE/INVISIBLE CHAINS

1. Greenham Common was a women's peace camp established in 1981 to protest against American cruise missiles being sited at Royal Airforce Greenham Common in Berkshire, England.

2. Greg Philo, *Seeing and Believing: The Influence of Television* (London: Routledge, 1990).

3. Mary Douglas Vavrus, "Opting Out Moms in the News," *Feminist Media Studies* 7, no. 1 (2007): 47–63.

4. In her study of the experiences of working-class young women, Valerie Walkerdine found that they often lacked any idea of how to act on a fantasy, how actually to move from the wish to being able to work it to do something different. In my study, I found this applied to both former working-class and middle-class women. See Valerie Walkerdine, "Neoliberalism, Working-Class Subjects and Higher Education," *Contemporary Social Science* 6, no. 2 (2011): 259.

5. See Helen's comment cited in chapter 4 of this book.

6. Sarah Banet-Weiser, *Empowered: Popular Feminism and Popular Misogyny* (Durham, NC: Duke University Press, 2018).

7. Everyday Sexism Project, http://everydaysexism.com; Hollaback Project, http://www.ihollaback.org; #MeToo, https://twitter.com/hashtag/metoo; #TimesUp, https://twitter.com/hashtag/timesup.

8. Rosalind Gill, "Post-postfeminism? New Feminist Visibilities in Postfeminist Times," *Feminist Media Studies* 16, no. 4 (2016): 610–630.

9. Banet-Weiser, *Empowered* (book proposal copy), 4.

10. Banet-Weiser, *Empowered* (book proposal copy), 4.

11. Sheryl Sandberg, *Lean In: Women, Work, and the Will to Lead* (London: WH Allen, 2013), 172.

12. Anne-Marie Slaughter, *Unfinished Business: Women, Men, Work, Family* (London: Oneworld, 2015), 217.

13. These are the titles of chapter 2 and chapter 3, respectively, in Ivanka Trump, *Women Who Work: Rewriting the Rules for Success* (New York: Penguin, 2017).

14. Richard Sennett and Jonathan Cobb, *The Hidden Injuries of Class* (Cambridge: Cambridge University Press, 1972), 152.

15. Catherine Rottenberg, "The Rise of Neoliberal Feminism," *Cultural Studies* 28, no. 3 (2014): 418–447.

16. BBC, "Facebook's Sheryl Sandberg in Call to Help Working Mothers," BBC Business, May 14, 2017, http://www.bbc.co.uk/news/business-39917277.

17. Slaughter, *Unfinished Business.*

18. Maggie Haberman, "Ivanka Trump Swayed the President on Family Leave. Congress is a Tougher Sell," *New York Times*, May 21, 2017, https://www.nytimes.com/2017/05/21/us/politics/ivanka-trump-parental-leave-plan.html; Jennifer Steinhauer, "Even Child Care Divides Parties. Ivanka Trump Tries Building a Bridge," *New York Times*, March 11, 2017, https://www.nytimes.com/2017/03/11/us/politics/ivanka-trump-women-policy.html.

19. Rosalind Gill and Shani Orgad, "Confidence Culture and the Remaking of Feminism," *New Formations* 91 (2017): 16–34; Rosalind Gill and Shani Orgad, "The Confidence Cult(ure)," *Australian Feminist Studies* 30, no. 86 (2015): 324–344.

20. Katty Kay and Claire Shipman, *The Confidence Code* (New York: Harper Business, 2014), xix.

21. Gill and Orgad, "The Confidence Cult(ure)."

22. Kay and Shipman, *The Confidence Code*, 101.

23. Sandberg, *Lean In*, 28.

24. See, for example, Cara Moore, "How to Be Confident at Work and Get Over Imposter Syndrome in 6 Steps," *Telegraph*, March 23, 2016, http://www.telegraph.co.uk/women/work/how-to-be-confident-at-work-and-get-over-imposter-syndrome-in-6/; Noopur Shukla, "The Hidden Power of Imposter Syndrome," MIT Management, March 19, 2017, https://emba.mit.edu/the-experience/executive-insights-blog/the-hidden-power-of-imposter-syndrome/; Westminster Briefing, "Supporting Women in the Workplace," event agenda, Manchester, UK, June 14, 2017, http://www.westminster-briefing.com/fileadmin/westminster-briefing/Agendas/supporting_women.pdf.

25. Samantha Simmons, "The Election—Is Imposter Syndrome to Blame?" *Huffington Post*, June 12, 2017, http://www.huffingtonpost.co.uk/samantha-simmonds/the-election-is-imposter-_b_17017264.html.

26. Luc Boltanski and Eve Chiapello, *The New Spirit of Capitalism* (London: Verso, 2007), 10.

27. Jill Treanor, "Gender Pay Gap Could Take 170 Years to Close, Says World Economic Forum," *Guardian*, October 25, 2016, https://www.theguardian.com/business/2016/oct/25/gender-pay-gap-170-years-to-close-world-economic-forum-equality.

28. Al Jazeera, "WEF: Gender Wage Gap Will not Close for 170 Years," *Al Jazeera*, October 26, 2016, http://www.aljazeera.com/news/2016/10/index-gender-wage-gap-close-170-years -161026071909666.html.

29. Associated Press, "Report: Women Won't Earn as Much as Men for 170 Years," October 26, 2016, https://apnews.com/114bfd7fb7f94d3085d353b94db689ab.

30. Lauren Davidson, "Gender Equality Will Happen—but Not Until 2095," *Telegraph*, October 24, 2014, http://www.telegraph.co.uk/finance/economics/11191348/Gender -equality-will-happen-but-not-until-2095.html.

31. Barbra Cruikshank, "Revolutions Within: Self-Government and Self-Esteem," *Economy and Society* 22, no. 3 (1993); Nikolas Rose, *Inventing Ourselves: Psychology, Power, Personhood* (Cambridge, Cambridge University Press, 1998); William Davies, *The Happiness Industry: How the Government and Big Business Sold Us Well-Being* (London: Verso, 2015).

32. Gill and Orgad, "Confidence Culture and the Remaking."

33. Catherine Rottenberg, "Happiness and the Liberal Imagination: How Superwoman Became Balanced," *Feminist Studies* 40, no. 1 (2014): 156.

34. Black Career Women's Network, https://bcwnetwork.com/; cited in Gill and Orgad, "Confidence Culture and the Remaking," 21.

35. Gill and Orgad, "Confidence Culture and the Remaking."

36. Trump, *Women Who Work*, 131.

37. See, for example, Angela Ahrendts, "Apple's Angela Ahrendts: Always Be Present," *Leaders and Daughters*, March 6, 2017, http://leadersanddaughters.com/2017/03/06 /always-be-present-read-the-signs-stay-in-your-lane-and-never-back-up-more-than -you-have-too/; Dana Smithers, "Enjoy the Present Moment," *Law of Attraction Blog*, March 12, 2014, http://www.empoweredwomeninbusiness.com/enjoy-the-present-moment/.

38. Catherine Rottenberg, *The Rise of Neoliberal Feminism* (Oxford: Oxford University Press, 2018), 130, 132.

39. Rachel Aroesti, "Take That, Patriarchy! The Horrific, Cack-Handed 'Feminism' of Netflix's Girlboss," *Guardian*, May 10, 2017, https://www.theguardian.com/tv-and-radio/2017 /may/10/girlboss-netflix-horrific-cack-handed-feminism-sophia-amoruso. For a related critique of a progress narrative that dominates contemporary popular feminism, see Clare Hemmings, "Resisting Popular Feminisms: Gender, Sexuality And The Lure of The Modern," *Gender, Place & Culture*,1–15 (2018).

40. McKinsey & Company, "Women Matter 2: Female Leadership, a Competitive Edge for the Future," 2008, 17.

41. Jessica Mairs, "Women Are the Salt of Our Lives. They Give it Flavour," *De Zeen*, February 17, 2017, https://www.dezeen.com/2017/02/17/women-salt-lives-architecture -gender-discrimination-santiago-calatrava/.

42. Erika Rackley, "So, Lord Sumption Says to Be Patient—We'll Have a Diverse Bench . . . in 2062," *Guardian*, November 20, 2012, https://www.theguardian.com/law/2012/nov/20 /judiciary-uk-supreme-court.

43. See Banet-Weiser, *Empowered*, on popular misogyny circulating alongside and as a response to popular feminism.

44. Mirra Komarovsky, *Women in the Modern World, Their Education and Their Dilemmas.* (Boston: Altamira Press, 1953), 66, cited in Betty Friedan, *The Feminine Mystique* (London: Penguin, 2000 [1963]), 104, 105.

45. Julie A. Wilson and Emily Chivers Yochim, *Mothering through Precarity: Women's Work and Digital Media* (Durham, NC/London: Duke University Press, 2017), 41.
46. Wilson and Yochim, *Mothering through Precarity*.
47. All three- to four-year-olds in England were entitled to 570 hours of free early education or childcare per year. These are usually taken as fifteen hours a week for thirty-eight weeks of the year. From September 2017, UK government increased its provision of free early education and childcare to thirty hours a week. See GOV.UK, "Help Paying for Childcare," http://www.gov.uk/help-with-childcare-costs/free-childcare-and-education-for-2-to-4-year-olds (accessed June 13, 2018).
48. Catherine Rottenberg, "Back from the Future: Turning to the 'Here and Now,'" conference paper, May 9, 2017, Goldsmiths, University of London.
49. Angela McRobbie, *The Aftermath of Feminism: Gender, Culture and Social Change* (Los Angeles /London: Sage, 2009), drawing on Judith Butler, *The Psychic Life of Power* (Stanford, CA: Stanford University Press, 1997).
50. See NationBuilder, "Women's Equality Party," http://www.womensequality.org.uk/about (accessed June 13, 2018).

CONCLUSION: IMPATIENCE

1. The term "retro housewives" is discussed in the introduction and appeared in Lisa Miller, "The Retro Wife," *New York* magazine, March 25, 2013, http://nymag.com/news/features/retro-wife-2013-3/; the term "new traditionalist" is discussed in chapter 3 and by Susan Faludi, *Backlash: The Undeclared War against Women* (London: Chatto & Windus, 1992), 70–71.
2. See Eli Zaretsky's discussion of the instrumental role of housewives and mothers in enforcing the split between the sphere of commodity production in the public world and social reproduction in the home, and the extension of the housewife's tasks in the nineteenth century to include responsibility for preserving the family's emotional realm. Eli Zaretsky, *Capitalism, the Family and Personal Life* (London: Pluto, 1976).
3. Betty Friedan, *The Feminine Mystique* (London: Penguin, 2000 [1963]), 44. See chapter 5 in this book.
4. Nancy Fraser, "Contradictions of Capital and Care," *New Left Review* 100 (2016): 114.
5. Sheryl Sandberg, *Lean In: Women, Work, and the Will to Lead* (London: WH Allen, 2013).
6. Katty Kay and Claire Shipman, *The Confidence Code: The Science and Art of Self-Assurance—What Women Should Know* (New York: Harper Collins, 2014).
7. Arlie Hochschild with Anne Machung, *The Second Shift: Working Families and the Revolution at Home* (New York: Penguin, 1989), 1. See discussion in chapter 2.
8. Tiffany Dufy, *Drop the Ball: Achieving More by Doing Less* (London: Flatiron, 2017).
9. See Sara Ahmed, *The Promise of Happiness* (Durham, NC: Duke University Press, 2010).
10. This is how Nancy Fraser frames this distinction, as mentioned before. Fraser, "Contradictions."
11. Rosalind Gill and Shani Orgad, "The Confidence Cult(ure)," *Australian Feminist Studies* 30, no. 86 (2015): 324–344; Rosalind Gill and Shani Orgad, "Confidence Culture and the Remaking of Feminism," *New Formations* 91 (2017): 16–34; Shani Orgad and Rosalind Gill, *Confidence Culture* (Durham, NC: Duke University Press, forthcoming).

12. Catherine Rottenberg, "Happiness and the Liberal Imagination: How Superwoman Became Balanced," *Feminist Studies* 40, no. 1 (2014): 156.

13. "Interview: Rebecca Asher, Producer and Writer," *The Scotsman*, April 3, 2011, http://www.scotsman.com/lifestyle/culture/books/interview-rebecca-asher-producer-and-writer-1-1572297; see also Rebecca Asher, *Shattered: Modern Motherhood and the Illusion of Equality* (New York: Vintage, 2011), 6.

14. Friedan, *Feminine Mystique*, 15.

15. This formulation is inspired by Sennett and Cobb's observation about the humbling of the workingmen they studied being "at once less brutal and more insidious." Richard Sennett and Jonathan Cobb, *The Hidden Injuries of Class* (New York: Knopf, 1972), 248.

16. For a similar observation on these conflicting discourses, see Valerie Walkerdine, Helen Lucey, and June Melody, *Growing Up Girl: Psychosocial Explorations of Gender and Class* (Basingstoke, UK: Palgrave, 2001), 81.

17. CNN, "Read Oprah Winfrey's Rousing Golden Globes speech," CNN, January 10, 2018, https://edition.cnn.com/2018/01/08/entertainment/oprah-globes-speech-transcript/.

18. This term is used in Emma Goldman, "The Tragedy of Women's Emancipation," in *Red Emma Speaks*, ed. Alix Kates Shulman (New York, 1972), 176.

19. Lauren Berlant, *Cruel Optimism* (Durham, NC/London: Duke University Press, 2011).

20. See, for example, Sheryl Sandberg and Adam Grant, *Option B: Facing Adversity, Building Resilience and Finding Joy* (London: WH Allen, 2017), 103.

21. Kristen Domonell, "Why Endorphins (and Exercise) Make You Happy," CNN, January 13, 2016, http://edition.cnn.com/2016/01/13/health/endorphins-exercise-cause-happiness/.

22. Zaretsky, *Capitalism*.

23. Todd Gitlin, afterword, in Charles Wright Mills, *The Sociological Imagination* (Oxford: Oxford University Press, 2000 [1959]), 230.

24. Gitlin, in Mills, *The Sociological Imagination*.

25. Here I draw partly on Friedan, who called on women in the 1960s to say no to the feminine mystique and refuse to act out their husbands' fantasies. Friedan, *Feminine Mystique*, 288.

26. Friedan, *Feminine Mystique*, 288.

27. For a critical view on the limitations of the current #MeToo-inspired debate on the gender pay gap, see Tania Branigan, "Sorry, Chaps, but Denial Won't Fix the Gender Pay Gap," *Guardian*, March 24, 2018, https://www.theguardian.com/commentisfree/2018/mar/24/gender-pay-gap-figures-inequality.

28. This pattern is corroborated by other research that shows a persistent gender inequality in the division of childcare within heterosexual families. *The Modern Families Index 2018* (London: Working Families, 2018), 27, https://www.workingfamilies.org.uk/publications/mfindex2018/.

29. For example, David Pedulla and Sarah Thbaud, "Can We Finish the Revolution? Gender, Work-Family Ideals, and Institutional Constraint," *American Sociological Review*, 80, no. 1 (2015): 116–139; Scott Schieman, Leah Ruppanner, and Melissa A. Milkie, "Who Helps with Homework? Parenting Inequality and Relationship Quality among Employed Mothers and Fathers," *Journal of Family and Economic Issues* 39, no. 1 (2018): 49–65; Ruti Galia Levtov, Gary Barker, Manuel Contreras-Urbina, Brian Heilman, and Ravi Verma,

"Pathways to Gender-Equitable Men: Findings from the International Men and Gender Equality Survey (IMAGES)," *Men and Masculinities* 17, no. 5 (2014): 1–35.

30. Charlotte Faircloth, "Intensive Fatherhood? The (Un)Involved Dad," in *Parenting Culture Studies*, ed. E. Lee, J. Bristow, C. Faircloth, and J. Macvarish (London: Palgrave Macmillan, 2014).

31. Tina Miller, "Falling Back into Gender? Men's Narratives and Practices around First-Time Fatherhood," *Sociology* 45, no. 6 (2011): 1094, cited in Faircloth, "Intensive Fatherhood?" 196.

32. Schieman, Ruppanner, and Milkie, "Who Helps"; *The Modern Families Index 2018*.

33. *The Modern Families Index 2018*; Fatherhood Institute, "UK Mums and Dads Are Worst in Developed World at Sharing Childcare," June 12, 2016, http://www.fatherhoodinstitute .org/2016/uk-mums-and-dads-are-worst-in-developed-world-at-sharing-childcare/.

34. *The Modern Families Index 2018*, 19.

35. Kim Parker and Gretchen Livingston, "7 Facts about American Fathers," June 15, 2017, Pew Research, http://www.pewresearch.org/fact-tank/2017/06/15/fathers-day-facts/.

36. Jack O'Sullivan, "The 'Dad Factor'—a Major Ingredient for Children's Successful Learning," *Bold: Blog on Learning and Development*, July 27, 2016, http://bold.expert /supporting-dads-is-key-to-improving-childrens-learning/.

37. Sarah Gordon, "Few Families Opt for Shared Parental Leave," *Financial Times*, September 17, 2017, https://www.ft.com/content/2c4e539c-9a0d-11e7-a652-cde3f882dd7b.

38. Zaretsky, *Capitalism*, 52, citing Kate Millett, *Sexual Politics* (New York: Doubleday, 1970), 105.

39. Fraser, "Contradictions of Capital," 117.

40. See Hannah Hamad's discussion of iteration of postfeminist fatherhood: Hannah Hamad, *Postfeminism and Paternity in Contemporary US Film: Framing Fatherhood* (New York/London: Routledge, 2014); see also Jan Moir, "Why Does TV Portray Every Dad as a Dimwit?" *Daily Mail*, June 13, 2013, http://www.dailymail.co.uk/femail/article-2340677/Why-does-TV -portray-dad-dimwit.html.

41. I thank Astrid Sanders for her advice on the legal aspect of this issue. See also Xpert HR, "Is There Anything to Prevent an Employer Making Informal Enquiries of an Employee on Maternity Leave about Whether or Not She Intends to Return to Work?" n.d., http:// www.xperthr.co.uk/faq/is-there-anything-to-prevent-an-employer-making-informal -enquiries-of-an-employee-on-maternity-leave-about-whether-or-not-she-intends-to -return-to-work/68326/ (accessed June 13, 2018).

42. Goldman, "The Tragedy of Women's Emancipation," 176.

43. A provocative anonymous letter published in the *Guardian* expresses a similarly strong resentment felt by a husband whose wife "won't get a job while he work[s] himself to death." Tellingly, the expression of his bitterness and discontentment at what he regards as a deeply unequal relationship and his wife's leisurely life is enabled by and conditioned upon his being anonymous. These strong feelings cannot be expressed openly. "A Letter to My Wife Who Won't Get a Job While I Work Myself to Death," *Guardian*, July 2, 2016, http://www.theguardian.com/lifeandstyle/2016/jul/02 /a-letter-to-my-wife-who-wont-get-a-job-while-i-work-myself-to-death.

44. Emily, whose story is discussed in chapter 5, reflected on a similar trade-off when she said that she "exited her job instead of exiting her marriage."

45. Hochschild with Machung, *The Second Shift*, 18.

46. Viv Groskop, "Do Young Women Really Crave the 1950s?" *Guardian*, April 8, 2014, https://www.theguardian.com/commentisfree/2017/apr/08/do-young-women-really-crave-1950s.

47. Stephanie Coontz, "Do Millennial Men Want Stay-at-Home Wives?" *New York Times*, March 31, 2017, https://www.nytimes.com/2017/03/31/opinion/sunday/do-millennial-men-want-stay-at-home-wives.html.

48. Sarah Macharia, *Who Makes the News? Global Media Monitoring Project 2015* (London: World Association for Christian Communication, 2015), 8, http://cdn.agilitycms.com/who-makes-the-news/Imported/reports_2015/global/gmmp_global_report_en.pdf.

49. Lauren Berlant, "The Female Complaint," *Social Text*, no. 19/20 (1988): 243.

50. Lauren Berlant, *The Female Complaint: The Unfinished Business of Sentimentality in American Culture* (Durham, NC/London: Duke University Press, 2008), 19.

51. Berlant, *Female Complaint: Unfinished Business*, 245.

52. Berlant, *Female Complaint: Unfinished Business*, 248–249.

53. See Gill and Orgad, "The Amazing Bounce-back-able Woman: Resilience the Psychological Turn in Neoliberalism," *Sociological Research Online* 23, no. 2 (2018): 477–495. Gill and Orgad, *Confidence Culture*.

54. Julie A. Wilson and Emily Chivers Yochim make a similar observation in relation to how happiness affectively overloads the mothers they studied. See *Mothering through Precarity: Women's Work and Digital Media* (Durham, NC/London: Duke University Press, 2017).

55. Owen Hatherley, "Keep Calm and Carry On—the Sinister Message Behind the Slogan that Seduced the Nation," *Guardian*, January 6, 2016, http://www.theguardian.com/books/2016/jan/08/keep-calm-and-carry-on-posters-austerity-ubiquity-sinister-implications.

56. Angela McRobbie, *The Aftermath of Feminism: Gender, Culture and Social Change* (London: Sage, 2009), 78.

57. See introduction.

58. The notion of the plea of my interviewees is inspired and influenced by Sennett and Cobb's conclusion of *The Hidden Injuries of Class*.

59. Lucy Stone, the prominent American orator, abolitionist, suffragist, and vocal advocate and organizer promoting rights for women, said in 1855 (and was cited by Friedan in 1963): "It shall be the business of my life to deepen this disappointment in every woman's heart until she bows down to it no longer." Elinor Rice Hays, *Morning Star: A Biography of Lucy Stone* (New York: Harcourt, Brace & World, 1961), 83, cited in Friedan, *Feminine Mystique*, 69.

APPENDIX 3: STUDY METHODOLOGY

1. Ted Palys, "Purposive Sampling," in *The SAGE Encyclopedia of Qualitative Research Methods*, ed. L. M. Given (Los Angeles: Sage, 2008), 697–698.

2. Pamela Stone, *Opting Out? Why Women Really Quit Careers and Head Home* (Berkeley: University of California Press, 2007), 242.

3. Mike Savage, Fiona Devine, Niall Cunningham, Mark Taylor, Yaojun Li, Johs Hjellbrekke, Brigitte Le Roux, Sam Friedman, and, Andrew Miles, "A New Model of Social Class? Findings from the BBC's Great British Class Survey Experiment," *Sociology* 47, no. 2 (2013): 219–250.

4. Yvonne Tasker and Diane Negra, *Interrogating Postfeminism: Gender and the Politics of Popular Culture* (Durham, NC: Duke University Press, 2007), 13.

5. This was influenced by the interview technique used by Valerie Walkerdine and her colleagues in their study of working-class and middle-class young women. Valerie Walkerdine, Helen Lucey, and June Melody, *Growing Up Girl: Psychosocial Explorations of Gender and Class* (Basingstoke, UK: Palgrave, 2001), 93–94.

6. Betty Friedan, *The Feminine Mystique* (London: Penguin, 2000 [1963]).

7. Walkerdine, Lucey, and Melody, *Growing Up Girl*, 94–107. The first and the third levels of my analysis correspond with the first and second levels of Walkerdine et al.'s study.

8. This discursive approach to public policy is outlined in Frank Fischer, *Reframing Public Policy: Discursive Politics and Deliberative Practices* (Oxford: Oxford University Press, 2003).

9. A "following the thread" strategy resembling the one I use was employed by Jo Moran-Ellis and her colleagues to analyze multiple datasets and follow their connections, and was replicated by Lara Descartes and Conrad P. Kottak in their study of images and realities of American middle-class mothers. See Lara Descartes and Conrad P. Kottak, *Media and Middle Class Moms: Images and Realities of Work and Family* (New York: Routledge, 2009); Jo Moran-Ellis, Victoria Alexander, Ann Cronin, Mary Dickinson, Jane Fielding, Judith Sleney, and Hilary Thomas, "Triangulation and Integration: Processes, Claims and Implications," *Qualitative Research* 6 (2006): 45–59.

10. George Marcus, *Ethnography Through Thick and Thin* (Princeton, NJ: Princeton University Press, 1998), 80.

11. Marcus, *Ethnography Through Thick and Thin*, 90.

12. Marcus, *Ethnography Through Thick and Thin*, 92–93.

13. See Shani Orgad, "The Survivor in Contemporary Culture and Public Discourse: A Genealogy," *Communication Review* 12, no. 2 (2009): 132–161.

14. Orgad, "The Survivor in Contemporary Culture," 93–94.

15. Shani Orgad and Sara De Benedictis, "The 'Stay-at-Home' Mother, Postfeminism and Neoliberalism: Content Analysis of UK News Coverage," *European Journal of Communication* 30, no. 4 (2015): 418–436.

16. Ronald Barthes, *Mythologies* (London: Paladin, 1973).

Index